TOMMY ATKINS'
CHILDREN

Frontispiece.   ARMY CHILDREN.

MINISTRY OF DEFENCE

Tommy Atkins' Children

THE STORY OF THE EDUCATION OF

THE ARMY'S CHILDREN

1675-1970

Colonel NT St John Williams BA

LONDON
HER MAJESTY'S STATIONERY OFFICE
1971

Published by
HER MAJESTY'S STATIONERY OFFICE

To be purchased from
49 High Holborn, London WC1V 6HB
13a Castle Street, Edinburgh EH2 3AR
109 St Mary Street, Cardiff CF1 1JW
Brazennose Street, Manchester M60 8AS
50 Fairfax Street, Bristol BS1 3DE
258 Broad Street, Birmingham 1
80 Chichester Street, Belfast BT1 4JY
or through booksellers

SBN   11 771016 4

Printed in England for Her Majesty's Stationery Office
by William Clowes and Sons, Limited, London and Beccles
Dd 501089 K40 1/71

Foreword

BY MAJOR-GENERAL H. H. EVANS, BA
DIRECTOR OF ARMY EDUCATION

This brief account of 300 years of education provided by the Army for its children tells of Army schools supported officially, at home and abroad, before the State made similar arrangements for its own children. It records much the Army has pioneered in children's education and periods when the Army arrangements have lagged behind those provided by the State.

It is most appropriate that this story should be written in 1970, the 50th Anniversary of the foundation of the Royal Army Educational Corps. The Jubilee year was graciously marked by Her Majesty the Queen with a visit to Eltham Palace, the home of the RAEC and the base from which 500 teachers leave annually for the Services' children's schools abroad.

The author, Col. N.T. St John Williams, has many claims to write this account. He joined the RAEC in 1947, after war-time service in Europe with the Sherwood Foresters and in the Far East with the Intelligence Corps. In his first RAEC appointment he was concerned with the re-opening of the children's schools in Singapore after the War. He has served the schools on the staff in Germany and as Commandant at the Institute of Army Education. Recently, as the Director of Army Education's principal staff officer for children's schools, he had a world-wide responsibility for them. He had much to do with the formation of the new tri-Service Children's Education Authority. Now, as Chief Education Officer, Far East, he has the task of closing down many of the schools he once helped to found.

In commending this book to all who study the history of children's education, I wish to pay tribute to the many thousands, both civilian and military, who over the years have made possible this story of massive achievement often in the most difficult circumstances.

London, 1970

Contents

Illustrations

Acknowledgements

I am indebted to the following for permission to quote extracts from the copyright material and to reproduce photographs indicated.

Associated Book Publishers (*Cromwell's Army*, by Sir Charles H. Firth)

William Blackwood & Sons Ltd (*The Last Post*, by Sir John Fortescue)

Butterworth & Co (Publishers) Ltd (*The New Law of Education*, by M. M. Wells and P. S. Taylor)

Cassell and Company Ltd (*Tommy Atkins*, by John Laffin)

Clarendon Press, Oxford (*Society and Industry in the Nineteenth Century*, by K. Dawson and P. Wall)

Councils & Education Press Ltd (*Education* of 23 September 1966)

The Director of Publications, Her Majesty's Stationery Office (*The Hadow Report, The Plowden Report, Hansard*, Code for Public Elementary Schools 1904)

The Editor DYRMS Chronicle (*DYRMS Chronicle*)

Hutchinson Publishing Group Ltd (*Sir John Moore's System of Training*, by Maj.Gen. J. F. C. Fuller)

Oxford University Press (*Education and the Army*, by Lord Gorell)

Penguin Books Ltd (*Government of Education*, by W. O. Lester Smith)

The Schoolmaster Publishing Co Ltd (*The Schoolmaster* of 4 December 1953)

Times Newspapers Ltd (*The Times* of 8 April 1944, *Times Educational Supplement* of 10 March, 4 August and 11 August 1967 and 5 January 1968)

University of Nottingham (*The Development of Educational Ideas and Curricula in the Army during the Eighteenth and Nineteenth Centuries*, by Major T. A. Bowyer-Bower)

University Tutorial Press Ltd (*History of English Education*, by S. J. Curtis and M. E. A. Boultwood)

British Museum (Etchings by Wenceslaus Hollar Nos. 2 and 3)

Central Office of Information (Nos. 20, 22, 23, 25–29, 32, 37, 38)

Army Public Relations (Nos. 6, 21, 30, 33, 34, 40, 41)

National Portrait Gallery (No. 4)

Ministry of Public Buildings and Works (No. 1)

Museum, Royal Army Chaplain's Depot (No. 13)

Illustrated London News 21 January 1865 (No. 17)

Army Department Library (M.O.D.) (Royal Warrant of 11 June 1920)

RA Mess, Woolwich (No. 14)

RAEC Museum, Beaconsfield (Nos. 7, 8, 10–12, 15, 16, 18, 19, 24, 31, 35, 36, 42, 43)

Eltham Palace (Nos. 5 and 9)

QVS, Dunblane (No. 39)

I am grateful to Maj.Gen. H. H. Evans, BA, Col. A. C. T. White, VC, MC, BA and Col. D. G. Washtell, MA for their critical reading of the text and for their many helpful suggestions; to Col. G. T. Salusbury, Curator of the RAEC Museum, Mr R. A. Wafer of the Army Central Library and to the staff of the Army Department M.O.D. Library for providing source material; to Mrs E. M. Theobald for secretarial assistance and to Mrs J. Neal and the Institute of Army Education staff for help in typing and duplicating the manuscript.

Time Chart

1946   Royal Army Educational Corps
       BFES formed
1948   Army schools in UK handed over to LEAs
       Seconded teachers' scheme started
1951   *GCE*
1952   Director of Army Education responsible for BFES
1954   Lathbury Committee on Secondary Boarding Schools
1955   Education Allowances for Forces
1958   *Beloe Report* (CSE)
1959   *Crowther Report* (Boys 15–19)
1960   *Albemarle Report* (Youth Service)
1963   *Newsom Report* (Non-academic 13–16 age group)
1964   *Department of Education and Science (Secretary of State)*
1966   *Plowden Report* (Primary Education)
1968   *Public School Commission Report*
1969   Youth Service for Germany
       Service Children's Education Authority

PART I:

1675–1914

CHAPTER I

The Regimental School

Military Education. The first record of a school for Army children is dated Tangier 1675. Two schoolmasters were sent there – one a Cambridge graduate, the other a writing master and Gunner – and employed in the school. It is probable that they taught the children on a part-time basis, their main task being the education of the garrison's troops, since that was the practice. To explain this practice and to show why the Army should pioneer an educational system for its children many years before the State did the same for its own, our story must start with the soldier and the regimental school.

The Army has always valued education, principally for its relevance to military training. It understands that education can contribute to morale and to a soldier's personal and social well-being and that a regiment benefits from both; but it was the professional and administrative needs of the Army which demanded literacy of its soldiers and especially of its non-commissioned officers. The mediaeval army did not need literacy to handle the bow or bill-hook; nor did the introduction of firearms require it, since weapon training was given by word of mouth – and still is. Military tactics and warfare from the sixteenth to the nineteenth century made few demands on individual thought and initiative. A military force, to be effective, had to move and fire as a unit, upright, in drill formation and in unison. For this the soldier required training for instant obedience, not education; but literacy was required of his leaders.

The NCO was the link between the soldier and his officers, the one who trained and administered him. Moreover, the soldier himself was a potential NCO and the ranks the only source from which the NCO could be selected. A soldier would memorise the disciplinary code, as it was read aloud to him at the pay table, but it was the NCO who had to read it. Furthermore, in an age when the troops were scattered round the town in billets, an officer's orders had to be hand-written and copied, also by hand, for circulation to the NCOs to read to the detachments of men for which they were responsible. Who but the Army could educate such men for their military duties, since little or no education was available in civil life? In Cromwell's New Model Army some men had been able to read the Bibles supplied to them, but 'the majority of the infantry could not even write their names. When petitioning or attesting the evidence given before courts-martial, most of them made their mark instead of signing.'[1]

It is not surprising that the bulk of the Army was illiterate, when one considers who was being recruited. Marlborough's army included convicted felons, able-bodied paupers, sons of debtors and a number of volunteers, whose motives were not always high minded, as Farquhar's scheming recruiter said in 1704:

'If any gentlemen, soldiers or others have a mind to serve her Majesty, and pull down the French king; if any prentices have severe masters, any children have undutiful parents; if any servants have too little wages, or any husband too much wife, let them repair to the noble Sergeant Kite, at the sign of the Raven.'[2]

– and who should know better than Farquhar, for he had served both as a soldier and as a recruiting officer! Nevertheless, many did volunteer for the duration of the war or for three years, instead of the normal engagement for life – 'men who craved adventure, excitement, loot and rape. A few, very few, were soldiers by instinct or patriots. All these types of men – yokels, criminals, drunkards, adventurers – were the raw clay from which armies were fashioned.'[3]

To fashion NCOs from such an Army, colonels began to establish regimental schools and appoint schoolmasters. In 1662, the officers of Fort St George, Madras, requested the East India Company to provide them with a schoolmaster; in 1675 there were at least two in the garrison at Tangier. Before permanent barracks were built, soldiers were billeted in local inns and taverns; their hosts were required by law to furnish them (in return for stoppages of pay) with straw, candles, food and drink. Only a literate NCO with some idea of writing and of simple accounts could hope to prevent his men from being fleeced at every turn. As Sheridan's character says, 'the Angel uses us like devils and the Rising Sun refuses us light to go to bed by.'[4]

That unit administration in the eighteenth century was beginning to make increasing demands on the educational skills of its NCOs

4

is clear from the qualifications required of them in the Queen's Royal Regiment.[5]

The Serjeant Major – 'should be a man of real merit, a complete serjeant and a good scholar ... and must be ready at his pen and expert at making out details and rosters'.

The Corporal – 'should have a quickness of comprehension with a knowledge of reading, writing and accounts'.

The first record of a unit school in England occurs in 1762, when the First Regiment of Guards (Grenadier) was stationed in the Tower of London.[6] But regimental schools, started unofficially during the seventeenth and eighteenth centuries, had become accepted practice by 1800, as various Regimental Standing Orders testified. They show that the schoolmaster's main task was to teach the troops and the 'enlisted boys', but between times and when these were away from camp, he was expected to teach the regiment's children for a stipulated fee, in a room set aside for that purpose, with coal and candles provided:

'A school will be established in the Rifle Corps for the instruction of those who wish to fit themselves for the situation of Non-Commissioned Officers. NCOs are expected to attend when not fully masters of the information which is required for their duties: every Serjeant is expected to be master of reading, writing, and the four first rules of arithmetic. The knowledge of these will also be much in favour of promoting the Riflemen.

'The Schoolmaster is to be a Serjeant of good character, and abilities: whenever his scholars amount to twenty, he will have a Corporal of abilities as his usher. The sum which is to be paid for schooling is to be as follows:

By Serjeants	6d per week
By Corporals	4d ,, ,,
By Buglers	4d ,, ,,
By Privates	3d ,, ,,
By Children	2d ,, ,,

These sums are to be collected by the Schoolmaster from the Pay Serjeants of Companies, every Saturday evening. The Schoolmaster will pay his usher, the Corporal, a sum of not less than one third of his profits.

'His school will be open every day, excepting Sundays and Saturday evening, from the rouse Bugle to the breakfast one, from eleven o'clock till dinner hour, and after dinner till evening parade; from 1 October to 1 April, the winter season, for two hours also before taptoo. At the intervals, *when for one hour the school is not likely to be occupied by the men of the regiment, the schoolmaster is to give instruction to the children.*'

5

'The school is to be under the immediate direction of the Adjutant and Serjeant Major: it will be daily visited by the senior Orderly Officer, and stated in his report. Whenever the Corps is stationed for a period, in any one quarter, the Quarter-master will arrange the school room in the most comfortable manner; he will also make a stoppage of companies' coal and candles sufficient for its use.

'The school-master and usher will be exempted from all duties; they will attend Sunday parades.'

(Regulations for the Rifle Corps, 1800)[7]

The Parents. But an age which had scant regard for its soldiers' characters or for their conditions of pay, quartering, food and health, could hardly be expected to be particularly solicitous about their dependants. Married quarters were not provided until after the Crimean War, and before 1792, when the first barracks were built, the best a soldier's wife and children could hope for was a share in a local cottage or tavern. After 1792, six wives per 100 rank and file, excluding sergeants, were allowed 'to live within the walls', screened from the unmarried men by blankets or canvas. Here a woman had her children, exposed to the twin evils of barrack life, profanity and drunkenness; here her children grew up, sleeping on the floor or in a bed vacated for the night by a soldier absent or on duty. Not for many years would conditions improve for the soldier's family. The women foraged, cooked, washed and mended for the men of their 'barrack', receiving in return a very small sum out of the men's stoppages of pay.* When the regiment went abroad, the same number, selected by lot, accompanied the troops overseas as camp followers under the orders of the provost staff. In the absence of medical facilities, they nursed the sick and tended the wounded. In the Peninsular War they lived side by side with the local women who were following the regiment, some of whom, if well-behaved, were allowed to embark for England with a view to being ultimately married.[8]

Not infrequently, a soldier married 'off the strength'; that is, without official permission, and the plight of such a family was frequently desperate, especially when the husband was posted to another station; unassisted, and usually without his pay, the wife would follow him as best she could. Some commanding officers were highly intolerant when it came to giving permission to marry. Their reasons might have been the fighting efficiency of the soldier or the

* In 1783 the soldier's pay was raised for the first time for 123 years from its level of 8d a day. For a hundred years from 1797 it remained at 1/- a day. Most was deducted for subsistence and off-reckonings,

6

size of the 'baggage train'. In Ireland and Tangier it was the fear of popery,[9] and during the siege of Gibraltar in 1727 the suitability of the woman.

'A soldier asked his officer's leave to marry a prostitute. As a measure of dissuasion the officer ordered him a hundred lashes. The man took his punishment without a murmur and presented himself next morning, with his back cut to pieces, to renew his request, when the officer had not the heart to refuse him.'[10]

Since most of the troops were on overseas service and for long periods at a time, it is not surprising that large numbers married local girls, some without the benefit of clergy. In India, for example, the soldiers of one regiment found an attractive source of supply of

'very pretty half-caste wives, whom they had got out of the Byculla orphan school at Bombay, where any soldier of good character and possessed of capital to commence house-keeping, may obtain a helpmate. These girls are tolerably well educated, and would make grateful and affectionate wives, were it not that soldiers in general make such bad husbands.'[11]

Such were the parents of the Army's school children. Since the State did not recognise its own children, it had no interest in the Army's. Commanding officers, therefore, began to concern themselves with their welfare and put them to school, partly for reasons of philanthropy, partly because they were a source of potential recruits, and perhaps for a more practical reason – to stop them from being a nuisance round the camp!

Tangier. Little is recorded of the Army's first known school for children at Tangier, when the town came into the possession of Charles II as part of the marriage dowry of his Queen, Catherine of Braganza, and had to be garrisoned. An entry in the Calendar of State Papers, dated 17 April 1675, states

'Whereas We have thought fit to employ Richard Reynolds Master of Arts and Fellow of the Sidney Sussex College in Our University of Cambridge in Our Service as Schoolmaster in Our Towne of Tanger. . . .'[12]

We know that George Mercer, Clerk, held the post in 1683.[9] Of the various petitions addressed to Lord Dartmouth as Governor of Tangier in 1683, one was from

'John Eccles, usher and writing master to the school, and gunner. Was appointed seven and a half years ago at a salary of £30 a year, in succession to Mr. Hughes, the first master there, with a convenient lodging; but for upwards of five years had been obliged to find his own lodging at a total cost of £30. 3s., for which he desires compensation.'[13]

When the garrison was evacuated in 1683–84 one of the chief cares of the Governor was for the many invalids 'and the many famelyes and their effects to be brought off.'[14] The hospital ship *Unity* sailed for home on 18 October 1683 with 114 invalid soldiers and 104 women and children, under the care of this same John Eccles, destined to be 'quartered at Falmouth on an allowance of 3d a day to each soldier's wife, until the arrival of the battalion.' We know that there were 342 children and 217 wives in the garrison on 30 December 1676,[15] of whom 173 and 129 respectively belonged to the Army. This was the source of the garrison's schoolchildren.

Routh gives a detailed picture of the garrison from 1661–84, the town, inhabitants, church and hospital, but nothing else about the school. The garrison consisted usually of about 1200–1400 soldiers, English, Irish and Scots, occasionally increasing to 2000 or more, chiefly supplied by 'the Old Tangier Regiment'.[16] There were also about 600 local inhabitants of various nationalities. Social distinctions were strongly marked. The Governor and his family, with the principal officers of the garrison, formed the small upper layer, while the next group in rank included the municipal dignitaries, the ministers, the doctors and the schoolmaster, together with the more important merchants and the subaltern officers. Conditions were hard, discipline strict, and punishments severe. One soldier, for example, was sentenced to death for making treasonable speeches against the King, namely for saying he was 'no Englishman, but Scotch or French'. Another was 'found in the streets most wickedly and beast-like drunk' and sentenced to walk round the city with pots and cups hung about his neck, a drum before and the Marshall's men behind 'to whip him smartly and who are to have the same, if they do not lay on hard enough'. Apart from sieges, sorties and sniping, there was dirt, hard drinking, bad food, 'flux and scurvy', or poverty to kill off the soldiers and their families and to ruin the health of the survivors.

Early Schools. The schoolmasters, then, would teach the children part-time, their main responsibility being the education of the soldiers. A century later, in 1768, Captain Simes[17] described the responsibilities of a schoolmaster in this same Tangier Regiment, The Queen's Royal Regiment. A Serjeant or Corporal, sober, honest and of good conduct, capable of teaching the 3 Rs, was

8

'to be employed to act in the capacity of a Schoolmaster, by whom soldiers and soldiers' children are to be carefully instructed: a room to be appointed for that use: and it would be highly commendable if the Chaplain, or his deputy, would pay some attention to the school.'

There are other references to children being taught in regimental schools. In 1774 Sgt Lamb of the Royal Norfolk Regiment (9th of Foot) taught writing and arithmetic to children of NCOs in the barracks,[18] and in 1779 the Royal Artillery School, Woolwich, was opened in a building on the Horse Artillery Square in Woolwich Barracks. The children of the garrison attended this school, which came under the management of the Board of Ordnance and of a headmaster named Serjeant Dougherty. The Duchess of York subscribed 20 guineas for the purchase of books and all the HQ officers contributed to its maintenance.[19] In 1802 the Rifle Corps had a school for soldiers at Shorncliffe Camp, but 'when the school was not occupied by the men the schoolmaster to give instruction to the children'.[20] References soon multiply – an inspecting general complimented the 80th Foot on a school for the soldiers' children, while the school of the Royal Scots was so efficient that the magistrates of Stirling requested that the local people 'might participate in its benefits'.[8] In 1811 Wellington established for the Base details, HQ of the commissariat and some coast artillery stationed at Belem, near Lisbon, a garrison school[21] attended largely by the children, since the troops had little time to think of improving their personal educational prospects. This is our first record of a children's school established on active service. But few officers can have resembled Lieutenant Peevor of the 18th Foot, who, being ordered to rest after the fighting in Nepal (1816), volunteered to take charge of the regimental school, and during the next 8 years gave all his spare time to teaching young soldiers and children, so winning each year a commendation from the inspecting general.[22]

Once begun, regimental schools flourished, without State aid or recognition, supported by 'the zeal, intelligence and liberality of the officers, and by private contributions'[23] (Palmerston). Meanwhile, two military schools were founded, which were to become famous for the education of Army children.

Royal Hibernian School, Dublin. On 18 April 1769, the following petition was addressed to King George III by philanthropic people in Ireland, appalled at the destitution of the families of soldiers serving in Ireland, and of Irish soldiers overseas.

'That upon the Death of NCOs and Private men of your Majesty's Army in Ireland and upon the Removal of Regiments to Foreign Service, great numbers of children, Boys and Girls having been left destitute without either Publick or private Aid for their Sustenance; and the number of these unfortunate children having increased very considerably by Drafting the Regiments during the late war,* and by Rotation for the Relief of Regiments upon Foreign Duty, a Subscription was set on Foot in the year 1764 for raising a Fund to support the Establishment of an Hospital, in Order *to preserve such objects from Popery, Beggary and Idleness, and to train them up so as to become usefull, Industrious Protestant Subjects*, and the subscribers to this usefull Charity have formed themselves into a Body under the Name of The Governors and Guardians of the Hibernian Society for maintaining the Orphans and Children of Soldiers only.'[24]

The Petition was granted on 14 July 1769. Thus was established in Dublin The Royal Hibernian School, the first English boarding school maintained by public funds. The public and regiments had already contributed generously and the Irish Parliament granted £3000 towards the erection of a 'Hospital', the site being the gift of the King. In an old minute book of the School is recorded its opening on 6 March 1770.

'This day the children in their new clothing appeared before the Committee and were afterwards received into the Castle Garden by His Excellency the Lord Lieutenant, and thence marched to the Phoenix Park, to the new Hospital, attended by the Artillery Musick.'

The original complement of pupils was 90 boys and 50 girls in the charge of an inspector and inspectress, with a chaplain and an assistant mistress.[25]

At first the school had to contend with financial difficulties and in July 1770 the Committee appealed to the Lord-Lieutenant for a further grant of the Royal Bounty, pointing out that, in consequence of falling subscriptions, they were unable to maintain 140 children, much less increase the number as they wished to do. This appeal produced £2000, to which was added in 1774 a legacy to the school of £3000 from the mother of General Wolfe, in memory of her famous son. In the same year the 40th Regiment (The Prince of Wales's Volunteers) gave a donation of one day's pay to the Society. In 1801 the Government made a grant of £3960 per annum to the school, increased in 1808 to £5000, when the

*The Seven Years' War, 1756–1763.

number of boys had risen to 424. Finally in 1809, as Chief Secretary for Ireland, Sir Arthur Wellesley, afterwards Duke of Wellington, announced that in future the school would be entirely maintained by Parliament. As a result, it was ordered that boys on reaching the age of 15 should be enlisted, if they were willing, into the regiments that applied for them.

At this time, the school was in effect an industrial establishment, since the boys were employed at gardening, tree-planting, weaving, net-making and other remunerative industries, and the girls at spinning worsted, weaving yarn, lace-making, making clothes and domestic work. The children followed a Spartan routine: Rise at 6am (7 in winter); wash and comb hair; Prayers, to be read by a boy: School for one hour in the one large hall, which also served as dining-hall and playroom. After breakfast ('grace before and after, also a psalm'), trades and the garden occupied the morning and part of the afternoon. Dinner was at 1 o'clock, supper at 7, bed at 8 (1780). To assist in instruction, 12 boys were selected in 1789 to act as assistant ushers, distinguished from the other boys by a blue worsted epaulette on the left shoulder and the weekly receipt of a small gratuity. The best boy and girl in the School wore a silver medal; the worst wore their coats turned inside out.

In 1801 the chaplain became directly responsible for the education of the boys. Two years later the governors passed a resolution of thanks to the chaplain for his extraordinary attention to the education of Mr Henry Fletcher, one of the boys of the school, whereby he was admitted a gentleman cadet of the Royal Military College – the first of the military schools to send a boy to Sandhurst! Then in 1808, the school was remodelled on that of the sister school at Chelsea, and adopted the monitorial system of Dr Bell, thus raising the educational standards considerably.

Royal Military Asylum, Chelsea. Meanwhile, the Royal Military Asylum, Chelsea (now the Duke of York's Royal Military School, Dover) had been established in 1801. The Royal Warrant dated 24 June was addressed by George III to

'our most dearly beloved Son Frederick, Duke of York, nominating Commissioners for the Government of our Royal Military Asylum, which we have been pleased to establish at Chelsea, for the maintenance and education of a certain number of Orphans and other Children of Non-Commissioned Officers and Soldiers of Our Army.'

By a Warrant of 1846 the following clause was added:

'None shall be admitted except the children born in wedlock.'

The school was built at Chelsea on a site acquired from a Naval captain called George, and equipped on a lavish scale.[26] The architect was John Sanders, who was later responsible for the buildings at Sandhurst. The original school still stands, now known as the Duke of York's Headquarters in King's Road. George Street has been renamed Sloane Gardens.

The organisation and curriculum of the early years of the Royal Military Asylum are not only of interest in themselves, as an example of one of the first English schools maintained at public expense, but also because of the school's influence on the English educational system. The first official mention of the school is to be found in the Journals of the House of Commons on 9 June 1800, when it was ordered that a Committee be appointed to consider a project for erecting a school. The Committee met the following morning in the Speaker's Chamber, but the school was not ready to open its doors to the first of the 150 boys and 50 girls until 29 August 1803. The number quickly rose to 1000 and the accounts for 1809–10, given at the end of the Chapter, list the number of children as 1140 and show on the staff a Chaplain, Reading and Knitting Mistresses, an Instructor Serjeant-Major, Serjeant Master-Tailor, a Serjeant Master-Shoemaker and nine Serjeant Assistants (these last were pensioners from Chelsea Royal Hospital, established in 1694 * for invalid soldiers, from whose out-pensioners were found soldier instructors for the Royal Military Asylum). Also, there were 36 Corporals and 18 Lance Corporals, receiving an additional 2d. and 1d. per week respectively – selected boys who probably acted as assistant teachers to the Serjeants, when the school assembled for instruction according to Bell's monitorial system.

The orphanage was self-supporting, a proportion of the boys learning cobbling or tailoring in the workshops and some of the girls working under the seamstress, or in the laundry. The children made more than their own requiremnts in clothing and shoes, the balance being sold to other similar institutions.[27]

The two principal educational figures on the establishment were the Chaplain or, as he was officially called, The Superintendent of Morals and Education, and Alexander Hodgins, the Serjeant-Major of Instruction. The Chaplain was required:

'to examine the children in the Church Catechism and instruct them in the meaning thereof according to their capacities every Sunday;

* Its foundation stone was laid by Charles II in 1682 and the buildings finished by Sir Christopher Wren in 1690.

and to read prayers to them every Wednesday and Friday morning. He is also to be responsible for the education of the children; to take care that they reverently attend public worship; to reprove them for any irregularities or vices which he shall observe, or know them to be guilty of, and if they do not amend, after admonition, he is to report their behaviour in writing to the Commandant. It will likewise be his duty to have a watchful eye over the moral and religious conduct of the Officers, Assistants and servants of the Institution, Workshops, Refectories and Dormitories and particularly to report to the Commandant if he hears any oaths or indecent expression made use of by the children, or by the under Officers or servants of the Institution. In fine he shall, in every respect to the best of his ability, endeavour that the children be carefully instructed in the principles of virtue and religion, and that a pious, sober and orderly conduct be observed by every person in the Asylum.'[28]

These duties of the Chaplain make it clear that secular education was secondary to religious training, closely reflecting the Church of England's attitude towards elementary education in charity schools in the country at large at this time. It was not until 1846, when the Asylum was reorganised and the Corps of Army Schoolmasters formed, that secular education was to take a much larger place in the curriculum of Army schools.

The Serjeant-Major, after rousing the children at 6 o'clock in summer and 7 o'clock in winter, had

'to read or cause one of the senior boys to read, such prayers as may be directed by the Chaplain; after which he shall cause them to proceed to the school business of Reading, Writing and the first four rules of Arithmetic or of such other employments as may be assigned to qualify them either for the duties of a soldier, or for other subordinate situations in life.'[28]

Every three months the Serjeant-Major had to deliver to the Adjutant for the Commissioners' attention a list of the boys by class, age, the length of time each had been at the school, his chosen trade and general progress. It was his responsibility to ensure the assistants taught their classes diligently, had a time-table prominently displayed, and found a convenient occasion for him to examine their pupils.

Discipline was the responsibility of the Commandant, the Drummer being nominated by regulation to administer such corporal punishment as was ordered by the Commandant. The Commandant in 1826 gave details to a Committee of the type of punishments awarded.

'If a boy is impertinent to a Serjeant or does not obey his orders or is caught throwing stones, the Serjeant is permitted to give him

13

two or three stripes with his cane. For all other offences his name is put on a report, which is sent to the Commandant every morning, who orders all the boys to be assembled in one of the schoolrooms, at 12 o'clock, when the boys are whipped with a rod at the discretion of an officer, who is always present, not exceeding however 6 stripes. If a boy is guilty of thieving or running away, the Commandant generally attends the punishment and whips him more severely. To vary the punishments they are sometimes put in a cage in the schoolroom, sent to drill, or prevented from going out to see their friends when applied for.'[28]

The co-educational nature of the school caused certain difficulties and the Chaplain reported to the Commissioners on 13 March 1821 that the usual precautions for keeping the children of each sex within their proper limits were not effectual and that further security had been adopted – a strong barrier wall and railing had been placed, so as to form a complete and total separation between the two branches of the establishment. But experience had proved that notwithstanding this additional barrier, and in spite of the utmost attention on the part of the officers and serjeants, it was found 'that the two sexes contrived to elude this vigilance'.

There were at this time 360 boys and 189 girls over the age of 12 in the asylum and this particular difficulty was finally solved in 1823, when the Southampton branch of the school (opened in 1817 and still known as Asylum Green) was made into a girls' school and the boys transferred to Chelsea. There was another branch establishment at the Albany Barracks, Parkhurst, in the Isle of Wight, which opened in 1810 for sixty infants and increased to 100 infants two years later. Both branch establishments were closed in 1840 and the few remaining girls were sent to Chelsea. The last girl left the school at the end of 1846, 'greatly to the advantage of the reputation of the school', according to an early brochure.

Official Recognition. The Duke of York's greatest contribution, however, to Army education was to be the official recognition he obtained for the regimental schools for adults and children. As already noted, regimental schools had been in existence for many years through the care and generosity of Regimental Officers, but now the Duke of York was to obtain official support for them. On 26 August 1811 he wrote (Appendix B) to Viscount Palmerston, Secretary-at-War,* asking for the establishment of regimental

*The Secretary of State for War and the Colonies and the Secretary-at-War were separate offices, which were merged in 1855. The latter sat in Par-

schools and serjeant-schoolmasters to instruct the soldiers' children gratis. He further requested a schoolroom, winter fuel and money for stationery and books.

Palmerston, supporting the request, issued Circular 79, dated War Office, 27 December 1811:

Sir,
The Prince Regent having had under his consideration the advantages which would result to the army from the establishment of regimental schools for the instruction of young soldiers, and of the children of soldiers, I have the honour to acquaint you that His Royal Highness has been graciously pleased to order, in the name and on behalf of His Majesty, that, in each battalion or corps, a regimental school shall accordingly be forthwith established.

The school is to be placed under the superintendence of a serjeant-school-master, and you are to select a person properly qualified for the situation, who is to be an attested soldier, and will be borne on the establishment, with the same pay and allowances as the paymaster-sergeant of the Corps.

When the corps is in barracks, a room will be appropriated for the school, with an allowance of fuel in the winter months.

The sum of 10/- per annum will also be allowed, from the 25th instant inclusive, on account of the charges to be incurred for stationery and other incidental expenses of the school, and may be stated, half-yearly, in the paymaster's regimental accounts.

Instructions as to the plan of education to be adopted in the regimental school will be issued by His Royal Highness the Commander-in-Chief.

Colonel of the   I have, &c.
Regiment of   (Signed)   PALMERSTON

The Duke of York could now issue his own Order to the Army, which he did on 1 January 1812. It required all Generals and Commanding Officers to take the regimental schools under their special protection. Regimental chaplains, as part of their duties, were to inspect and diligently supervise the schools and the conduct of the serjeant-schoolmasters.

'The aim is to give the Soldiers the Comfort of being assured, that the Education and Welfare of their Children are objects of their Sovereign's paternal Solicitude; and to raise from their Offspring a succession of Loyal Subjects, brave Soldiers, and good Christians.'

Writing a fortnight later, in a less noble vein, he stressed the importance of children being trained

liament, was responsible for Army finance and presided over the War Office administration; the former planned operations and raised recruits.

'in the means of making themselves useful and earning their liveli-hood, which might be effected at a cheap rate, by employing the best qualified and best behaved Women of each Regiment, in instructing the Girls in Plain Work and Knitting, and employing the Tailors and Shoe-Makers of each Regiment, in instructing the Boys.'

Finally, on 24 July 1812 a Warrant was issued by Lord Palmerston to the Barrack Commissioners, empowering them to issue the requisite coal and candles and to appropriate a suitable room

'for the purpose of a regimental school, to be kept open during the day-time only, and to be marked "the school-room". The room shall be provided with such moveable desks, tables and forms as may be necessary. The school-room so set apart is to be for the accommo-dation of young soldiers, and of the children of those soldiers whose wives (to the extent of the number limited by the King's regulations in this behalf) shall be allowed to accompany their husbands.'

In 1812, Lord Palmerston, in presenting the Army Estimates, asked Parliament to authorise £20,000 to cover the expenses of the schools for soldiers' children,

which had been established in every battalion in the Service. Out of this the charges for the pay of the Serjeant Schoolmasters, for books and contingencies were met and he thought that this expense would neither be deemed useless nor lavish, when the benefit thence de-rived to the country was considered and the advantages it afforded to the Army.'[23]

This was, as Palmerston said, a small beginning but the English educational system as a whole had to wait until 1833 for Parlia-ment to approve a financial grant to establish its elementary schools, 20 years after the Army had won its case for the official provision of schools for Army children.

REFERENCES

1. C. H. Firth, *Cromwell's Army*, Methuen, 1902.
2. G. Farquhar, *The Recruiting Officer*, 1704.
3. John Laffin, *Tommy Atkins*, Cassell.
4. Sheridan. *St Patrick's Day or The Scheming Lieutenant*, Act 1, Sc 1. 1775.
5. Captain Thomas Simes, *A Military Course for the Government and Conduct of a Battalion 1777*. Simes was a Governor of the Hibernian Society.
6. PRO WO 47/59, 1762. Vol. 26 (Folio 42), Minute dated 15 January 1762. 'Mr. Alcock having by letter of this date signified that the Officers' Guard Room at the Spur Guard at the Tower which is at present un-occupied, may be lent as a school room to the Battalion of the first Regiment of Guards till further Orders. The same was ordered accord-ingly.'

7. Col. Coote-Manningham's Article V, *Regulations for the Rifle Corps*. Blatchington Barracks, 25 August 1800.

8. Col. A. C. T. White, VC, *The Story of Army Education 1643–1963*, Harrap.

9. E. M. G. Routh, *Tangier 1661–1684*, Murray, 1912.

10. Sir J. W. Fortescue, *The Last Post*, Blackwood, 1934.

11. S/Sgt J. MacMullen, *Camp and Barrack Room* (quoted in MacGuffie *'Rank and File'*).

12. PRO *Calendar of State Papers, Domestic Series, 1661–1678, Entry Book 47*, p. 6.

13. PRO Historical Manuscripts Commission Reports, *MSS of the Earl of Dartmouth 1887*, Appendix, Part 5, p. 104.

14. PRO Colonial Office Papers 279 (1–49), *Lord Dartmouth to Sir L. Jenkins 19 August 1683*.

15. PRO Survey by John Bland, CO Papers 19, 371.
(Army Wives 129: Children 98 Male and 75 Female: Wives of citizens and Molemen 88 and 169 children.)

16. 2nd of Foot. The Queen's Royal Regiment, so named after Catherine of Braganza. The Regiment's badge, the Pascal Lamb, was her crest.

17. Simes, *The Military Medley*, Dublin, 1768, p. 2.

18. Sgt Lamb, *Memoirs*, Dublin, 1811, p. 69. After his discharge in 1784, Lamb became schoolmaster of the Free School at White Friars Lane, Dublin.

19. Duncan, *History of the Royal Artillery*, Vol. II, p. 82, Murray, 1819.

20. Fuller, *Sir John Moore's System of Training*, pp. 39 and 161. Hutchinson, 1924. See also (7) Part II, ss. 4 and 5.

21. Wellington, *General Orders*, dated Freneda, 25 February and 8 May 1812.

22. Webb, *A History of the Services of the 17th (Leicestershire) Regiment 1911*. Quoted in Hawkins and Brimble. *The History of Army Education*, MacMillan, 1947.

23. Palmerston. Speech on the *Army Estimates*, 22 February 1812. Hansard.

24. A copy of this Petition is held in the RAEC Museum.

25. *Rules and Regulations of the Royal Hibernian Military School*, Dublin, 1854, p. 6. Most of the School's original documents were destroyed during the Second World War at Arnside Street Record Office, Walworth.

26. DYRMS MSS. *Accounts of General Receipts and Disbursements 1801–1811*. Quoted in a thesis on *The Development of Educational Ideas and Curricula in the Army during the 18th and 19th centuries*, 1954, by Major T. A. Bowyer-Bower, RAEC. The ground was purchased for £4,687. 8. 2d., "including £46., being the exact amount I paid for the fixtures, garden utensils, Green House, plants, two cows, a cart, clock and some inferior articles of very little value" (Letter from Capt George dated 1799. PRO WO40 12/9). Alexander Copland, the builder, received £88,716. 18. 2½d. for his work. Furniture and fittings cost £6,808. 0. 11¼d. The purchase of leases in Garden Row for a new Infirmary brought the total bill to £104,189. 2. 3d.

27. For example in a letter dated 14 May 1813 one thousand pairs of shoes in the stores were offered to the Committee of the Foundling Hospital 'at 1/- a pair for making by the boys, over and above the cost of leather at contract price'.

28. DYRMS MSS. RAEC and DYRMS Museums hold a large collection of Commissioners' Minute and Letter Books, Registers and Offence Books, etc., covering the period 1805–1907.

APPENDIX A

Estimate of the Money necessary to defray the Expence of the Royal Military Asylum, Chelsea, for the present Establishment of 1140 children for 365 Days, from 25th Dec: 1809 to 24th Dec: 1810, both Days inclusive.

Pay, Salary, and Wages £3,337 15 0

Examples:				
	Commandant	£500.	0.	0 p.a.
	Chaplain	£350.	0.	0 p.a.
	Reading Mistress	£ 43.	5.	0 p.a.
	Serjeant-Major	£ 54.	15.	0 p.a.
	Master-Tailor	£ 42.	11.	8 p.a.
	Master-Shoemaker	£ 42.	11.	8 p.a.
	Cook	£ 20.	0.	0 p.a.
	Surgeon	£273.	15.	0 p.a.

Provisions
48 Serjeants, Nurses,
   Cooks, and
   Laundresses . . each £21. 6. 11 p.a. £1,024. 12. 0
1140 Children . . . . . each £ 9. 17. 8½ p.a. £11,269. 7. 6
                         —————£ 12,293. 19. 6

Clothing and Repairs . . . . . . £ 3,717. 3. 1½

Fuel and Candles . . . . £   915. 10. 0

Lighting Lamps . . . . £   104. 0. 4

Laundry Expences . . . . £   584. 3. 4

Utensils: Porringers; Plates; Spoons, Knives & Forks:
      Ladles; Chamber Pots; Brooms; Brushes;
      Mops; Pails etc. . . . . . £   180. 0. 0

Bedding . . . . £   524. 12. 1

House Linen . . . . £   190. 10. 5

Books, Printing and Stationery
Newspapers, postage, etc. . . . . . £   417. 18. 0½

                             £22,265. 11. 10

Infant Asylum in the Isle of Wight
   for 60 children . . . . £   820. 12. 0½

                             £23,086. 3. 10½

APPENDIX B

Letter from Duke of York to Viscount Palmerston

Horse Guards, 26 August 1811

My Lord,

The advantages, which must attend the establishment of regimental schools throughout the service for the education of young soldiers and soldiers' children, are so apparent that I feel it incumbent upon me to request your Lordship will submit the measure to the immediate consideration of the Lords Commissioners of the Treasury.

When I state the few wants in which the present difficulty originated, I trust the Lords Commissioners of the Treasury will be induced to sanction the expense, which will be trifling comparatively with the benefits attending such an establishment. In the first place, it is essential that a sergeant-school-master should be appointed to each battalion, and I would recommend that he should be paid according to the rate of pay now attached to the paymaster's clerk; and it would be the duty of this person to instruct the boys receiving pay, and also the soldiers' children, gratis.

It will also be necessary that the Commissioners for the affairs of barracks shall be authorised to appropriate one room in each regimental barrack for the use of the school, with a proportionate amount of fuel in the winter months, and it will be essential to allow an extra charge upon the contingent account of each regiment, for the articles of stationery and books which may be requisite for the use of the boys and children.

As the future discipline of the service is much involved in the importance of this subject, I shall be glad to be furnished with the decision of the Lords Commissioners of the Treasury, in order that in the event of their approval I may take the earliest opportunity of carrying the necessary arrangements into execution.

I am, &c.

(Signed) FREDERICK
Commander-in-Chief

CHAPTER 2

The Beginnings of

Elementary Education

The Beginnings. In 1812, when the Army had gained official recognition and financial support for its children's schools, similar provision was not available for the poorer children in UK. Their chances of being educated at all were slight and depended on whether there was a school in their district and on whether their parents had either the money or the inclination to have them educated. Such schools as were in existence relied on endowments, voluntary subscriptions and fees. For the rich or middle class child a tutor could be engaged, or he could be sent to one of the old grammar schools, mostly Tudor foundations. The very wealthy might send their sons to one of the nine great public schools,* which provided the classical background indispensable for a gentleman. Although a few lads of ability had been able to rise to the top in law, in scholarship and in the Church, a man was expected to remain in the social class into which he was born:

> The rich man in his castle,
> The poor man at his gate,
> God made them, high or lowly,
> And order'd their estate.

Education was certainly not to be provided at public expense to help him to rise above his station. Nineteenth-century England was largely an agricultural country, so what need was there for schools and literate farm labourers?[1] Teaching a ploughman to read would not improve his ploughing. As for an educated maidservant, she would only spend her time writing her own letters and

* Winchester, Eton, Westminster, Harrow, Rugby, Shrewsbury, St Paul's, Merchant Taylors' and Charterhouse.

reading other peoples' (Cobbett). In the debate in the House of Commons on Whitbread's Parochial Schools Bill 1807[2] one opponent explained:

'Giving education to the labouring classes of the poor would, in effect, be found to be prejudicial to their morals and happiness: it would lead them to despise their lot in life; instead of teaching them subordination it would render them factious and refractory; it would enable them to read seditious pamphlets, vicious books and publications against Christianity: it would render them insolent to their superiors.'[1]

The state of elementary education can be seen from the reports of the Parliamentary Select Committees established between 1818–37. 'It appears clearly from the returns, as well as from other sources, that a very great deficiency exists in the means of educating the poor, wherever the population is thin and scattered over country districts.'[1] Opportunities in S.E. England were better than in the North and West, in England better than in Wales. The population shifts left the new centres of industry and the larger towns especially badly served. Even where facilities existed, low wages and the soaring cost of food and clothing denied most parents the means to take advantage of them. As soon as children reached the age of 5 or 6 they laboured in the mines or factories to supplement the family income. Few working-class children, even if fortunate enough to be able to attend school, could remain there after 9 or 10 years of age. In general terms, it is true to say that 'not only were there insufficient schools, but only a small proportion of children of school age, about one in thirty, received any organised education'.[3]

The types of elementary school varied greatly. In London and the large towns and in certain rural areas there were charity schools, the first institutions to provide education on a large scale for both sexes. These schools spread from the latter half of the seventeenth century and were endowed either by wealthy landowners or supported by private charity and Church collections. They provided the three Rs and the Church catechism free or on payment of a few pence a week. Boys were apprenticed to a variety of trades and girls became seamstresses or domestic servants. Those schools which survived were taken over by the National Society in 1811.

Not unlike the charity schools, but with an industrial bias, were the schools of industry, where boys were taught useful occupations such as gardening, carpentry, cobbling and printing and the girls spinning, knitting, sewing and straw-plaiting, the produce being sold to support the school. The girls' schools were better attended than the boys', since their products were more easily saleable! One James McPhail, learning that Pitt supported these schools, pleaded in a letter to Lord Hawkesbury in 1796 for schools of morality to be established also, since

> 'not one in 20 of the lower class attends public worship – but instead we too often find many of them on the Sabbath day frequenting the ale-house etc., pilfering from the fences, hedges, turnip fields, etc. A great many of your Lordships' turnips were stolen last year and I find it a difficult task this year to prevent them from a like disaster.'[1]

But as the demand for industrial hands accelerated, parents preferred to send their children to work in mine and factory. For these children there was one day free – Sunday – on which they created such 'hell' that Robert Raikes opened his first Sunday School in 1780 with the declared intention of 'preventing their growth into habitual criminals by bringing them under Christian influence'. Many Sunday Schools provided secular instruction. Kay-Shuttleworth said of them,

> 'the idea of education for the poor sprang from a religious impulse. . . . It regarded the school as a nursery of the Church and congregation and confided its management to the chief Communicants, to the deacons, elders and class teachers. Thus the Sunday School became the type of the daily school.'[4]

There were also the Ragged Schools for the really destitute and, for parents who could afford a few pence a week, there were the private schools. Teachers eked out a living with cobbling or some other trade, a number being ex-soldiers, who, since no Army pensions were paid in those days, turned to teaching for a livelihood. By far the greater number were Dame Schools, conducted by women nearly as ignorant as the children they taught.

> 'None are too old, too poor, too ignorant, too feeble, too sickly, too unqualified to regard themselves, and to be regarded by others, as unfit for school-keeping. There are few, if any, occupations regarded as incompatible with school-keeping – unemployed domestics, discharged barmaids, vendors of toys or lollipops, keepers of small eating or lodging-houses, needle women who take in plain or slop work, milliners, advanced consumptives, cripples almost bed-ridden, persons of doubtful temperance, outdoor paupers, persons who spell badly (mostly women, I grieve to say), who can scarcely write and who cannot cipher at all.'[5]

Not all private schools were inefficient but the majority were little more than child-minding establishments. On a higher level were the private academies, offering groups of studies leading to the professions and to careers in the Army or Navy.

Voluntary Societies. The main sources of schools were the two big religious organisations – the National Society, founded in 1811, and the British and Foreign School Society (1812), the former supporting the Church of England and the latter the Nonconformists. The Nonconformists resented the claims of the Church to control education, but both agreed that religion was an essential part of it.

'The National Society, supported by the established Church, contend that the Schoolmaster should be invariably a churchman; that the Church Catechism should be taught in the school to all the scholars; that all should be required to attend Church on Sundays, and that the schools should be in every case under the superintendence of the clergyman of the parish.

The British and Foreign School Society, on the other hand, admit Churchmen and Dissenters equally as schoolmasters, require that the Bible should be taught in their schools, but insist that no Catechism should be admitted.' So wrote Lord John Russell to Lord Lansdowne in 1839.[4]

Very few people believed in a purely secular education. The fact that the National Society controlled by far the greatest number of schools did not cause any serious problem in the large towns which possessed schools run by both Societies. In rural districts, however, it was often the case that the parish school was the only one available and Nonconformists objected to sending their children to be taught the doctrines of the Church of England. But such was the popular clamour for educational reform that at last in 1833 a newly-formed House of Commons, elected under the extended franchise of the Reform Act, approved by a vote of 50 against 26 the first State Grant to education, viz. 'That a sum, not exceeding £20,000, be granted to Her Majesty, to be issued in aid of Private Subscriptions for the erection of School Houses for the Education of the Children of the Poorer Classes in Great Britain.'

The money was to be divided between the National Society and the British and Foreign School Society. Half the estimated cost of building a school had to be raised by voluntary subscriptions before any of the State's money would be given to either Society. Preference was given to applications from large towns and cities.

Bell and Lancaster. Two major problems faced the two societies. They had to make the best use of the few teachers available and at the same time to find the most economical method of organising and maintaining a school. They both found the answer in the schemes advocated by Andrew Bell and Joseph Lancaster who, working independently, evolved a similar system, popularly known as the 'monitorial system'. The teaching methods used in the National Schools followed Bell's ideas, while the British and Foreign Schools used those advocated by Lancaster.

Lancaster,[6] the son of an old soldier, was led by his natural love of teaching to adopt the calling of an usher. Longing to own a school of his own he established in 1801 a school in Borough Road. Always in financial difficulties, he capitalised upon the idea of making use of older children to teach the younger. He explained his system in his book *Improvements in Education* (1803).

'My school is attended by 300 scholars. The whole system of tuition is almost entirely conducted by boys. . . . The school is divided into classes, to each of these a lad is appointed as monitor: he is responsible for the morals, improvement, good order, and cleanliness of the whole class. It is his duty to make a daily, weekly, and monthly report of progress, specifying the number of lessons performed, boys present, absent etc., etc. As we naturally expect the boys who teach the other boys to read to leave school when their education is complete, and do not wish that they should neglect their own improvements in other studies, they are instructed to train other lads as assistants, who, in future, may supply their place. To be a monitor is coveted by the whole school, it being an office at once honourable and productive of emolument.'[6]

Bell was in many ways the exact opposite of Lancaster. Life as a clergyman in the Episcopal Church of Scotland did not offer sufficient outlet for his ambitions and he went to India to seek his fortune. Within a short space of time he collected a number of regimental chaplaincies and was appointed Superintendent of the Military Male Asylum in Madras – a school for the orphan sons of soldiers. In Madras he came across a native teacher who made use of sand for teaching his children writing. His attempt to introduce this into the Asylum was resisted by his assistants. He therefore selected an 8-year-old boy to teach the class. The experiment was successful and Bell developed his system in 1791–92, some years before Lancaster adopted his monitorial idea. He returned to England a comparatively wealthy man and published an account of his work in Madras in 1791 under the title of 'An Experiment in Education'. Bell and Lancaster exchanged ideas. Mrs Trimmer, resenting the success of Lancaster whose schools were undenominational, published a pamphlet in which she stated that Bell had originated the monitorial system and Lancaster had copied it. Although unimportant in itself, the quarrel was the beginning of a bitter struggle between the two parties which was so disastrous in later years to the cause of national education.

The truth was that both developed their systems independently. Lancaster, at least, had no doubt about this and, in his 'Improvements in Education', generously admitted the debt he owed to Bell.

'I ought not to close my account, without acknowledging the obligation I lie under to Dr Bell of the Male Asylum at Madras, who so nobly gave up his time and liberal salary, that he might perfect that Institution which flourished greatly under his fostering care. He published a tract, in 1798, entitled, "An Experiment of Education, made at the Male Asylum at Madras, suggesting a System whereby a School or Family may teach itself, under the Superintendence of the Master, or Parent".... From this publication I have adopted several useful hints. I much regret that I was not acquainted with the beauty of his system, till somewhat advanced in my plan; if I had known it, it would have saved me much trouble, and some retrograde movements....'

The schools of Lancaster and Bell had many points in common. Both used monitors. Lancaster boasted that one of his masters could teach 1000 pupils, whilst Bell went one better, maintaining that under his system one master could conduct ten schools of 1000 pupils, if the premises were close together. Both systems achieved great popularity because of their cheapness. Expenditure on books was unnecessary. Bell's system was more flexible than Lancaster's. There were fewer monitors and larger classes. The desks were placed near to the walls leaving the centre free for monitorial groups. (See 5.) This was marked out in hollow squares for the classes. In both systems the monitors were pupils drawn from the upper classes of the schools, who received the lesson they had to teach from the master and then passed it on to the pupils. Both systems appealed to the spirit of emulation. The Head Monitor or Inspector examined the classes at regular intervals and promoted those who were efficient to the next class. Lancaster believed in the salutory effect of public disgrace but for cases of serious misbehaviour ingenious forms of punishment were given, e.g. a heavy log was worn round the shoulders as a pillory, or a boy's legs were shackled to keep him from wandering. Sometimes a pupil was put into a cage which would be suspended by a rope from a beam in the roof. Bell, despite the almost universal belief in the efficacy of corporal punishment, instituted a jury system, by which the form of punishment was decided by the boys themselves – confinement in school or expulsion, but the use of the cane was forbidden.

Whatever the criticisms of the monitorial system for its cheapness, the narrowness of its curriculum and its mechanical methods. it represented a sincere attempt to provide through voluntary effort mass education for the children of the poorer classes. It proved, too, that the task was beyond the capacity of the philanthropic societies, unless substantial help from the State was forthcoming.[3] What is of particular interest in the story of Army children's education is that Bell, having tried out his system on soldiers' children in Madras, now introduced his system to England at the Royal Military Asylum, Chelsea, where his methods were so successful that they were subsequently developed in the Army's schools overseas and in the English educational system at large.

REFERENCES

1. Aspinall & Smith, *English Historical Documents*, Vol. XI, Eyre and Spottiswoode.
2. To give parish vestries or magistrates power to raise money for parish schools, which would give two years' free education to children whose parents could not afford to pay fees. The Bill was rejected in the House of Lords. Hansard 1807.
3. *An Introductory History of English Education Since 1800*, Curtis and Boultwood.
4. Dawson and Wall, *Society and Industry in the 19th Century (Education)*, OUP.
5. Report of the Newcastle Commission 1861.
6. Salmon, *The Practical Parts of Lancaster's 'Improvements' and Bell's Experiment*, CUP, 1932.

CHAPTER 3

Dr Andrew Bell and the

Army's Monitorial System

Bell and the Army Schools. The Duke of York, having obtained authority to establish regimental schools, whose objects would be to 'implant in the children's minds early habits of Morality, Obedience and Industry and to give them that portion of learning which may qualify them for Non-Commissioned Officers',[1] and having instructed Commanding Officers to select 'a person properly qualified for the situation of Serjeant-Schoolmaster', had to provide a method of training them. He had also to issue his promised instructions as to the system of education to be adopted in the regimental school. This he did through the General Order issued on 1 January 1812.

The Commander-in-Chief first asked Commanding Officers to take the regimental schools under their constant personal care and attention, since the schools, with proper guidance and management, would be of great benefit not only to the children themselves, but to the Army and to the nation in general. He continued:

'It is extremely essential that children's minds should be impressed with early habits of order, regularity, and discipline, derived from a well-grounded respect and veneration for the Established Religion of the Country. With this view, the Commander-in-Chief directs, that the Regimental Schools shall be conducted on Military principles; and that, as far as circumstances will permit, their establishment shall be assimilated to that of a Regiment, and formed on a system invented by the Rev Dr Bell, which has been adopted with the most complete success at the Royal Military Asylum.

'His Royal Highness has directed, that extracts shall be made from Dr Bell's "Instructions for Conducting a School, through the Agency of the Scholars themselves", which, having received Dr Bell's approbation, are subjoined, as the best directions His Royal Highness can give for the conduct of the Regimental Schools of the British Army.

'It is necessary to observe, that, although, in the Instructions, Boys only are mentioned, yet the Female Children of the Soldiery are also intended to partake of the benefits of this system of education, wherever the accommodation, and other circumstances, will permit.'[2]

The 'subjoined extracts' to this letter set out Dr Bell's monitorial system and the following examples show its military application.

'Doctor Bell's system rests on the simple principles of Tuition by the Scholars themselves: the boys teach one another, however numerous they may be, under the superintendence of one Master.

'It is a great advantage of this system, that, by economizing time, it allows an opportunity of establishing a drill, implanting in children's minds an early predilection for the profession of their fathers, which, it may be presumed, the generality of them will adopt, when arrived at an age to make their option.

'The first object is to model the school, by arranging it into classes, or companies. As many boys as appear to have made the same progress, or nearly so, are to be placed in the same class; the fewer classes, the better.

'Each class or company is to have a Serjeant Teacher, being one of the boys; and, if numerous, a Corporal, or assistant teacher, being also one of the boys; chosen from a higher class, or from the head of his own. The rest of the class is to be paired off into Tutors and Pupils; the best or most trusty boy takes the worst, the next best, the next worst; and so on.

'The business of the teacher is to instruct and help the tutors in learning their lessons, and teaching their pupils; to prevent idleness among the class, while learning their lessons; and to hear them, when ready.

'When a boy has held a high rank in his class for some time, the master should make him an Assistant Teacher, or advance him to a superior class, where he is placed at the foot; and if, in a few days, he rise near the middle, he continues in the new class; if not, he must go back into his old class. Also a boy, who fails, for some time, in saying his daily lessons well, is to be degraded to an inferior class.

'The master or teacher should never set a lesson or task, which can require more than a quarter of an hour in the lower classes, and half an hour in the higher for the learner to be completely master of it, and to say it well. The scholars, having said one lesson well, immediately read over the next, and are required to tell, which are the hardest words, before going to their seats to learn it – the teacher proportioning its length to its difficulty. Hard words, and words which have not occurred before, are to be particularly attended to, and first learnt; and, after a while, only these will require to be learnt; as the great bulk of the lesson will be already familiar.

'When the lesson has been thus prepared or learnt, it is said by the scholars in portions, to the teacher, who names the boy who shall begin, the rest following in turn: and if well said, they proceed to the next lesson; if not, they must repeat the same lesson (even shortened, if need be) till it be well learnt. The rule of the school is – short, easy, frequent, and perfect lessons.'[2]

Training at Chelsea. Bell had introduced this system into the Royal Military Asylum, Chelsea, and, therefore, it was to this school that the Adjutant-General directed that prospective teachers should go for training.[3] Arrangements were made to billet the serjeants in taverns nearby and by 6 February 1812 the first course had finished its training. The Commandant of the Royal Military Asylum sent the following report.

To: Lt.General Calvert,*
    Adjutant-General.   6th February 1812

'I have the honour to transmit to you the following list of Serjeant Schoolmasters who have attended at the Royal Military Asylum for some time past for the purpose of receiving information explanatory of the mode adopted at this Institution on instructing children according to Dr Bell's system; and who are now reported by the Doctor sufficient enough to join their respective Corps. . . .

'I beg leave to report to you that the above 22 Sjts. during their attendance at this Asylum have conducted themselves orderly and in a soldier-like manner.'[4]

The first two courses produced eighty-seven serjeant-schoolmasters, who were reported upon by Dr Bell himself. Others followed, each lasting about four weeks and practically every regiment in the country was represented. Students came from such varied units as the Royal Horse Guards, the Royal Wagon Train, Foot and Dragoon Guards and from thirty different regiments of Foot, and from stations as far apart as Waterford, Oxford and Inverness. Nearly all of those nominated were Serjeants, though the lists included three private soldiers and two corporals.[5] Doctor Bell's reports must have been brief and to the point, for the Commandant in his letters to the Horse Guards on the conclusion of each course followed the nominal role with the plain statement: 'I have the honour to acquaint you that the Sjts. are reported by Doctor Bell sufficiently acquainted with his system of education and capable of conducting their regimental schools.'[4]

Following the fifth course, which ended on 2 July 1812, a further thirty-two Serjeants were trained. Reports show that students were

---

*Sir Harry Calvert was a Commissioner of the Asylum from 1801 to his death in 1826. The School's Minute Books show he seldom missed one of the Board's monthly meetings.

now under the direct control of the Chaplain Headmaster and that Dr Bell was no longer personally supervising the instructor training, as he had done initially. From 1814 onwards only an occasional student was sent to the Asylum for teacher training and there were no more large courses, until the formation of the Corps or Army Schoolmasters in 1846.[5] Since these serjeant-schoolmasters were members of the regiment, wearing its uniform and subject to its regulations, it depended on the will of their Commanding Officers whether or not they received any training. Their quality varied considerably, the school having frequently to compete for the more talented with the more insistent claims of the orderly room or of the paymaster.

The responsibilities and duties, for which these Serjeant-Schoolmasters were trained, were set out in Bell's Instructions:

'The Serjeant-Schoolmaster has the immediate care, management, and direction, of the whole school; gives life and motion to every member of it; and is occupied wherever there is most occasion for his services, and where they will best tell. He is to encourage the diffident, the timid, and the backward; to check and repress the forward and presumptuous: to bestow just and ample commendation upon the diligent, attentive, and orderly, however dull their capacity, or slow their progress; to regulate the ambitious, rouse the indolent, and make the idle bestir themselves; in short, to deal out praise and displeasure, encouragement and threatening, according to the temper, disposition, and genious of the scholar. He is occasionally to hear and instruct the classes himself: and still oftener, to attend to and direct the teachers, while hearing their respective classes.'

Reading, writing and arithmetic formed the curriculum, reinforced with morality and religion. The alphabet was to be taught by tracing individual letters in sand, first with a copy and then without: progress was to be rewarded by the issue of a personal slate. Spelling of words of one syllable followed, then punctuation, and so by drill and repetition the pupil progressed to longer words, until he was reading the whole book. Another advantage of this method, according to Bell, was that the first principles of Moral and Religious Instruction were equally capable of being taught in this way.

'As the Alphabet is taught letter by letter, and the Addition and Multiplication tables are learnt column by column, so the same division of labour, by short, easy and frequent lessons, and the same perfect knowledge of every lesson, are to be observed and required in this most important branch of instruction.'

Bell's final instructions to all concerned with the direction of the school were to watch over the moral and religious conduct of the children and to protect them from 'the vices to which their condition is peculiarly liable'.

In order to teach his system at the Asylum and to form new schools overseas, Bell used the senior boys, who had been trained as Assistant Teachers and designated Corporal, as models. For example, John Duckett and Patrick Doyle, aged 12 or 13, were 'approved by the Asylum Committee on 8 October 1811, to go to Portugal (undoubtedly Wellington's school at Belem near Lisbon) to assist in forming a school of the soldiers' children on Dr Bell's principles.'[4] Thomas Allcock and James McLeod were sent in September 1815 to Gibraltar to superintend a school upon the Madras system,[5] while a letter dated 18 February 1817 requested authority for "two boys to go to Canada for the purpose of assisting in the regimental schools in that Colony'.[6]

Requests for such boy Assistant Teachers to help civil schools were also received and accepted. For instance, Dr Bell took an Asylum boy named Thomas King to Sunderland, at the request of the Bishop of Durham that

'a boy should be spared from the Institution, to accompany the Reverend Dr Bell, who is going into the county of Durham, for the purpose of introducing his system of instruction, (which has been adopted with so much effect in the Royal Military Asylum) into two large schools forming in the populous parishes of Sunderland.'[7]

Thomas Bunny was sent to Northamptonshire at the request of Lord Spencer and did so well that he later went to the parish of Lutterworth in Leicestershire to do the same task.[8]

Thus the success of Bell's teacher training methods at the Military Asylum, Chelsea, began to be noised abroad, just as his methods had already been acclaimed at home. The National Society, impressed by this success, asked for his assistance in training their schoolmasters, as the following extract from the Minute Book of the National Society's School Committee shows.

'At their first meeting in 1812 the General Committee invited Dr Bell to advise the Committee on the best way of training Masters. He attended on 22 January 1812, and was empowered to engage suitable persons for training. Training arrangements were made in the Society's schools at Lambeth, Marylebone and Gowers Walk and the corresponding Committee were to advertise for people desirous of engaging themselves for the purpose of being trained to act as schoolmasters upon the Madras system.'[9]

But not everyone praised his methods. Some considered they tended to lower still further the teacher's social position

'by requiring little else of him than an aptitude for enforcing discipline, an acquaintance with mechanical details for the preservation of order, and that sort of ascendancy in his school which a sergeant-major is required to exercise over a batch of raw recruits before they can pass muster on parade.'[10]

At least, they were the first attempts to grapple with the country's shortage of teachers, without whom popular education could not have spread. His monitors may have been 'instructors, but never educators',[11] but the standard of training provided at Chelsea for these serjeant-schoolmasters was on a higher level than was prevalent among schoolmasters in general in England at the time.

One reason for the low standard of the country's schoolmasters was their poor salaries. Whatever little money was available to the religious societies was needed more for the construction of schools and for teacher training. 'The wages of one who is fit to teach the children of the poor fall below those paid to the humble mechanic'[12] and attracted chiefly those semi-skilled craftsmen, shopkeepers, clerks or superior domestic servants who had tried other trades and saw in teaching a second best.[13] But the sheer difficulty, experienced by this first generation of teachers, of bringing discipline, morality and learning to the children of the poor, and their low professional status were hardly likely to keep them in the schools, once recruited and trained. 'The elementary schoolmaster is thought very little of; in fact, so much despised, that men of respectable attainments will not undertake the office of schoolmaster.'[12] This question of status would also face the Army schoolmaster – but that was a problem for the future.

Meanwhile, momentous events were taking place at the Royal Military Asylum, Chelsea, whose local inhabitants were roused from their Sunday morning slumbers by the sound of drums beating an alarm. *The Times*, in its edition of 1 April 1816, explained why.

'We are sorry to learn that at five o'clock yesterday morning the schoolroom of the Royal Military Asylum at Chelsea was discovered to be on fire: providentially, both as regards time and place, the part of the building where the flames broke out was not near the apartments occupied as sleeping rooms, and it was so near morning that immediate assistance was afforded by the active exertions of

1. *Frederick, Duke of York and Albany (1763–1827).*
   Commander-in-Chief, 1798.

2. *Contemporary view of Tangier Harbour and Upper Castles by Wenceslaus Hollar.*

3. *Site of first Army children's school, 1675. Tangier. Army barracks in centre.*

Prospect of ye Innerpart of Tangier, with the upper Castle, from South-East.

1. The Governours House.
2. Peterborow Tower.
5. Head Court of Church.

4. The Market place.

4. *Dr Andrew Bell (1753–1832).*

5. *Bell's Monitorial System – Royal Military Asylum, Chelsea, 1810.*

7.   *Army Schoolmaster, First Class, 1854.*

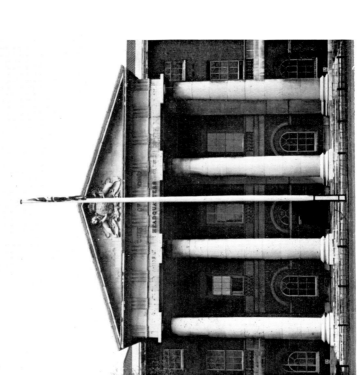

6.   *Royal Military Asylum, Chelsea, as it is today.*

8. *RMA, Chelsea, 1900. Note teaching gallery above.*

9. Uniforms of boys and girls of RMA, Chelsea, 1813.

10. RMA, Chelsea, 1805.

the little objects of this noble charity, who to the number of several hundreds were employed in procuring water; and by the speedy arrival of engines from town, by ten o'clock in the morning the fire was extinguished, but not until a considerable portion of the interior of the southern extremity of the main edifice was consumed from the dining hall to the roof.'

The same newspaper reported another interesting event on 22 February 1823. The school had pioneered and introduced into its curriculum a system of physical education under a Frenchman, Monsieur Clias, which aroused considerable interest, since Gymnastics and Physical Training did not form part of the Army's Training Scheme for Soldiers until 1861, nor organised physical exercises a part of the curriculum of most civil schools until 1890.*

'We looked into the School of the Military Asylum on Tuesday morning to observe a course tuition, which lately has been introduced there. It was a matter of considerable disadvantage to our troops during the late war that, being chiefly enlisted at full age from among the manufacturing classes, they lacked (for a time) that alacrity of body, which would have been inherent to men bred to more active employment. Weavers and shoemakers must be converted into soldiers and they cannot immediately have either the strength or alertness of gamekeepers. Where there is leisure to attend to such considerations there can be no question about the expediency of encouraging such bodily exercises, as by rendering our soldiers more vigorous shall make them more formidable in the field. The superiority of our cavalry in appearance and deportment to our infantry is obvious; and it can only be ascribed to the more active discipline of the riding school. We are glad, therefore, to see something in the shape of gymnastic exercises going on among the incipient warriors of the Military Asylum, and we should be glad to learn that the principle is carried into our military depots generally.'

In 1825 the Military Asylum was honoured in another way, when King George IV gave the School the distinction of carrying Colours, similar to those borne by Infantry regiments, and presented it with the Colours which were to be carried by the boys for the next seventy-two years and which today proudly hang in their chapel at Dover.

But perhaps the most momentous event for the School was the death of its founder, Frederick, Duke of York, on 5 January 1827. On 19 January one thousand boys from the School, in undress military uniform, were admitted into St James's Palace, where his

---

* The Educational Code of 1871 recognised military drill (frequently taught by a military serjeant) varied by Indian club and dumb-bell exercises.

body lay in state, at 10 o'clock in the morning before the doors were opened to the public, preceded by their band, the drums muffled with black cloth, and followed by their thirty-six nurses, in uniform, straw hats and red gowns, to pay their last respects to their benefactor, who had been a frequent visitor to their school and chapel. A few months before his death he had paid his last visit, when the children crowded round him and gave him three hearty cheers. The Duke was much moved and, putting his hand on the head of the foremost boy, exclaimed with tears in his eyes, 'God bless you, my lads!'

REFERENCES

1. War Office Library. General Order and Circular Letter Collection, 1811–1833, Folio 592, Letter dated 14 November 1811.
2. War Office Library. General Order 216 of 1 January 1812. Dr Bell's Instructions are attached.
3. War Office Library. General Order and Circular Letter Collection, 1807–1812, Folio 605. Letter dated 28 December 1811, addressed to 31 different regiments.
4. Royal Military Asylum (DYRMS), Commandant's Letter Books, 1805–1818.
5. Bowyer-Bower, 'Army Education 18th and 19th Centuries'. Degree Thesis. Nottingham University.
6. The Bill for expenses came to £39. 17. 0. Letter addressed to William Merry, Deputy Secretary at War.
7. Minutes of Commissioners' Meeting, 30 March 1808.
8. Minutes of Commissioners' Meeting, 24 December 1808.
9. Minutes of School Committee, Vol. I, p. 2.
10. Educational Expositor, March 1853.
11. R. W. Rich, 'The Training of Teachers in England and Wales during the 19th Century'.
12. British Parliamentary Papers, 1845. XXV, Minutes 1843–44. Quoted by Tropp, *The School Teachers*, Heinemann.
13. BPP 1841. XXXIII, Minutes 1842 (Inspectorate Reports).

CHAPTER 4

Clerical Influence in
Army Children's Schools

Army Chaplains and the Schools. The Order of 1 January 1812, which established the Army children's schools and issued Bell's system of teaching for world-wide adoption in them, also required the Army's chaplains to lend their active support.

> 'The Commander-in-Chief considers it peculiarly incumbent on the Chaplains, and other clergymen engaged in the Clerical Duties of the Army, to give their aid and assistance to the Military Officers in promoting the success of these Institutions, by frequently visiting the Regimental Schools of their Divisions and Garrisons; by diligently scrutinising the conduct of the Serjeant Schoolmasters; examining the progress and general behaviour of the children; and reporting the result of their observations to the Commanding Officer of the Regiment.'

Bell, himself a Churchman, in his Instructions considered it was 'highly desirable that an examination of the school should take place weekly, by the Commanding or other Superintendent Officer of the Regiment or the Chaplain of the Division, Garrison or Regiment.' Since it was also the view of the Establishment that children's education in England should be controlled by the Church and largely consist of its teachings, it is not surprising that the Army should also put the education of its children under its Chaplain's Department and that the school curriculum should be based on religion. Lord Brougham expressed the view that 'a parson was a Clerical Schoolmaster': Bell and the Army Chaplain's Department echoed this concept during the next forty years.

The chaplains had a greater influence on Army education during this period because they were the only source through which 'Approved Books' could reach the soldier and his children.[1] The

35

Duke of York, otherwise most liberally minded, was not so where the supply of reading matter to the troops was concerned. He and the country at large feared the spread of the doctrines of the French Revolution into the Army, which might be needed to protect property and its owners, whose interests appeared to be threatened by the rising tide of Chartist discontent and political agitation. Secular libraries for troops, which included books for children, were not officially sanctioned until 1840,[2] when libraries and reading rooms were authorised for the Army at each of the principal barracks throughout the United Kingdom and the Colonies 'to encourage the soldiery, to employ their leisure hours in a manner that shall combine amusement with the attainment of useful knowledge, and teach them the value of sober, regular and moral habits'.

In 1840 the Adjutant of the Royal Military Asylum was complaining to one Thomas Holt about quite a different matter:

'I am directed by Colonel Brown, Commandant, to acquaint you that from an advertisement which appeared in the "Times" newspaper, saying the boys of the Royal Military Asylum are to be reviewed by Tom Thumb at the Juvenile Fete at Vauxhall Gardens on Tuesday next the 23rd inst, and that as such an announcement has been inserted without authority or permission, and would be viewed as bringing the Boys into ridicule and burlesque, and has been an abuse of the permission which was granted to the application for their attendance, they cannot under such circumstances be permitted to be present.'[3] (Vauxhall Gardens had been a fashionable resort from the reign of Charles II. Dr Johnson described it as 'that excellent place of amusement, there being a mixture of curious show, gay exhibition, vocal and instrumental music not too refined for the general ear, for which only a shilling is charged – and last, though not least, good eating and drinking.' It was also noted for its walks, so intricate that even the most experienced mammas could get lost while looking for their daughters. The Gardens were demolished in 1859.)

A report about the same date (1845) disclosed that all was not well at the Royal Hibernian School, Dublin. The military staff were not qualified to instruct the boys, the books were unsuitable, classes too large, and arithmetic, English grammar and geography were omitted from the curriculum. As a result of this Report, Mr Henry Gibbons was appointed Headmaster, to be for 46 years the revered head of generations of Hibernians, and to be a legend to their successors.[4] It was during his headship that the girls left for the Drummond School at Chapelizod, but not before some had sailed from Dublin to take up jobs in Australia as domestic servants. Nineteen such immigrants, aged 14 to 19, listed as Female Orphans, arrived on 14 May 1849 on the *Pemberton* – all able to read and write, except four who could read only. It is interesting to speculate how much the descendants of Jane Anderson, Mary Burton, Ann Gordon, Marianne Ryan and Mary White, etc., owe to the literacy of such girls as these, rare in England, probably non-existent among women in the Colonies at that time![5]

Meanwhile, Gibraltar was laying the foundations of a pattern of Army schools which would flourish for over 100 years. In 1843 there were six regimental schools, belonging to the 1st of Foot (Royal Scots),* 7th (Royal Fusiliers), 38th (South Staffordshire Regiment), 48th (Northamptonshire Regiment) and 79th of Foot (Cameron Highlanders) and the Royal Artillery, each under its own regimental schoolmaster and assistants. By 1910 the number would increase to ten and bear names familiar to present-day education officers. There were infant schools at Castle Road (later Line Wall Military School), Buena Vista, Europa and Casemates and one in South Barracks for the infantry and another for the REs. The elder children went to schools at Castle Road (the present St George's School), Casemates (moved in 1903 to Montague Bastion), Buena Vista and Europa, both demolished in 1969 to make way for the Army's new Europa Point Primary School.

So far the story of Army children's education has been one of voluntary provision, through the foresight and generosity of regimental officers, leading in 1811 to the official recognition of schools; to the training of regimental personnel as schoolmaster serjeants in 1812; to the introduction of a world-wide system of teaching and of an educational curriculum in the basic subjects, on lines laid down by Dr Bell; and to the establishment of library facilities, including books for children, in 1840. Regimental schools were now to be found wherever the Army had its stations, established and controlled by the Regimental Commanding Officer. The death in 1827 of the Duke of York, the Commander-in-Chief, of his Adjutant-General, General Sir Harry Calvert, the previous year, and of Doctor Andrew Bell in 1832, marked the end of an era. Together they had achieved much. The next decade would see the schools pass from regimental control to inspectors of education, representing the military authorities, and the formation of a professional Corps of Schoolmasters. The man who would shape this generation of

* Numbers changed to Regimental names in 1881.

schools would be the Army's Principal Chaplain, the Rev G. R. Gleig.

Rev G. R. Gleig and the RMA Chelsea. In 1844 Gleig became Principal Chaplain to the Forces. At the age of 16 he had been simultaneously an Exhibitioner of Balliol and an Ensign in the 85th Regiment; before he went on half-pay at the age of 20 he had been wounded six times in action. From Oxford he was ordained; financial needs turned him into a professional writer, made him a national figure and brought him in 1834 at the age of 38 the Chaplaincy of the Royal Hospital, Chelsea.[4] In 1844 he became Chaplain-General and continued in this office until 1875. During the period 1846–57 he acted as Inspector-General of Army schools and worked indefatigably to improve the range and quality of Army children's education, supported by such influential Parliamentarians as Sidney Herbert (Secretary at War, 1845–46) and Mr B. Baring, Lord Ashburton (Paymaster-General, 1845–46).

Gleig was soon convinced that the educational standards in the schools needed improvement. He doubted the continued effectiveness of Bell's system. Ten years of first-hand knowledge, while living as Chaplain at the Royal Hospital next door, had convinced him that the Military Asylum, Chelsea, also 'stood in need of a good shaking up'. In the summer of 1846 he met by chance on the deck of a river steam-boat the Paymaster-General, who was one of the Commissioners of the Asylum, and persuaded him to accompany him on the first unannounced visitation that it had known. In his own words this is what he found:

'It was school-hour, yet to and fro numbers of boys were passing along the walks and about the corridors some laden with baskets of coal or carrying filthier utensils, some bearing provisions, some sweeping out the colonnade in front of the building. A large wheel was then used for the purpose of raising water, by the process of the forcing-pump, from certain underground tanks to the top of the house. Three or four unfortunate boys were at work on this wheel, straining beyond their strength and in constant risk, should they lose their hold, of having their limbs broken; while others, in the kitchen, seemed to be kept to the tether by the not very euphonious oratory of the cook, and an occasional box on the ears. Our visitors penetrated through the door-way, and were greeted by sounds of the strangest and most discordant kinds. The harsh voices of men rose occasionally about the hub-bub of children, both being from time to time drowned in the crash of many ill-tuned instruments. Then there would come the sound of a smart blow, followed by a shriek and succeeded by what startled and shrieked as much as either, a brief but profound silence. They mounted the stairs, opened the school-room door, and became witnesses of a scene which neither of them is likely to forget in a hurry. The school-room was a huge hall, measuring perhaps 60 or 80 feet in length by 30 in breadth. Two enormous fireplaces, so constructed as to burn an enormous amount of fuel without diffusing any proportionate amount of heat, testified to the good intentions of the architect. In other respects, the fitting up was meagre enough.

'A single platform, whither, when the writing lesson came on, the children by classes were supposed to repair, occupied about 20 feet in the middle of the room. All the rest were void, except where chairs stood for the accommodation of the masters, and cages for the punishment of the boys. For in addition to the cane, the ser-jeant schoolmasters had at their command four instruments of tor-ture, in the shape of iron cages, each occupying the centre of the room. Observe that these cages were constructed so as to render it impossible for the little prisoners to stand upright: who were re-quired, nevertheless, to turn a heavy handle, and whose diligence, or its opposite, was marked by a process, which, if they did not see it, they never failed to feel.

'Four or five groups of boys were gathered round as many ser-jeant masters, some bawling out sounds which were not words, though they were intended to represent them; some roaring forth arithmetical tables; some repeating the Church Catechism at the top of their voices; some conversing, and all shuffling and struggling amongst themselves. There was no order, no regularity, no atten-tion; indeed the latter would have been impossible, inasmuch as in the heart of the classes was one, more numerous than the rest, which seemed to be taking the lessons on the fiddle. As to the acquirements of these poor lads, their proficiency proved on examination to be such as might be expected. They could not read, they could not write, they could not cypher, they could not spell. They did not know whether Great Britain was an island, or how, if divided from France, the two nations were separated. "We can't help it, sir" said one of the Serjeant Schoolmasters. "We never learned these things ourselves. How can we pretend to teach them?" '

(Edinburgh Review, April 1852)

The sequel to their visit was an official inspection, ordered by the Privy Council, the report of which was startling and incontro-vertible.

'Physically the boys were in good condition, but the teaching stood utterly condemned. The Serjeants were untrained, none of them having any scholarship beyond what was expected of the boys them-selves; of the Serjeant-Major, or Headmaster, it was said that all strictures passed on the staff applied equally to him. The Asylum had adhered to Dr Bell's orders without swerving one hair's breadth. In over 40 years all that had been accumulated in the way of text books were Bibles, Catechisms, Spelling Books, Mrs Markham's "History of England" and a volume entitled "Manners of the Jews".[6]

The necessary reforms did not take long to materialise. On 4 May 1846 a special Board of Commissioners met to consider

'whether it would not be possible with the assistance of the present Military Asylum to bring about a more uniform and efficient course of education, by providing for the periodical inspection of Regimental Schools, and by prescribing some rules to ensure the competency of the teacher previously to his appointment by the Commanding Officer.'[7]

They discussed the desirability of arranging for a 'Model School' and a 'Normal School' or training college of the type established at Battersea by Kay-Shuttleworth some five years earlier. Finally, they sent to the Commander-in-Chief their recommendations for the reorganisation of the RMA Chelsea and of the regimental schools and for an inspector,

'a gentleman of acknowledged ability, conversant with the different systems of education in practice and willing to devote much time and attention to this object.'[8]

They claimed that their recommendations, when carried into effect, would secure 'an extensive and effectual system of education in the Army'. That these claims were fully justified the following pages will show.

Formation of the Corps of Army Schoolmasters and the Normal School, Chelsea. On 22 June 1846 the Commissioners were informed that the Commander-in-Chief, the Duke of Wellington, 'has attentively read the paper sent to him having for its object the improvement of the boys' school at the Royal Military Asylum and the annexation thereto of a training school for the education of schoolmaster serjeants . . . and fully concurs.'[9]

Two Royal Warrants, bearing the signature of Queen Victoria, followed. The first on 2 July 1846 provided the authority for the formation of the Corps of Army Schoolmasters, which was to be responsible for education in the Army until replaced by the Army Educational Corps in 1920. The Warrant read:

'Whereas with the view of improving the system of instruction in the Regimental Schools, we have deemed it expedient to introduce into our Army a class of men better calculated to perform the duties of Schoolmaster in the several Regiments of Cavalry and Infantry. Our Will and Pleasure is that such persons as, after having obtained a Certificate of fitness from the Training School, established by our authority, shall be appointed Schoolmaster Serjeants, shall be allowed the Pay of two shillings and sixpence a day, with an increase of sixpence a day to be granted by Our Secretary at War at his discretion for efficiency and Good Conduct.

'In order to secure an efficient superintendence over the Regimental Schools it is Our Will and Pleasure that an Inspector of Regimental Schools shall be appointed by Our Secretary at War.

'Given at Our Court at Buckingham Palace, this 2nd Day of July, 1846, in the tenth year of Our Reign.'

The second established the Normal School at Chelsea to train these schoolmasters and a Model School for regiments to copy.

'With the view of securing efficient School Masters in our several Regiments of Cavalry and Infantry – Our Will and Pleasure is that there shall be established at our Royal Military Asylum at Chelsea, a Normal School for the instruction of persons to be appointed Schoolmaster Serjeants in our Army, and also a Model School, which shall consist of the Boys maintained in Our said Asylum, and upon which all the Schools in Our Regiments of Cavalry and Infantry shall be formed.

'Given at Our Court at Windsor, this 21st day of November, 1846, in the 10th year of Our Reign.'

A headmaster was to be appointed to the Normal or Training School at an annual salary of £350, with an assistant at £200 to control the Model School. Two other masters were appointed to the Model School with salaries of £200 and £120 respectively and another master for the Infant School at £120 p.a.

Establishment of Army Schoolmistresses. Before continuing the story of Gleig and the training of the Army schoolmaster, another event should be noted, which was to have great importance to primary education in the Army. In 1839, Lt.Col. Somerset took over command of the Cape Mounted Rifle Corps, which had a vacancy for one of its two authorised schoolmasters. In a letter to General Napier, then GOC at the Cape, he requested, instead of a man to fill the vacancy, a schoolmistress to be sent out to instruct the female children, quoting the good work done by such a woman in his previous unit (evidently officially engaged). He suggested, furthermore, that a schoolmistress should be authorised for each regiment for this purpose. His letter was referred by T. B. Macaulay, the historian (at that time Secretary-at-War) to Lord Hill, the Commander-in-Chief, who replied on 14 January 1840 that he had 'great pleasure in concurring in a measure likely to become in every way beneficial'.

Macaulay lost no time in putting to Parliament the proposal to establish a schoolmistress in each infantry battalion and cavalry regiment to teach 'the female children of the Soldiery' at a cost of about £3500. He rebuked the amused Opposition by reminding them that

> 'perhaps they were not aware, as indeed he himself was not aware until a few weeks ago, that . . . the number of *female* children actually accompanying our regiments was not less than 10,000.* Those children were in the most emphatic manner called "The children of the State". For the public service they were hurried from place to place – from Malta to Gibraltar, from Gibraltar to the West Indies – from the West Indies to Halifax, as the common weal might require. It would, therefore, be inexcusable, if we did not provide these, at a small expense, with some means of instruction.'
>
> (*Hansard*, 9 March 1840)

Having obtained Parliamentary authority, Macaulay drew up the necessary Warrant for Queen Victoria's signature:

> 'Whereas Our Forces in every part of the World are accompanied by many Female Children of Our Soldiers and Whereas such Female Children, being, in consequence of the exigencies of Our Service, subject to peculiar disadvantages, are therefore peculiarly entitled to Our Royal Care and Benevolence, and Whereas no adequate means have yet been provided for bringing up such Female Children to be useful and respectable Members of Society; and Whereas it hath appeared to Us that the defect can be supplied only by means of Female tuition; Our Will and Pleasure is, that in every Regiment of Cavalry, and in every Regiment, Battalion and Regimental Depot of Infantry, there shall be a Schoolmistress, qualified to instruct the Female Children of Our Soldiers as well in reading, writing and the rudiments of arithmetic, as in needlework and other parts of housewifery, and to train them in habits of diligence, honesty and piety.
>
> 'And in order to provide for the remuneration of such Schoolmistresses, We are pleased to grant an allowance of £20 per Annum for each Regiment of Cavalry, and after the rate of £3 per Annum for each Company of Infantry in Our Service: and We are also pleased to grant £5 to every Regiment of Cavalry and to every Regiment or Battalion of Infantry, in Our Service, for the expenses attending the first formation of the Regimental Female Schools.
>
> 'Given at Our Court of Windsor, this 29th day of October, 1840, in the 4th Year of Our Reign.
>
> 'BY HER MAJESTY'S COMMAND T. B. MACAULAY'

* There were 213 of them in the Cape Mounted Rifle Corps alone.

It is interesting to note that the Corps of Queen's Army School-mistresses thus originated from a Commanding Officer's concern for the children of his regiment – even though the majority of them were Hottentot!

Inspection and Training of Army Schoolmasters. The Commissioners' recommendations for the staffing and inspection of Army schools, fully supported by Wellington, could now be implemented. Gleig was appointed on 2 July 1846 the first Inspector-General of Military Schools, in addition to his duties as Chaplain-General. His letter of appointment instructed him to select candidates for appointment as schoolmasters and assistants; to examine and certify them; to recommend to the Secretary-at-War a general system of education and the necessary books to be adopted in regimental and depot schools and where new schools should be built, enlarged or adapted; and to have a general supervision over the barrack and regimental libraries.

To obtain candidates for training as Army schoolmasters Gleig inserted a notice in *The Observer*, outlining the conditions under which 30 unmarried men between the ages of 19 and 25 could be accepted at the Royal Military Asylum, Chelsea. They were required to be 'of irreproachable moral character, good constitutions and not under the standard of military height. The literary qualifications of candidates are – that they shall read fluently, write good hands, be conversant with the principles and practice of arithmetic, be well grounded in sacred and profane history, and have received in other respects a plain but liberal education.'

The applicants, who underwent a rigorous competitive examination lasting several days, were, according to Gleig, well-connected sons of clergymen, surgeons, Army officers and such like, or as the Press put it, 'the parents of some of the applicants had moved in the superior ranks of life'. If successful they would receive their keep but no pay during their two years' training and no pension at the end of ten years of service in the Army. They had also to find a £50 bond to ensure their good behaviour and eventual enlistment into the Army.

The Normal School opened in March 1847 with 24 civilian students. Some had been former teachers, others clerks and tradesmen: one was a partly qualified surgeon and one a 'maker of philosophical instruments'. One withdrew during the course to join the East India Company, and one to take up a commission, which his father had purchased for him.[4] Only 13 completed the second year. Five had proved unsatisfactory, as the register showed:

'Clerk to Warehousemen in London City – dismissed 1847 for drunkenness.'

'Clerk in Stores, London – dismissed for being slovenly, sullen and smoking.'

These were replaced by corporals of two years' service in the Army. The Duke of Cambridge made no secret that he preferred these men, as being more amenable to discipline. But not many were able to pass the examination and others were deterred by having to lose all previous service for pension on becoming a 'student'. But it was in this way that the system of double entry began from civilian or military life, which continued as an essential feature in the recruitment of Army schoolmasters.

The remainder of the students were youths of 16 years of age, recruited either from the Asylum, Chelsea, or from the grammar schools, who were given a two-year preliminary course before they began their real training. James Thomson, the poet, was an example of this class of student. He entered the Asylum in 1850 at the age of 16 and was first appointed in 1854 as an Army schoolmaster at Ballincollig, near Cork.

The register of the first year's candidates shows that, on entry, they had little knowledge of geometry and algebra, but more acquaintance with the other subjects required – English Literature, Religious Knowledge, English and Ancient History, Geography and Arithmetic. Those who presented themselves were thus older and more experienced than those who had entered, in February 1840, the Battersea Training College, organised by Kay-Shuttleworth and Carlton Tufnell. The students on Battersea's first course were pupil-teachers, aged 13, from the Poor Law Schools at Norwood, indentured as apprentices for seven years and destined to teach in schools of industry for pauper children. The minimum age was raised a few years later to 18 for entrance to a course of two years.

Kay-Shuttleworth's students at Battersea were subjected to a modest, realistic curriculum and to an austere regime, so that they would be attuned to the actual conditions they would find in their schools amongst the poorest section of the population. But the Rev Derwent Coleridge* at St Marks thought the better the schoolmaster was bred, the more highly trained, the more socially

* Son of the poet and the first principal of St Mark's College, Chelsea.

respected, the more ready he would be 'to combat the difficulties, to submit to the monotony and to move with quiet dignity in the humbleness of his vocation'.[10] Admitted at the age of 15 for a 3 year course, his students, too, had to become practically acquainted with the conditions of the poor among whom they would have to labour and followed a daily schedule of 8 hours' study, $3\frac{3}{4}$ hours of work in the garden or on the farm and were allowed only 30 minutes for leisure.

Gleig visited both the Battersea and St Mark's Training Colleges in 1844 and it is probable that what he saw there influenced the training scheme he devised two years later for the Army's Normal School at Chelsea. The Army schoolmasters needed a liberal background, because their future duties would include not only teaching children but also providing for soldiers and NCOs the basic subjects of a sound general education. It is clear from the comprehensive book list (Appendix A), discovered written in pencil on the cover of the Normal School's register, that Gleig did provide this and so helped to free the regimental schools from the limitations of Bell's monitorial system. Gleig was an author himself* and edited for Longmans a cheap and useful library of 45 titles, called 'Gleig's School Primers'. It is hardly surprising that these books were high on the list he officially prescribed for use in Army schools.[11]

In 1849 Gleig issued a set of regulations for the training of schoolmasters at the Normal School, Chelsea (see Appendix B).[12] Before he could practise the art of teaching there, the future schoolmaster had to become proficient in a wide range of academic subjects – English Language, Religious Knowledge, English and Ancient History, Geography, Mathematics, Astronomy, Mechanics, Natural History and Military Fortifications, together with Singing and Drawing. The course, lasting two years, had four terms of six months each. The academic subjects occupied the first three terms and 'learning how to teach' the fourth. The method of instruction was to be oral lectures of one hour each, prepared 'to interest and excite the curiosity of the pupils'. The first half hour of each lecture would recapitulate the previous day's lesson 'by an oral examination of the students' remembrance'. Each lesson was supplemented by prescribed reading, private study and an examination of notebooks.

The students rose in summer at 5.15am, assembled for Roll-call

* Including a well-known *Life of Wellington*.

45

at 6.15am and Drill at 6.30am; 8am Breakfast; 8.45 Prayers; 9–12-noon Study; 12–1pm Recreation; 1–1.45pm Dinner; 2–5pm Study; 5–6pm Gymnastics or Fencing; 6–7pm Recreation; 7pm Supper; 7.30–9.30pm Private Study and Reading; 9.30pm Prayers; 10pm Bed.

The first of the thirteen Army Schoolmasters to complete their training and survive this Spartan programme was Mr Frederick Scrivener. The War Office asked the Duke of Wellington in April 1849 to authorise his posting to the Garrison School at Preston. The letter (see Appendix C) reminded the Duke that certain arrangements had been agreed in 1846 to encourage the recruitment of schoolmasters and to enhance their standing. They were to rank next to the serjeant-major and, although on enlistment they came under military law, they were not to be subject to corporal punishment 'in the very improbable case of gross misconduct'. They were to receive a higher salary than their civilian colleagues, but both were to lack a pension scheme for some years to come. The Corps of Army Schoolmasters would have the additional attractions of foreign travel and a smart officer-type military uniform, which later incurred the wrath of the Duke of Cambridge. 'They consider themselves more like gentlemen than anything else', he complained to the Royal Commission of 1870.[14]

Chapel-Schools. Gleig next turned his attention to the provision of school accommodation. From his tours he had reported that in nearly all barracks the chapel and the school were still the men's original living-rooms, put to new purposes but still unconverted. Despairing of financial support for a new building programme, he submitted a plan for a dual-purpose building, the chapel-school. He took a temporary church building he had seen at St John's Wood as a model, which was being used temporarily by the Guards at a cost of £900, while their permanent church was under construction.[13] He decided the chancel could be cut off by a movable screen, and the nave divided into six classrooms by baize curtains slung on wires, whilst small outbuildings could serve as vestry and school stores.

In one such chapel-school, provided at the Manchester Barracks, a Major Foster of the Royal Engineers reported:

'The West end of the chapel is fitted with desks and drop curtains to separate the boys and girls and to enclose the space to be used for school purposes. The additional fitment required to make the room available for schools as well as for Divine Worship may cost about £30.'[15]

In May 1848 Gleig prepared two detailed memoranda: one for 'an apartment which shall be fitted up as a School Room only' and the second on 'the fitting of a Room which shall serve the double purpose of Chapel and School Room'. These documents received the approval of the Ordnance Office (responsible for planning and building) and the Secretary at War, and were issued for guidance when building in old barracks or constructing new ones. These chapel-schools were still being erected in barracks as late as 1876, and one can still be seen in use as the Garrison Church of the South Staffordshire Regiment at Lichfield (see illustration 15).

Gleig's Achievements. In 1852 Gleig wrote a lengthy article for the *Edinburgh Review* covering his work for military education between 1846–52. Perhaps it gave a somewhat exaggerated account of the deficiencies of Army Education at the end of the Dr Bell era 1830–45, but it showed what he thought of his own achievements during that time, the place of religious instruction in the curriculum, and of other educational problems.

'The British Army is composed of men taken, generally, from the lower orders of society. With few exceptions our recruits are composed of agricultural labourers and operatives out of work; to whom may be added a small sprinkling of tapsters, clerks, scriveners, serving men, and broken down young gentlemen. They come to us from all parts of England, Scotland and Ireland and profess as many forms of Christianity as are to be found in the population of the United Kingdom. After four or five years' service a large proportion of them marry, and their children are of course brought up in the religious opinions of their parents. So that, upon the whole, you could not find gathered together in any one place, a more perfect epitome of religious England, Scotland and Ireland than in a regiment of the line.

'To introduce into the Army an educational system which, without putting in abeyance religious instruction, should yet deal with it in such a manner as to gratify all without offending the prejudices of any, was an undertaking from which timid or bigoted theorists would have shrunk. Yet the men themselves would reject, especially for their children, any system of education which was avowedly divorced from religious instruction. What had been done? That which we are satisfied might be done in every town, district and parish throughout the kingdom.

'The business of the children's school opens every morning in barracks at a quarter before nine o'clock with prayer. This may occupy, perhaps, five minutes, after which the trained master reads to his scholars, collected together, a portion of Scripture, and explains it in its grammatical and historical bearing; deducing from the whole such a lesson in moral and religious truth as it seems to convey. He touches, in so doing, upon no topic of sectarian controversy. He has been trained to speak as the Scriptures speak, without casting about for inferences which lie beneath the surface.

'At the close of the bible lesson the children fall off to their classes. The subjects taught, besides elementary reading are:

Scripture history; England; Colonies; India; Greece, Rome; France; Arithmetic – slate and mental; Geography; Natural History; Object lessons; Grammar, dictation and composition writing; all from Gleig's series.

'Nor does it interfere with, or take the place of, that more dogmatic teaching which Churches and their Ministers have an undoubted right to control. On the contrary, the children trained in regimental schools, under masters qualified morally as well as intellectually to conduct them, are noted for the attention which they pay to the catechising of the minister, whether it takes place on Sunday or any other day in the week. What is there to prevent the adoption of this system, modified of course, in its details, to the acknowledged wants of a nation, composed, like its army, of persons professing many creeds, yet all alike willing to be taught, provided their favourite opinions be dealt with tenderly?'

Gleig, apart from initiating a revised scheme of education in the Army, made changes in its educational organisation and administration. On 19 April 1850 there appeared the first of a long series of education training manuals. It was entitled 'Regulations for the Guidance of Regiments to which a Trained Schoolmaster is appointed by the Secretary at War'.

Some of these regulations were:

1. All schoolmasters had to be trained at the Royal Military Asylum.
2. The appointment was to rank next to that of the Sergeant-Major.
3. The schoolmaster's pay was to be 2s. 6d. a day and beer money, 'with an extra 6d. a day after such a period as the Secretary at War may decide'.
4. When the regiment paraded for inspection, muster, or to attend divine service, he had to take his place at the head of the children wherever they were positioned.
5. Schoolmaster wishing to marry had to apply for permission to the Commanding Officer, who forwarded the application for

the consideration of the Secretary at War, accompanied by his opinion of the character and responsibility of the person, whom the schoolmaster was desirous of marrying.

6. Assistant schoolmasters were to be appointed to help the schoolmaster, when the numbers on the school roll warranted it.

These regulations were amended in 1852 and required applicants for admission to the Royal Military Asylum to be full corporals and unmarried. In June 1854, schoolmasters were no longer to be regarded as garrison, regimental or assistant schoolmasters, but were to be divided into four classes, the fourth class being assistant schoolmasters. Beer money was stopped and instead of the usual colourful uniform, which 'resembled too much the undress uniform of a commanding officer', a plainer one, a blue-frock coat, was provided 'more in accordance with the military rank of the Schoolmaster'. (See illustration 7.)

A Royal Warrant of 30 March 1850 brought into existence two new types of children's schools. These were: Infant Schools, 'of which the Schoolmistress shall have sole charge', where both sexes were to be instructed in reading and writing, until they were sufficiently advanced to receive instruction under the trained schoolmaster or his assistant; and Industrial Schools under the schoolmistress, where the girls were to be instructed in knitting, needlework and household occupations.

The younger boys could also attend the industrial schools, which were not separate establishments, but merely the name given to the afternoon activities of the children's school. Today these activities would be called Handicrafts. The NCOs, Drummers and Privates had to pay for the attendance of their children at the infant and industrial schools on a sliding scale of 2d. per month per child to 1d. per month per child if three or more children of the same family attended. This money was 'appropriated to the use of the schoolmistress'.

The years 1855–57 saw further additions to Army School Regulations, but Gleig had now completed his reorganisation of Army education. His achievements had been great, especially for the schools and schoolmasters, but the disasters of the Crimean War (1854–56) underlined the need for urgent reforms in officers' education and training to meet the new technical and scientific requirements of the Steam Age. Gleig resigned in 1857 and the War Office decided that the direction of Military Education would be better placed in the hands of a military officer and therefore offered the appointment to Lt.Col. J. H. Lefroy, an artillery officer known in scientific circles for his work in magnetic and meteorological observations. He had entered the Royal Military Academy, Woolwich, in 1831 and while stationed there had opened with a group of young brother officers an evening Sunday school for soldiers' children. This early example of his concern for the well-being of the soldier and his family was to characterise his service throughout a long and brilliant career. He was to become a General, a Colonel Commandant of the Royal Artillery, Fellow of the Royal Society and Governor of Bermuda and Tasmania.

REFERENCES

1. War Office Library, General Order and Circular Letter Collection, GOs Nos. 414 and 417 of 18 May and 24 June 1824.
2. General Order No. 544, dated Horse Guards, 5 February 1840. War Office Library.
3. RAEC Archives, letter to Thomas Holt, Vauxhall Gardens, dated 20 June 1840.
4. Col. A. C. T. White, *The Story of Army Education*, Harrap.
5. 4/4816 Immigration Lists, Port Phillip, Vol. 4, 1848–49. Letter from The Michell Library, Sidney, dated 19 October 1961, in RAEC Museum.
6. See 4 and the Privy Council Report, PRO (WO/OS/84).
7. Minute Book of the Commissioners, 1833–1846.
8. PRO WO 33/OS/108290/1 of 7 April 1846, Report on the state of the RMA, Chelsea.
9. MS Letters Vol. 3. Board of Commissioners, June 1846.
10. Rich, *The Training of Teachers during the 19th Century,* CUP.
    Charles Dickens in *Hard Times* (1854) gave his picture of teachers and their training and concluded: 'if only they had learnt a little less, how infinitely better they might have taught much more.'
11. 'My Predecessor in Office' by Rev Jarvis in *The Journal of the Royal Army Chaplain's Department*, 1935. The full series covered Algebra, Arithmetic, Astronomy, Geography, Health, History, Chemistry, Physics, English, Sacred and Ancient History.
12. PRO WO 43/OS/109100, dated 16 May 1849.
13. PRO WO 423.OS 111451, letter from Gleig to Sidney Herbert dated 10 November 1845.
14. The professional journals of the day expressed the same opinion. 'It is no strange thing that men who in education, tastes and habits, have all the qualifications of "gentlemen" should regard themselves as worthy of something very much higher than the treatment of a servant and the wages of a mechanic.' (*The School and the Teacher*.)
15. PRO WO 43 OS papers 111451 dated 22 January 1846.
16. PRO WO 43/85. These proposals were incorporated in the Regulations issued on 19 April 1850.

APPENDIX A

Book List for Normal School, Chelsea

Grammatical and Literary Studies

Hunt's Parsing
Ross's Etymology
*Reid's Grammar
*Reid's Dictionary

Readings in Poetry
Readings in Prose
Paradise Lost
*Magon's Milton

Historical/Geographical Studies

History of England
Browne's History of Greece and
  Rome
Antiquities of Greece and Rome
Gleig's Military History

Cornwall's Descriptive Geography
McLeod's Geography of Palestine
*White's Abstract of Gaul
Atlas

Mathematical Works

Tate's Arithmetic
Tate's Algebra
Hunt's Arithmetic

Pott's Euclid
Tate's Mechanisms
Hunter's Tables

(* Listed on a bill dated 4 September 1849 found in the register.)

APPENDIX B

'The System of Study and Instruction to be Followed in the Normal School of the Royal Military Asylum.'

1. Pupils educated in the Training Institution at Chelsea shall be considered fit to pass into the Military School to practise the art of teaching when they have been sufficiently instructed in the following subjects.

   a. A general knowledge of the scriptures of the Old and New Testaments.
   b. The English Language including the power of reading correctly any work in prose, etymology, grammar, composition and accuracy in spelling and punctuation.
   c. The History of England.
   d. The Histories of Greece and Rome.
   e. The Outlines of General History – Ancient and Modern – the former partially, the latter more in detail.
   f. Geography (Mathematical, physical and political), of the British Empire, e.g. Colonies and Dependencies.
   g. The descriptive Geography of the World with a general view of the physical features and political state of its several portions.
   h. The simplest Elements of Astronomy.
   i. Arithmetic.
   j. Four books of Euclid or else Tate's Geometry.
   k. Algebra as far as Equations.
   l. The elements of Mechanics, or rather the application of Mechanical powers, as taught by Tate.

   To these may be added as being very attractive to British soldiers, the nature of whose Service in all parts of the World offers abundant opportunities of indulging the tastes:

   m. Natural History including Botany, Zoology and Mineralogy.
   n. Military Drawing and Field Fortifications.

   Singing and Drawing are to be taught likewise, but both and especially the former, must be regarded as subsidiary to other and more important matters – lessons in Singing twice a week and in Drawing once a week will, for the present, be sufficient.

2. The mode of communicating information on all these subjects, shall, as much as possible, be by oral lecture.

Gleig advised that the students should be divided into two departments and each department into two classes. He detailed which subject should be taken by the Headmaster and which by the Second Master, leaving Military Drawing and Fortification to be taught by the Adjutant. He considered that the Masters should – 'so manage their lectures that a course complete in itself shall be comprised within each half-yearly term, on satisfactorily going through the lowest of which (and not before) the pupils shall be advanced to a higher course. The fourth half-year to be spent in learning how to teach.'

He advised the Masters to write out a course of lectures, – 'so expressed as that in the delivery they shall interest and, as much as possible, excite the curiosity of the pupils. For a lecture lasting an hour, not more than half-an-hour should be given to the delivery of the lecture, the first half being devoted to an oral examination of the students' remembrance of the previous day's lecture.' At the end of each lecture they had to prescribe a textbook reading on the subject.... 'The pupils will thus be doubly instructed, first by the information which the Master communicated to them orally in the classroom and next by private studying and the examinations arising out of it. The Master will also carefully inspect their notebooks.'

APPENDIX C

To Field Marshal, His Grace   War Office
     The Duke of Wellington KG   2 April 1849

My Lord Duke,

I have the honour to announce to your Grace that I propose to send Mr Frederick Scrivener whose education has been completed at the Royal Military Asylum to be Schoolmaster to the Garrison School at Preston.

I enclose a certificate from the Inspector of Schools of Frederick Scrivener's fitness to undertake this duty and a testimonial from the Head Master of the Royal Military Academy School to his character and conduct during his continuance in that Institution.

I request that your Grace will give directions to the Adjutant-General to enlist Frederick Scrivener in accordance with the provisions of the Mutiny Act.

It was arranged in 1846 that the new schoolmasters should rank next to the Sergeant Major and your Grace has assented to . . . their Dress, position and Messing.

With a view to obtain the services of a valuable class of persons and uphold the position of the Schoolmaster, without in the remotest degree comprising Military discipline, there was an understanding that these Schoolmasters, who are to be enlisted Soldiers, should not be made subject to Corporal punishment if in the very improbable case of gross misconduct it should be deemed proper to bring any one of them to a Court Martial.[16]

CHAPTER 5

Military and Civilian Schools
in the mid-Nineteenth Century

Control of Army Education. Before Lefroy could start work, one
important question had to be answered – an issue raised by Lefroy's
appointment. Who should control education in the Army? Was it
the responsibility of the civilian Secretary of State at the War
Office * with the power to decide policy or was it more properly the
concern of the Commander-in-Chief, who represented the prerogative of the Crown, with the right to issue orders? Gleig had had no
doubts about the answer. He believed the welfare of the soldier was
best kept in civil hands and had opposed every attempt to associate
commanders and staff with the soldiers' education.[1] He had been a
professional writer and his views on social reform were progressive
and forceful. His reports on what he had seen of the mental and
moral state of the men had been vastly different from the conven-
tional inspection reports and 'struck consternation into the Horse
Guards', as he related in later years with evident pleasure.

Lord Panmure (Fox Maule), the Secretary at War, in offering the
responsibility to Lt.Col. Lefroy, had also offered to create for him
a new appointment of Inspector-General of Military Education,
directing him to take Sandhurst away from its Commissioners and
the regimental schools away from the Chaplain-General in order to
unify education in the Army and bring it more directly under the
Secretary of State. The Commander-in-Chief, the Duke of Cambridge, objected to the appointment. He had no intention of
surrendering control of education and proposed a new Department
of Education to regulate all educational training, and to be
responsible to himself.

*The War Office, until 1907, was situated in Pall Mall. The office of
the Commander-in-Chief was in the Horse Guards in Whitehall.

At this point Queen Victoria intervened. The Duke was her cousin and had her confidence, whilst she was on the worst of terms with her Prime Minister, Palmerston, and had no intention of allowing him to take over her prerogative of appointing officers. 'If for his military proficiency and moral discipline', she wrote to Palmerston,[2] 'the officer is to be responsible to his military chief, and for his mental requirements to a civil department, the unity of the system will be broken and the Army ruined.' The argument could not be refuted, and Lefroy appeared in the Gazette in February 1857 as Inspector-General, not of Military Education, but of Military Schools. The next day a War Office circular reminded all chaplains that 'Regimental and Garrison Day Schools are no longer entrusted to their charge'. These were ungracious words to use to Gleig and to the Army Chaplain's Department, which for more than a generation had made a great and lasting contribution to Army education, both adult and children's.[1]

A very British compromise followed. A new advisory body was formed, 'The Council of Military Education', responsible to the Secretary of State, though its President was the Commander-in-Chief. Members represented arms of the Services, with the exception of Canon Moseley, an HMI. In April 1860 the Council took over control of the Army schools and libraries and became responsible for the selection, training, promotion and discipline of the Corps of Army Schoolmasters. Lefroy's office was abolished, but not before he had become immensely popular with Army schoolmasters and made a report to the Secretary of State for War on 31 December 1858,[3] which gave a most comprehensive and intensely interesting account of children's education in the Army world-wide at that date.

Lefroy's Inspection Report 1858. During the first year of his Inspectorate, Lefroy had visited children's schools at twenty-four military stations in England and twelve in Ireland. Periodical inspections had also been carried out at all stations by his assistant inspectors and the Report included the state of the regimental schools both of the Queen's Army in India and of the armies of the East India Company.* Assistance was given by Her Majesty's

*The British Government first sent a British regiment to India in 1754 and for a hundred years afterwards there were two organised forces in India, engaged upon different terms and subject to different discipline and authority.

Inspectors and memoranda were submitted by isolated school-masters in the Colonies. The Report included the schools established at Gibraltar, Malta, Corfu, China, Africa, the West Indies, Australia, New Zealand and North America.

In 1858 there were 12,000 children under instruction in regimental schools, the majority being between 5 and 12 years of age and a small proportion rising to 15. They were divided into two classes, infants and grown children, the latter comprising all children of either sex who could read words of two syllables. Separate schools for girls existed only at Woolwich. 'It is, however, desirable to divide the girls from the boys wherever they are numerous enough to form a separate school.'[3]

Soldiers were not obliged to send their children to the regimental school; some parents, on religious or other grounds, preferred to send them elsewhere. But

'the convenience of the barrack school, the trifling amount of the school fee, and a well founded confidence in the means of instruction provided, suffice to induce parents, with insignificant exceptions, to send them there. Should any parent fail to do so, and at the same time neglect to provide otherwise for their education, leaving them in idleness and vice, to the annoyance of others, it would undoubtedly be competent to a commanding officer to withdraw from such parent the indulgences allowed to the well-conducted married soldier. I am not aware, however, of any such case having arisen.'[3]

Lefroy then discussed an educational problem, which is even today one of the Army's most difficult problems to resolve – the migratory child and the effects of 'turbulence' on its education.

'Irregularity of attendance arising from truantships is probably not more frequent than in all common schools, but there are other causes of irregular attendance peculiar to Army schools, which operate unfavourably on the progress of the children; such are the incessant changes in the stations of the troops, the movements of detachments, and the transfers of old soldiers from the service to the depot companies, or vice versa, and it is due to these that few children advance beyond the elements. The same causes on the other hand develop their intelligence, while the discipline in which they are brought up gives them an early notion of obedience, order, and cleanliness. Instances of misconduct are not frequent; the children are generally neatly dressed; very few instances of bare feet have come under my observation, and I have been much struck at the modest ingenuous countenances which issue from homes but little calculated to preserve the innocence of childhood.'[3]

Lefroy's biggest criticism was levelled against children learning by rote 'without the exercise of their own faculties' and he gave the following example of the Lord's Prayer, as written at Canterbury by a girl of 11, who could read and write perfectly well:

'Our Father beechart in heven alwed be they
name they kindom they will be dun in earth our tis
inheven and forgives this day our daly bred and
forgives they tresments again us and lead us not
in temtachen but lievers from evil for thine kingdom
the powyer the glory for ever and dever. Amen.'[3]

He praised the systematic instruction in needlework, introduced in 1854 by his predecessor the Rev G. R. Gleig, Chaplain-General, by which all female children, and a considerable number of the younger boys, were assembled for two hours every afternoon under the schoolmistress, for instruction in needlework, marking, knitting, etc., for which materials were provided to an amount not exceeding five shillings a head per annum. But singled out for exceptional commendation was 'the excellent attempt, recently made at Colchester, to teach household duties'.

'Eighteen children are divided – six girls washing, six cleaning plates, knives etc., six boys cleaning boots, candlesticks etc. The use of a women's wash-house has been granted every Wednesday for this instruction, the coppers of which are filled by a fatigue party, and the fires lighted by two of the girls. The girls for washing are allowed to bring six articles each from home to be washed, and the children bring six articles each to be cleaned.

'The girls for washing commence at $8\frac{1}{2}$ A.M., and are instructed by the mistress in washing, preparing blue-water, starch, &c., until 10 o'clock. By this time the girls are able to proceed with their work with less assistance from the mistress, giving her an opportunity of attending to the girls told off for cleaning. These girls commence cleaning at 10 A.M., and continue until 12 o'clock, using rouge and whiting for plate, rotten stone and oil for copper and brass, bathbrick for knives, and bees'-wax and turpentine for furniture. At 11 A.M. the six boys commence cleaning boots, shoes, candlesticks, &c., and continue until 12. The girls who were cleaning and the boys now carry the clothes to the drying ground, and put them up to dry. The girls go to their homes and assemble again at 2 o'clock, but each boy in his turn watches the clothes for half an hour, one boy being appointed to see that this duty is done properly. At 2 o'clock the girls who have been washing begin to iron and get up the clothes, while the articles which have been cleaned are laid out in an orderly manner for inspection. At $3\frac{1}{2}$ P.M. the children take the articles that have been cleaned and washed to their respective homes, pleased at being able to show their parents how well they have done their work. The wash-house is put in proper order by the children, and the key given over at 4 o'clock. Before commencing to wash or clean, the materials to be used are neatly laid out by the children under the superintendence of the mistress, and when done with are carefully put away.'[3]

He hoped that at a future date the elder boys also 'will receive industrial instruction, a measure long advocated by Mr Gleig, and recognised in the Queen's Regulations, but nowhere realised, so far as I am aware' (probably for want of barrack accommodation). He thought the trades and callings of tailor, shoemaker, carpenter, tinsmith, armourer, basket-maker, mat-maker, straw-plait worker, collar and harness-maker and groom were 'readily teachable'.

He found the schools essentially secular, but

'it is not to be supposed that any conscientious schoolmaster or ministers have access to the children of their respective congregastruction, to whatever denomination of Christians he or she belongs; it is left to the clergy alone to impart specific religious instruction, at hours set apart for that purpose, and at which all recognised ministers have access to the children of their respective congregations.'[3]

Lefroy found this arrangement admirable, since it recognised the necessity of seeking the divine blessing on even secular instruction and provided for those children, whose parents had no objection, a little simple explanation of the Bible history and of the moral lessons it conveyed; and at the same time it left all other parents at liberty to keep their children away even from this, and it impartially excluded chaplains of every denomination from the management of the schools.

Lefroy also reported on the Model School at Chelsea and found the school had improved considerably, thanks to the exertions of the Headmaster and his staff, since the adverse report made in 1849 (See Appendix A) by the Rev Dr H. Moseley, one of the first HM Inspectors of normal schools and colleague of Matthew Arnold.

'It cannot be questioned', [said Lefroy] 'that these boys ought to compare very favourably with those of the same age in any other common schools whatever; they remain on an average six or seven years in the institution; the military discipline to which they are habituated is highly favourable to habits of regularity and attention, and is not unfavourable to mental activity. The musical instruction they receive quickens their taste and intelligence, and the union of industrial employment, in moderation, with intellectual culture is, perhaps, the most favourable condition for the latter. I am happy to believe that they will so compare, and that the state of things observed by Dr Moseley has quite passed away.'[3]

The boys were still wearing the same uniform as they had worn for sixty years, since the foundation of the school. It consisted of a red bob-tailed coat with two brass buttons at the back, blue knee-breeches, white starched collar, blue stockings, low shoes with brass buckles and leather caps (see illustration 9). The serjeants' uniform was a red coat, white waistcoat and breeches, long black gaiters, greatcoat, cocked hat with a cockade, sword, and a white wig with a queue. In 1865 the peaked cap, buttoned tunic and trousers of a modern type were introduced for the boys and this uniform lasted until replaced by the khaki of 1915.

In 1858 Queen Victoria assumed full sovereignty over India and one result was the transfer to the Corps of Army Schoolmasters of the schoolmasters of the East India Company, which had previously existed as a separate Corps. While the Indian Mutiny prevented Lefroy from obtaining full information about educational work in India, it was evident from the report of the Army Schoolmaster who was Superintendent of Army Schools, Bombay (the same Frederick Scrivener, whom we met in the previous chapter as the first trained Army Schoolmaster to be posted from Chelsea in 1849), that much good work was being done in the children's schools, both of the Queen's Army in India and of the Company's armies.

Schoolmasters and assistants were recruited from the regiments locally and underwent a course of training at the central school of military instruction, Poona. Most of the schools were conducted in the same manner as the regimental schools at home. There was a general lack of school-books and materials and great delays in obtaining replacements. Arrangements had been made with contractors in India to meet demands locally, instead of awaiting shipments from UK. School accommodation had been defective. The schools were usually held in barrack rooms, unfurnished, except with ordinary barrack tables, and sometimes the schoolroom and the canteen were in adjacent rooms. But since 1853 new buildings and adaptations were in hand in almost every area. The hours of attendance prescribed were 'Male children from 6.30–8.30am and 2 to 4.30pm, the younger children and girls to attend the female school from 9am to 12 and from 2 to 4.30pm. All schools to be closed by 5pm.'

Scrivener thought the trained schoolmasters were of much more use than schoolmaster-serjeants, for with rare exceptions all the schoolmaster-serjeants he had met in India were of very little use as teachers: they were generally incapable of maintaining order in their schools, and in several instances their conduct provided a poor example to the children entrusted to their care.

'I have felt it my duty to mention this thus prominently, as in consequence of the great temptation to drinking arising from the cheapness of spirituous liquors in this country, I regret to say that a very great number of men fall into habits of dissipation immediately they are placed in the receipt of a larger salary than they have been accustomed to receive.'

'If thoroughly trained masters from Chelsea, men of respectability, of conciliating manners towards their equals and juniors in rank in the regiment to which they may be appointed, of respectful and soldierly bearing towards their commanding and other officers, imbued with a love of their profession, of strict sobriety and of good moral conduct, are appointed to the various stations in India where their services are likely to be required, I am convinced that very great benefit will result therefrom. There is always a very large number of children in regiments in India urgently requiring instruction and training.'[3]

Lefroy's inspection of the Normal School, Chelsea, during 1858 showed that 178 Army schoolmasters had been trained there since 1846, of whom 19 had died, been dismissed or discharged and 3 had deserted, leaving 156 still in the service. Of the 178, 48 had previously been NCOs; the remainder had entered from civil life, 37 having previously been monitors and these monitors were required to serve two years as assistant schoolmasters in regiments or garrisons before returning as students. He found the generality of young men who offered themselves as students possessed very little previous education, but he did not recommend raising the entry standards, in order to accommodate the NCO entry from the Army, who formed one-third of the students. His chief complaint about the course was that it had too little reference to the future duties of the students, the most important of which was the education of soldiers to fulfil the duties of every grade of non-commissioned officer. 'Young men quit the institution as ignorant of everything connected with the discipline, duties, pay and administration of a regiment as they enter it, and are rarely led to consider these subjects as in any degree their concern afterwards.'[3] Nevertheless, he found the general conduct, attention and application to work of the students, both civil and military, to be excellent: in fact, they applied themselves to study too closely and neglected proper physical exercise and recreation. This needed remedying forthwith.*

Kay-Shuttleworth. The same problem of teacher training had been exercising the minds of leading educationists in England at the same period. After experimenting with pupil-teachers at the school he founded at Norwood, Kay-Shuttleworth hoped, especially on his appointment as Secretary to the Committee of Council, that he would be able to persuade the Government to sponsor a training college for teachers. This did not happen; so in 1840 he started a college at his own expense at Battersea. This pioneering adventure was invaluable and when the college ran seriously into debt in 1843 it was handed over to the National Society, which was stimulated to open more training colleges. There were 22 by 1845. In 1846, when the education grant had been increased to £100,000, Kay-Shuttleworth was able to establish his pupil-teacher system, which Matthew Arnold was to call 'the sinews of our popular education'. It helped to bridge the gap between the early school-leaving age of 11 or 12 years for boys who were potential schoolmasters and the minimum age of admission to a training college.

When he had served his 5 year apprenticeship as a pupil-teacher from 13 to 18, a suitably qualified student could go on to a training or normal school. These colleges were supported by per capita grants from the Government and outstanding pupil-teachers could win the proud title and frugal emoluments of 'Queen's Scholars' with a grant of £20 or £25 to attend them.

These young and newly *certificated* teachers were placed in complete charge of schools at the age of 19 or 20 for about £90 p.a. and house. They might have 200 to 300 scholars and, at most, a staff of 5 or 6 young pupil-teachers, whom they had also to prepare for an annual examination. There was an increased demand, too, for certificated schoolmistresses and many female pupil-teachers were attracted to the profession (since the alternatives were limited to domestic service, dressmaking or the factory), with the hope of abandoning it on marriage. With these conditions of entry, training, remuneration and employment, those offered by the Army to its own schoolmasters and schoolmistresses bore very favourable comparison.

In 1849 Kay-Shuttleworth had to resign from the Committee of Council through ill health, but by then there had been great changes

* The Newcastle Commission said exactly the same of the civil training colleges of this period.

in the education system. Each elementary school was obliged to have a Board of Managers, not all of which were like the board which reported on one of its teachers 'he is very incompetent but we like him, for he gives us no trouble and is very civil – duly touching his cap and never troubling us for money for books or maps etc.' The size of Government grants was increasing, being subject to a favourable report from the Inspectors, and the pupil-teacher system was helping to provide more and better qualified teachers. There were, however, certain basic problems remaining to be solved. Large numbers of children still had no education and for the rest schooling was neither compulsory nor free. Most schools were still run by the two large religious societies, the denominational teachings of the one being completely unacceptable to the other. Many schools were still dirty and inefficient. There was also the problem of the factory children. The 1844 Factory Act had introduced compulsory education for the first time, by insisting that children between 8 and 13 who worked in factories should spend three full or six half-days at school. These children, known as 'half-timers', produced new problems in the schools and the system was only finally abolished by the Education Act of 1918.

'They are dirty and labour-soiled, in ragged and scanty clothes, with heavy eyes and worn faces. ... The master professed himself unable to include them in the various classes, without materially injuring the progress of the other children.' (Inspectors' Minutes 1844)[4]

Newcastle Commission 1858–1861. During the 1850s the Government, faced with the expenses of the Crimean War (1854–56), tried to reduce spending, and education, as always, was a popular target for economies, especially as the country at large believed that the education grant was not being well spent. When the Committee of Council was reorganised in 1856 to become the Education Department with a Vice-President responsible for it to Parliament, a closer control over expenditure was possible.

The state of education was investigated by a Royal Commission established in 1858 under the Chairmanship of the Duke of Newcastle, which reported in 1861. Included in its terms of reference was the requirement to report on any further measures necessary for the extension of 'sound and cheap elementary instruction to all classes of the people'. This report, based on extensive enquiries, both in England and Europe, presented a full picture of conditions in education in the middle of the nineteenth century.

'The children in our public elementary schools do not, in fact, receive the kind of education they require. We have been obliged to come to the conclusion that the instruction given is commonly both too ambitious and too superficial in its character, and that (except in the very best schools) it often omits to secure a thorough grounding in the simplest but most essential parts of instruction.'[5]

The Report criticised the shortcomings of teachers. It recognised that the profession of schoolmaster was not suited 'to a young man of an adventurous or ambitious character. It is a life which requires a quiet, even temper, patience, sympathy, fondness for children and habitual cheerfulness'. Although they were superior by character and training to their predecessors,

> 'it is equally clear that they fail, to a considerable extent, in some of the most important duties of elementary teachers, and that a large proportion of the children are not satisfactorily taught that which they come to school to learn. . . .'[5]

The main concern of the Commission was to provide a firm 'grounding' for as many children as possible. Elementary education should consist of the three Rs; more schooling was unnecessary, especially if the child's wages were needed to keep its parents off the poor rates. In evidence before the Commission the Rev James Fraser, one of the Assistant Commissioners, gave his opinion of the limited aims necessary for elementary education and the Commission agreed with him.

> '. . . Even if it were possible, I doubt whether it would be desirable, with a view to the real interests of the peasant boy, to keep him at school till he was 14 or 15 years of age. But it is not possible. We must make up our minds to see the last of him, as far as the day school is concerned, at 10 or 11. We must frame our system of education upon this hypothesis; and I venture to maintain that it is quite possible to teach a child soundly and thoroughly, in a way that he shall not forget it, all that is necessary for him to possess in the shape of intellectual attainment, by the time he is 10 years old . . . He shall be able to spell correctly the words he will ordinarily have to use; he shall read a common narrative – the paragraph in the newspaper that he cares to read – with sufficient ease to be a pleasure to himself and to convey information to listeners; if gone to live at a distance from home, he shall write his mother a letter that shall be both legible and intelligible; he knows enough of cyphering to make out, or test the correctness of, a common shop bill; if he hears talk of foreign countries he has some notion as to what part of the habitable globe in which they lie; and underlying all, and not without its influence, I trust, upon his life and conversation, he has acquaintance enough with the Holy Scriptures to follow the allusions and the arguments of a plain Saxon sermon, and a

sufficient recollection of the truths taught him in his catechism, to know what are the duties required of him towards his Maker and his fellow man. I have no brighter view of the future or the possibilities of an English elementary education, floating before my eyes than this.'[5]

These limited aims pleased those who wished to have cheap education and the report suggested a way of preventing a waste of public money. It advised that in future the education grant should depend upon the efficiency of schools, which would be tested by examining the pupils. Robert Lowe,* appointed the first Vice-President of the Education Department, incorporated this recommendation in his revised Code for Education in 1862. He explained the new principle behind Government aid to education, when he introduced it in the House of Commons in 1861:

> 'I cannot promise the House that this system will be an economical one and I cannot promise that it will be an efficient one, but I can promise that it will be one or the other. If it is not cheap, it shall be efficient; if it is not efficient, it shall be cheap.'

The new system, known as 'Payment by Results', was to remain in force until 1897.

Council of Military Education. In 1860, then, the Council of Military Education took over responsibility for children's education from Lefroy, until the Council was abolished in 1870.

Its curious composition was not its only weakness. It lacked executive and financial powers and it had few agents. There were three assistant inspectors in UK, who covered respectively 58 Grown Children's and 59 Infant and Industrial Schools in London and SE England; 43 and 37 in Scotland, NW & SW Military Districts; and 35 and 34 in the Military Stations in Ireland. In the larger garrisons overseas, such as Gibraltar, Malta and Corfu, staff or regimental officers inspected and examined the schools and, from May 1863, six Superintending Schoolmasters, selected by merit and with the relative commissioned rank of ensign, were appointed from the ranks of the 238 Army non-commissioned schoolmasters for inspection duties. The Royal Warrant of 1863 made service in the Corps of Army Schoolmasters pensionable, but it dashed their hopes of warrant rank by only giving them the status of non-commissioned officers next below the serjeant-majors.

* He had previously been Paymaster to the Forces. Unsympathetic to education, he was said to have possessed an aptitude for giving offence, which amounted to genius.

The Council's first Report, published in 1862,[6] contained reports at the request of the Secretary of State for War, Lord Herbert, from each of the assistant inspectors of schools and from a few of the most experienced of the schoolmasters on the effects and cost of the more recent changes in the management of the regimental schools, both adult and children's and asked for their suggestions for improvement. From these reports, which were characterised by plain-speaking, it was clear that the changes had not met with universal approval, especially those concerned with the soldiers' education. A court case had shown that the attendance of soldiers at school could not be legally required as a military duty under the Mutiny Act, and therefore attendance at school could no longer be made compulsory, as the Duke of Wellington had ordered in 1849. ('All recruits, until dismissed drill, should attend the garrison or regimental schoolmaster daily for two hours'.) Consequently, educational provision and attainment now varied greatly between regiments, depending as they did on the interest and support of each commanding officer. Irregularity of attendance once again became the greatest difficulty with which the schoolmaster had to contend and systematic instruction became impossible. Not all COs were persuaded that education was necessary: some considered standards too high or that time for study could not be found in the face of military and recruit training, guards and fatigues. While some could see the advantages of a uniform system of practical standards linked to promotion, others could see few advantages accruing from the increased educational expenditure. A number regarded the system as designed simply to impart the greatest possible degree of education in the shortest time and under the most disadvantageous conditions. The abolition of adult fees was welcomed, but not the young schoolmasters.

> 'The men prefer the old serjeant schoolmaster to the young men from Chelsea. However able the latter, they do not take the same interest in their work nor feel to the same degree responsible for the progress of their pupils as older men who have risen in the regiment and who are identified with it.'[6]

There was no doubt that the Corps of Schoolmasters as a body felt frustrated in the classroom and dissatisfied with their status and conditions, especially of rank, pension and promotion. They were not commissioned officers nor serjeants eligible for promotion to commissioned rank.

> 'Placed in the middle of the rank structure, they were neither fish,

66

flesh, nor fowl, disowned by all, having affinity with none, exciting the prejudice of every class. . . . Two-thirds of them are regarded by Commanding Officers as a nuisance, by the officers generally as upstarts and by the NCOs as men who are above them in education and tastes, who are too-well paid, have too many privileges and consequently think too much of themselves.'[6]

The Council itself considered there were strong military, personal and social reasons why the soldier should at least be able to read and write and that this was a matter of sufficient importance to justify a place in the regular programme of military instruction and to form an integral part of the discipline of the Army. The Council recommended a beginning should be made with every recruit and, without pressure on the old soldiers, encouraging the rest to volunteer for advanced instruction linked to a scheme of certificates at the various levels to qualify for promotion. It felt the machinery, prepared at so much cost, was good and ample; it commended the schoolmasters for their conduct and ability, and was confident that the extension of elementary education among the men would be carried beyond its acknowledged, unsatisfactory state as soon as the one great impediment, namely irregularity of attendance, could be wholly, or even partially, removed.

There was general satisfaction with the education of the children. The shared accommodation in chapel-schools was frequently inadequate but there was much support for continuing the regimental school, instead of adopting larger garrison schools, despite their better staffing, better grouping of children and higher standards of attainment. The regimental school was more immediately under the eye of the CO and permitted a greater interest on the part of the officers and ladies of the regiment. One General did not agree and protested to the Council.[7]

'By mixing the children of several regiments in the same school emulation is excited among the schoolmasters as well as the scholars. There is no reason why the Commanding Officer or his lady should refrain from visiting the garrison school. Surely it ought to be a matter of greater pride to witness the superiority of their own children and of their own schoolmaster, than to be satisfied by thinking them so, without trial.'

The best examples of garrison schools at this time were those established at Woolwich for the infants and grown children of the various regiments of the Royal Artillery. In July 1849 the Rector of Woolwich wrote to the Lord Bishop of London praising their high standards of discipline, moral and religious training and the general instruction, which bore comparison with the best conducted of the national schools. He praised, too, the great interest taken in the welfare and progress of the children by the garrison and school staffs. A typical garrison occasion in January 1865 is shown in illustration 17, when

> 'about 1,000 children aged between 6 and 14 were regaled with tea and cakes, while their schoolmasters and mistresses, with the numerous staff of subordinate teachers, partook of the repast. A large company of visitors, including many officers of the Garrison, with their families and friends, were present at this agreeable scene.'
> (*Illustrated London News*)

The cost of these children's education for the year 1860 is given at Appendix B. It worked out at about 36s. a head.

State of Children's Schools. The Newcastle Commission in its deliberations on the educational state of the country also reported on the Army's educational system and expressed approval of the efficiency of its garrison and regimental schools after the 1856 modifications. Official statistics for 1861 showed 3440 boys and 2691 girls were attending the grown children's schools, 3110 and 3005 respectively the infant schools, and there were 7052 attending the industrial schools.

The elder children, comprising those able to read words of two syllables, were classed according to attainment, without reference to sex, and taught by the schoolmaster and his assistant. In European climates, all attended from 9.00am to noon; in the afternoon boys alone attended for one or two hours according to the requirements of the adult school, as a separate classroom was seldom available. The staple diet consisted of the three Rs, to which in most schools the elements of English history, general geography and English grammar were added, and in some schools music found a place.

The infant school, under the sole charge of the schoolmistress, was for children of both sexes, but boys were not kept after the age of 8. The Council, in order to make the infant school as extensively used as possible, gave instructions to admit children 'as soon as they are able to be without assistance'. Times of opening were from 9–12noon and 2–4pm. The industrial school was organised in the afternoon for all the girls of the grown children's schools and as many boys and girls from the infant school as could profit by the instruction in plain needlework, which was given by the schoolmistress and her assistants.

'The custom of giving to the child the article of dress she has made gives additional interest to her work and reconciles mothers to the loss of their daughters' services at home, when they find their time is so profitably employed at school.' Distribution was usually made at Christmastime and the clothing was of special benefit to the poorer families.

Inspector reports of the period provide interesting and often amusing cameos of life in the schools. One inspector complained of the 'falling off from that excellent penmanship that was at one time the characteristic of regimental schools' and of 'puzzling the brains of the pupils with rules of grammar, which should be confined to the most advanced scholars, as young children learn better by ear and habit than by abstract rules'.[8] The standard of singing varied according to country and teacher. In Ireland,

'the singing, both in the grown children and infant schools, continues to be indifferent. Whether it is that soldiers' children are naturally unmusical, or that the teachers generally have not the ear and taste to qualify them for giving instruction in singing successfully, or that they do not bestow sufficient time and attention upon it, I cannot determine.'

In Malta 'the singing of the Royal Artillery classes at St Elmo . . . eclipses everything of the kind which I have ever heard before in the service and is listened to with pleasure by the officers on guest nights after mess.' While in Montreal, 'singing was nominally taught, but not with much science or theory; still, it helped to amuse the infants, and prevented the school hours becoming tedious; therefore the effects were good, at least, in a practical, though not in a musical way.'

Another Inspector noticed much improvement in the past ten years in the social habits of soldiers and their families, partly due to the general progress of education. Their wives and children had become more comfortable at home, better dressed and mannered abroad. The slatternly woman, so well known as typical of their position in life, was in many stations now the exception rather than the rule: while the appearance of the children at the Sunday Schools bore favourable comparison with that of the best country parishes. The satisfactory change was due largely to the warm, unflagging interest taken by many wives of officers and varied from regiment to regiment in direct proportion to that interest.

In India, an Inspector complained of the poor results being achieved in some infant schools, where 'much labour appears to be expended to small profit'. Perhaps his opinion was influenced by 'the excessive and exceptional heat, which during the past two months has greatly interfered with my inspections and delayed my report!' Another found in his Gloucestershire industrial schools that knitting was considered an effeminate occupation for boys, but the Inspector knew 'of no other acquirement, which conduces to give a man occupation in his blind old age, when most of his faculties are so impaired as to preclude him from taking part in every other kind of useful labour.'

Normal School, Chelsea, 1861. In 1861 among the thirty-nine students, at the Normal School, Chelsea, were two non-commissioned officers of the Royal Marines, 'admitted at the request of the Lords Commissioners of the Admiralty'. Thirty were studying at the Normal School and nine doing teaching practice at the Model School. An experiment had been tried the previous year of reserving three out of the ten places in the half-yearly competitive examinations for NCO candidates to encourage those who held back from the competition under the erroneous impression that they were unequally matched with civilian schoolmasters and pupil-teachers, who had better opportunities for preparation. In 1861 competitive examinations without distinction were resumed. The success of the military candidates prompted the Council to invite commanding officers to encourage more of their candidates to come forward. Examination papers were set in Scripture, English language, Indian and Colonial History, Geography, Arithmetic, Algebra and Euclid. One is tempted to ask how many members of the profession today could tackle papers, which included such questions as:

'What were Noah's prophecies about his three sons, and how were they fulfilled?'

'Give some account, with dates, of Caesar's two invasions of Britain. Name the Romans who subsequently commanded armies in Britain, and give a short account of the exploits of each.'

'Parse completely the following sentence; The Prince of Wales concluded a two years' truce with France, which was become requisite, that he might conduct the captive King with safety into England.'

'Define the following terms, and illustrate each definition by four examples, one from each of the four great divisions of the globe: Island, peninsula, plain, tableland, straits, gulf, lake.'

'Find the simple interest, at the rate of $3\frac{1}{2}$ per cent per annum, on £385 12s 0d for two years 146 days.'

(August 1865)[7]

Students remained one year in the Normal School, after which, if successful in the terminal examination, they transferred to the Model School for twelve months' training practice. Students 'with superior qualifications' could pass out in less than two years. Each student at the training school was supplied, free of cost to himself, with some twenty-seven books covering his course of study, maps, slate, drawing board, box of mathematical instruments, a portfolio and set of scales, all of which he retained on becoming a schoolmaster and which he was required to produce for inspection every quarter.

Army Schoolmistresses 1860s. Since 1858, unqualified candidates for the appointment of Army schoolmistress had been sent at public expense to one of the following civilian institutions for a six-months' or twelve-months' teacher training course:

LONDON	Home and Colonial School Society's Training Institution, Grays' Inn Road; Wesleyan Training Institution, Westminster.
DUBLIN	National Society's Training Institution.
EDINBURGH AND GLASGOW	Free Church National Training Institution.

Candidates had to be between eighteen and thirty-five years of age and had to produce a certificate of moral character from a clergyman of the religious denomination to which they belonged, and evidence of their fitness for the duties of an infant schoolmistress in disposition and temper.

'They had to be able to read any English book correctly and fluently, without mispronunciation: to write a good clear hand: to write from dictation with correct spelling: to understand the elementary rules of arithmetic, simple and compound: to be acquainted with the outlines of sacred history, both of the Old and New Testament, and likewise of English geography and of the great divisions of the globe. They had to be good needlewomen, competent to cut out and make any part of a child's dress; to teaching knitting, marking, getting up linen, and similar female work and to possess a taste and ear for music, especially singing.'[3]

Lefroy had commented

'the supply of trained schoolmistresses to regiments is attended with difficulty. There are abundance of candidates for training, chiefly wives and daughters of NCOs, and generally of a low standard of educational qualification, although often possessing those personal qualifications which are more important. The difficulty is, that if married they are liable to all the movements incident to the service: if unmarried, their employment is restricted by considerations of prudence, and they are also liable by marriage to transfer themselves from a regiment or station where they are wanted to one where they are not.'[3]

The Regulations of 1863 improved the pay* and the system of appointment for schoolmistresses as they did for the schoolmasters. The minimum age for admission as pupil-teachers was raised from 15 to 17 and they were required to pass a pre-admission examination in elementary subjects and in needlework. Pupil-teachers were appointed to assist the schoolmistress, whenever the number of children in the infant and industrial schools exceeded 50. Monitresses (14–16 years of age) replaced the former pupil-teachers in classes exceeding 25 and a new class of Assistant Schoolmistress was established, being selected NCOs' wives appointed to assist on the same pay and conditions as pupil-teachers. Like them they were eligible for admission to training institutions or for direct appointment to the Third Class. The declared objects of these changes were to produce a more effective teaching staff and more recruits to the ranks of the Army schoolmistress. On 31 March 1865 there were 443 female teachers engaged in conducting the Army's infant and industrial schools, including 209 trained schoolmistresses. The Council commented, 'The Schoolmistresses as a body are well qualified for their positions. They have imbibed correct notions of system and of discipline, and they appear to be interested in their work.'

An interesting product of this system was Mrs Pinkerton, who was left a widow with three young children at the age of 24. She was persuaded by the Colonel of her husband's regiment – the Buffs – to study for the examination for Army schoolmistress. She joined their Model School on 20 November 1874 and her first posting was to the 21st Brigade, RA, then at Portsmouth. The pay at that time was £30 p.a. plus 8s. 6d. per week for lodging, fuel and light allowance.

When Queen Victoria visited Aldershot in June 1869, she visited the

---

* The Newcastle Commission had an answer for the civil schoolmaster's complaints about his low salary. 'If the emoluments of the young schoolmaster were smaller, those of the older schoolmaster would appear greater and there would be no complaint of the absence of promotion.'

families of the Buffs, who were at that time under canvas on Cove Common, and talked with Mrs Pinkerton (then Mrs Woodman). An extract from an Aldershot paper of that date related

'Her Majesty next visited the encampment of the married people of the 2nd Battalion the Buffs. The Queen visited the tent occupied by Quarter-Master Sgt Woodman and entered into conversation with Mrs Woodman, saying she thought Mrs Woodman looked very comfortable and enquired how she liked camp life. Mrs Woodman informed Her Majesty that she was very comfortable, and enjoyed camp life very much in dry weather, but that in wet weather it was anything but pleasant.'[9]

The Council of Military Education summed up its achievements at the conclusion of its last report on 31 March 1870. It made the not unjustified claim that

'considerable progress has been made in the Army school system, since it was placed under our superintendence in March 1860.

'The proportion of uneducated men in the Army, i.e. all those who can neither read nor write, or who can read but not write, has been reduced by one half; special classes and certificates of education have produced in almost every Corps a small body of non-commissioned officers and privates possessed of an amount of useful knowledge which qualifies them for the duties of the higher grades; the number of trained schoolmasters has increased from 191 to 270; the number of children under instruction has increased 70%; and the number of volumes in Garrison Libraries is 48% greater than it was at the time of the Council's first report.

'The Council consider that the system has, on the whole, progressed satisfactorily and that the Army has benefitted in no small degree by the means of improvement provided for it.'

(Signed)   WILLIAM NAPIER, Major-General
Vice-President[10]

The Council had finished its work and was now to be replaced by a Director General of Education.

REFERENCES

1. Col. A. C. T. White, VC, *The Story of Army Education*, 1643–1963. Harrap.
2. Letter of Queen Victoria. Letter dated 18 December 1856.
3. Report on the Regimental and Garrison Schools of the Army, HMSO, 1859.
4. Dawson and Wall, *Society and Industry in the 19th Century*, OUP, 1969.
5. Newcastle Report 1861.
6. First Report by the Council of Military Education, HMSO, 1862.
7. Report by the Council of Military Education, 1865.
8. Report by the Council of Military Education, 1868–69.
9. *The Army Schoolmistress*, July 1925.
10. 7th Report on Army Schools, 1870.

APPENDIX A

Report on Model School, Chelsea

'I have been impressed with an idea that these children bring to the business of the school a lower standard of general intelligence and aptitude for the acquisition of knowledge than is to be observed in other schools, and that the schoolmaster's work among them is, for this reason, one of more than ordinary difficulty.

'I know not whether it is attributable to this, that they do not appear to listen to the instructions they receive with much interest, or answer the questions put to them with much animation, or whether to the fact that the first attempts at teaching of the students of the Normal school being addressed to them, they have the frequent experience of having things said to them that they cannot comprehend, and thus acquire the habit of not attending to them.

'Some feebleness of the general intelligence is perhaps to be expected from boys separated, as these have been, at an early period from their parents, as compared with others of the same class, whose minds are brought into constant contact with those of persons of mature years, and whose intellects are quickened by a daily walk through the streets, and by the intercourse of a home.

'Such an intellectual condition of a mass of boys as this will not be remedied by teaching them geography or history, or English grammar; all such teaching as at present (1849) applied to the business of elementary instruction is mere fact teaching; there is no impregnation of the understanding in it. Nothing, for instance, which corresponds to that discipline which the minds of our own children are subjected to, when they are made to construe a passage from a Latin or a Greek author, or to study a proposition of Euclid.

'The impression I derived from the second and third divisions of the school corresponds to that I have recorded of the first. I recommend in both a careful attention to good reading.

'The fourth division is composed of children whose experience of the school commenced with the present system. This is a hopeful class. Under the care of a very able and zealous master, Mr Dexter, the children who compose it are making excellent progress. When they reach the upper divisions, I trust that they will establish for the school that character which may be justly expected of it.'

24 August 1849.   H. MOSELEY

Rough estimate of the expense of the Royal Artillery Schools at Woolwich for the year ending 31 December 1860

	£.	s.	d.
Pay and allowance of superintendent	162.	19.	2.
1 first-class schoolmaster	146.	0.	0.
5 third-class ditto	365.	0.	0.
1 fourth-class ditto	36.	10.	0.
7 schoolmistresses and 9 pupil-teachers	300.	0.	0.
Allowance to soldier assistants	200.	0.	0.
Materials for industrial schools	80.	0.	0.
School books and materials	100.	0.	0.
Fuel and light, schools, schoolmasters, schoolmistress, and superintendent	160.	0.	0.
Rent and repairs of school buildings and quarters	250.	0.	0.
Lodging allowances to schoolmistresses	100.	0.	0.
Schoolmasters clothing	45.	0.	0.
Allowances to school orderlies	15.	0.	0.
	£1,960.	9.	2.
Deduct school fees	83.	0.	0.
	£1,877.	9.	2.

This total divided by 1,007 being the number of pupils (350 Adults and trumpeters; 380 Grown Children; 277 Infants) in daily attendance, shows the expense of each pupil's instruction for the year 1860 to be about £1. 16s.

(Signed) C. WHARRY,
Quartermaster

(Given in the First Report by the Council of Military Education, HMSO 1862.)

CHAPTER 6

1870: The Forster Education Act and the Royal Commission on the Army's Schools

Forster's Education Act, 1870. Army children were fortunately spared the system of 'Payment by Results', which governed civil schools from 1862–97. The Army's financial support did not come from capitation grants, the payment of which depended on

> 'certain conditions, such as the state of the school premises, and a satisfactory report of the inspector upon the discipline and religious instruction of the school; ... One third, however, of the sum thus claimable is forfeited if the scholar fails to satisfy the Inspector in reading, one third if in writing and one third if in arithmetic. For the purposes of examination, the children will be grouped according to age, and their failure in any of these subjects will render the school liable to lose one third of the allowance, and, if they fail in all, the State will contribute nothing towards the maintenance of the school.'[1]

Although popular with some because it was clear and simple to operate, this system and its effects on education, on the teachers and their salaries and even on the Inspectors,* were severely criticised by many educational thinkers. Matthew Arnold wrote

> 'In the game of mechanical contrivances the teacher will in the end beat us; and it is now found possible, by ingenious preparation, to get children through the Revised Code examination in reading, writing and ciphering ... I feel sure, from my experience of foreign schools as well as of our own, that our present system of grants does harm to schools and their instruction.'[2]

In 1867 a Parliamentary Reform Act gave the vote to most workers in the towns, who in turn demanded educational reform. As Robert Lowe put it

---

* A Durham inspector, a hunting man, used to arrive at a school in his pink coat, tie his horse to the railings, examine the children and be off in time for the meet.

76

'I suppose it will be absolutely necessary to educate our masters. From the moment you entrust the masses with power, their education becomes an imperative necessity. You have placed the Government of this country in the hands of the masses and you must therefore give them an education.' (Education and the Franchise 1867)

Other reasons besides political forced the Government to take a greater part in providing education. The population of England and Wales had grown rapidly over the previous sixty years. In 1801 it was nine million; in 1861 it was twenty million. There were too many children for the voluntary organisations to educate properly, even with some State aid. The industrialisation of the country demanded literate and skilled workers and made education for all even more necessary than ever.

The result was the Forster Education Act of 1870. Forster had been appointed by Gladstone to become Vice-President of the Education Department to sponsor the Bill. *The Times* in a leading article (18 February 1870), discussing the main provisions of the Bill, stated

'If it is proved that the school accommodation of a neighbourhood is deficient the duty will be thrown upon a local Board of Education of supplying the deficiency by the erection of a new school or supplementary schools. It this way there shall be within reach of every home in England a school to which the children may be sent to receive the elements of education. In schools with religious foundations the Conscience Clause shall exempt from religious instruction the children of those parents who signify their desire that they shall be excepted. The Bill thus provides that education, sufficient, efficient, and unsectarian, shall be within the reach of every man's child.'

The Act gave the new school boards wide powers. They could levy a local rate and acquire land in order to build new schools where such were necessary. Forster incorporated the clause, 'no religious catechism or religious formulary, which is distinctive of any particular denomination shall be taught in the school'. Parents were permitted to withdraw their children from religious instruction (if they wished) which was given at the beginning or end of the school session so that the time-table would not be upset. The school boards were empowered to pay all or part of the school fees where parents could not afford to send their children to school. Finally, they could make education compulsory, as London did between the ages of 5 and 13, with exemptions for children over ten who had passed Standard 5 and who were obliged to go to work to support their parents.

The Act of 1870 did not provide free nor compulsory nor secular education, but it was a landmark in the history of English education. By introducing schools which were independent of religious bodies and which were maintained by public money, local and national, it spurred the voluntary bodies also to provide more school places. It instituted the Dual System which was to remain a feature of education until the middle of the twentieth century. On the one hand, there were the board schools, undenominational and supported by government grant, the rates and fees; on the other were the denominational schools which could not receive rate aid but which were dependent on the government grant, fees, subscriptions, and the income from any endowments they possessed – a disadvantage not resolved until the Education Act of 1902. Nevertheless, it was to Forster, as his London statue records, that we owe a national system of elementary education.

Royal Commission 1870. The Army, too, had a landmark in education in 1870 when a Royal Commission was appointed to enquire 'into the present state of military education'.[3] It was to report whether the existing system of Army schools, including the Royal Military Asylum, Chelsea and the Royal Hibernian Military School, Dublin, 'afford a sound elementary instruction to Army children and what improvements are necessary'.

The Commission first considered the general superintendence and inspection of the Army's children's schools and observed that there was an inspector concerned with the general inspection of all Army schools in Great Britain, who had an assistant responsible for Ireland. For the nine districts of Great Britain there were nine commissioned superintending schoolmasters (with two for Ireland and one for Canada), whose duty it was to conduct an examination annually of the pupils in every regimental school within his district and to visit his schools as frequently as possible. The Commissioners felt that examinations were too frequent and interfered unduly with the working time of the schools. They felt it unnecessary that every school should be personally visited in the course of the year by the Inspector: instead a thorough inspection and examination of each should be made half-yearly by the Sub-Inspector of the district alone.

The Commission noted that the system of Army schools in India was not under the control of the Director General of Military Education as in other parts of the Dominions and that he had no direct authority over the local inspectors of schools in India, resident in each of the three Presidencies. The Commissioners considered that it was

'extremely desirable that the general system of Army schools, the method of inspection and superintendence, and the training and appointment of teachers should be conducted on uniform principles in India and in other parts of your Majesty's Dominions.'

The Commission looked into the arrangements made for the organisation and administration of the children's schools, mainly intended for the children of the non-commissioned officers and soldiers but also open to the children of officers, of subordinates employed in the military departments, of pensioners, and of civilians immediately connected with the Army. The payment of fees was required from all children, except those of soldiers serving abroad who had been prevented from accompanying their fathers. (Twopence per month for one child of an NCO or soldier, with reductions for additional children of the same family: threepence per week for each child of parents not in actual military employment: and 5s. per month per child of an officer, whose children received exactly the same instruction and treatment as all other children.) The autocratic nature of military discipline solved the problem of school attendance.

'The attendance at school of the children of NCOs and soldiers, married with leave, is compulsory, Commanding Officers of Corps being directed by your Majesty's Regulations to require "that all married soldiers shall send their children to the school of the Regiment or Garrison, on pain of being liable to be deprived of the privileges attendant on the residence of their wives in Barracks." '*

Twenty thousand children were in the Army schools at home and in the colonies, divided into infant and grown children's schools. The elder children of both sexes attended school together in the morning under the schoolmaster but were separated in the afternoon, the boys remaining under the master, while the girls joined the infants for special instruction under the mistress. The infant schools were entirely under the charge of the schoolmistress, generally, though not always, in a room set apart for the purpose. In one or two large garrisons, such as Woolwich and Chatham, where the regimental school reached an unusual size, there were special girls' schools but co-education was the normal practice. Discipline

* Compulsory attendance in civil schools remained a myth, in spite of the 1876 and 1880 Acts, until Balfour's Act of 1902.

was excellent; corporal punishment was forbidden, but no one objected to the odd cuff round the ear. No age limit was fixed for admission. Children were frequently sent to the infant school with their elder sisters, so young that they could not derive any benefit from the instruction. Similarly there was no fixed age for transfer from the infant to the grown children's school. Although by the regulations children had to remain in the infant school until they were able to read words of two syllables at least, this rule did not appear in practice to be observed. The transfer of a child from one class to another was left to be arranged between the schoolmaster and schoolmistress; boys, however, were *not* allowed to remain in the infant school after 8 years of age. In a few large garrisons, such as Aldershot, where a number of regiments were quartered, a system of garrison schools was tried, whereby the infant schools of several different regiments were combined, and placed under the charge of a single schoolmistress.

School hours were normally from 9–12 in the morning and from 2–4 in the afternoon. On Saturday there was no afternoon school. The schoolmaster was assisted by a certain number of soldier assistants, appointed from soldiers of the regiment or battalion to which the school belonged. The schoolmistress received similar assistance from pupil teachers and monitresses, the latter being selected from the more advanced girls attending the school. The monitresses joined the grown children's school for a short period every day, for instruction under the schoolmaster.

The subjects of instruction in the 161 grown children's schools (1871) comprised reading, writing, dictation, singing, grammar, English history, geography, arithmetic, and in some cases algebra. In the infant schools spelling, reading and singing were the subjects chiefly taught. (Typical time-tables for both schools are given at the end of the chapter.) The afternoon school attended jointly by the infants and girls was termed an 'industrial school', in which the pupils were taught various kinds of needlework. In religious instruction careful attention was paid to the religious predilections of the parents.

'The school is opened each morning with prayers and a simple Bible lesson, lasting for half an hour, but attendance at this is voluntary with children not of the same religious persuasion as the teacher. On two days in each week an hour is specially set apart for the purpose of instruction by the Chaplains of the several denominations to which the children belong. Sunday schools are likewise formed for religious instruction, but the arrangements

11. RMA, Chelsea. Battery firing salvoes.

12. RMA, Chelsea. Boxing, 1901.

13.   *Rev. G. R. Gleig (1796–1888). Inspector-General of Army Schools, 1846–57.*

14.   *Lt. Col. J. H. Lefroy (1817–90). Inspector-General of Military Schools, 1857–60.*

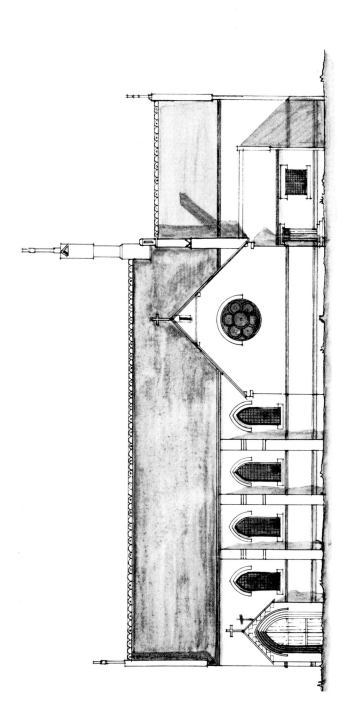

15. *Lichfield Chapel School, 1876. Still stands in the depot of the South Staffordshire Regiment.*

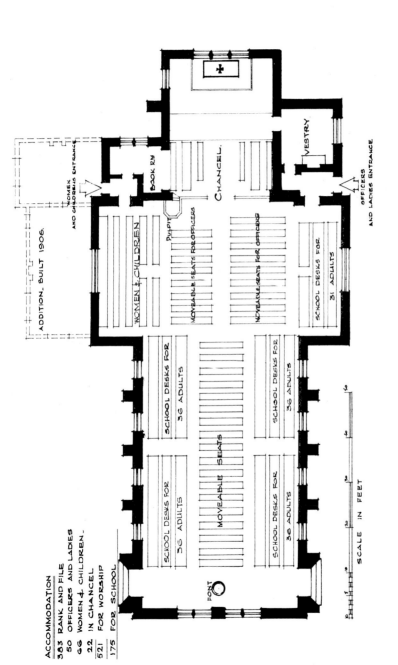

16. *Lichfield Chapel School was designed for 521 worshippers and 175 schoolchildren.*

17.   *Prize and Annual Feast Day for 1000 Woolwich Garrison schoolchildren, 1861.*

18.   *Regimental School, Poona, 1897. 2 Royal Irish Rifles.*

*19.   Boy orderlies, under the monitor, washing up after dinner.
RMA, Chelsea, 1888.*

connected with them are left in the hands of the Chaplains of the Forces. Schoolmasters and Schoolmistresses are, however, liable to be required by the Chaplain of the denomination to which they themselves belong to assist him in the Sunday school instruction. In some cases, though not universally throughout the Army, a special service for children is conducted on Sundays by the Chaplain.'

Having thus briefly reviewed the existing arrangements for children's schools, the Commissioners felt bound to express their belief 'that they are on the whole such as to provide the means of sound and useful elementary education to the children of the non-commissioned officers and soldiers of your Majesty's Army. The evidence we have received leads us to believe that the educational results of the schools are decidedly successful as compared with those of civil schools of a similar class. Colonel Pocklington, a member of the late Council of Military Education, expresses his belief that "the educational status of our Army schools is far beyond that of village schools"; and the Chaplain-General says "I have had many opportunities of examining schools both in London and in the country, and I think that nothing approaches the generality of our military schools." Instances are also mentioned in which the pupils of Army schools have proved their superiority over those educated at civil schools in competitive examinations held in connection with the Society of Arts. The regularity of attendance, which is enforced by the authority of Commanding Officers, gives the instructors a distinct advantage over those of the National Schools of the country, and contributes greatly to the satisfactory progress of the pupils. The subjects taught appear to us in general well adapted to the social condition and future wants of the children, and the system of instruction seems to be well devised and practically successful in its results. It is also evident that the advantages afforded by the schools are highly appreciated by the parents. We therefore find it necessary to recommend but few changes in the children's schools.'

While recommending a reduction in the capitation grant from 5s. to 2s. 6d. 'a sum amply sufficient for the purpose of an adequate supply of materials for instruction in needlework',* the Commissioners strongly recommended that opportunities for further industrial training should be afforded both to boys and girls. Whenever practicable, girls should receive instruction in domestic duties

* 'The 5/- is regarded by parents as a fund for giving the children extra clothes at Christmas and they demand their money's worth.'

and advantage should be taken of the regimental workshops and other existing means to give the elder boys, for whom no kind of industrial occupation was provided, some insight into trades such as tailoring, shoemaking, carpentry, farriery, saddlery, armourers' and smiths' work, engineering, etc. In spite of this form of training being authorised, the Commissioners found little evidence of its being systematically attempted. The Commissioners felt that it was unnecessary for them to indicate

> 'the great benefit that would accrue to children in the class of life of the pupils of an Army school from some kind of industrial training in youth, whatever may be their future career; while, as the sons of soldiers in numerous cases enter the military service, the arrangement we propose may help to extend an acquaintance with trades among the rank and file of your Majesty's Army'

and pointed out that such instruction in trades 'though only to a limited extent and an unsatisfactory system' was already enjoyed by the boys at the Royal Military Asylum, Chelsea – a model school for the regimental schools of the Army. The 2s. 6d. saved from the capitation grant should be devoted to this extra industrial training.

The Commission recommended that schoolmasters and schoolmistresses should not be compelled to take part in Sunday School instruction. However, they could not agree to allowing teachers a free Saturday morning, in spite of the fact that the attendance of children on Saturdays was so irregular, large numbers being kept at home by their parents for domestic duties. They felt 'it would be inadvisable to deprive those, who are in the habit of attending, of the opportunity of instruction, and to throw them for the whole day entirely on their parents' hands.' To a Commanding Officer who expressed his belief that the present class of teachers paid less attention to the children out of school than in former days, when a Regimental Serjeant was appointed schoolmaster, the Commissioners replied,

> 'Although it is certain that much good may be effected by the example and influence of individual teachers, it does not appear to us possible to require schoolmasters, as a matter of general regulation, to exercise any special control over the children out of school hours. The direct responsibility for the moral welfare of their children out of school, we consider, is a duty which must in a regiment, no less than in civil life, devolve mainly upon the parents.'

The Commission were strongly of the opinion that in all cases in which advantage had been taken of the privilege of admission to a regimental school regularity of attendance should be strongly enforced and recommended that a child's name, having once been placed upon the school books, irregularity in attendance, without sufficient cause,* should be stringently visited with forfeiture of the privilege of admission to the school.

On the payment of fees the Commission felt that there should be no change in the fees required of those not actually serving in the Army, but they recommended that no payment should be required for the children of either officers, NCOs or soldiers actually engaged in military service.

'The expense entailed by the remission of these fees would be trifling. At present the motive of saving the fee undoubtedly in some cases acts as a temptation to parents to keep their children absent from school for the whole month when they have lost a part of it, and the system of fees insists a multiplication of returns which imposes an unnecessary labour on the schoolmaster. The argument that people in general only value what is paid for does not appear to us to be applicable to soldiers in the same degree as to civilians. There can be no reason why a soldier should feel any sense of dependence or pauperism in availing himself of what would be considered one of the natural advantages of his military service. The privilege of free education has already been granted, in our opinion most wisely, to the soldier himself; and we strongly recommend that the same privilege should be extended to his children.'

The Commission examined the very early age at which infants were attending school and the complaint of the schoolmistresses that they were not only too young to benefit by the teaching but that their presence interfered with the instruction of the other children. They strongly recommended that a separate room should be put aside for these younger children. Of infant education in general the Commission underlined its paramount importance. 'It is impossible to attach too much importance to the necessity of paying strict attention to the instruction given in Infants Schools, as experience has shown that the successful results of later education depends, to a very great extent, on the care bestowed upon infant teaching.'

It did not favour dual purpose chapel schools by which the same building was used both for secular and religious purposes and recommended that, where practicable, special accommodation for the schools should be provided.

* A Devon schoolmaster found that every harvest, fair, hunt or chapel function encouraged his pupils to play truant or to supplement the family income. 'This is the fifth harvest thanksgiving they have attended this year. Truly, we are a thankful people!' he exclaimed.

Army Schoolmasters and Schoolmistresses, 1870. The Commission considered the position of the 258 established Army schoolmasters. On 31 March 1870 there were also 135 acting and detachment schoolmasters and 713 soldier assistants. Evidence showed clearly that there was a widespread feeling of dissatisfaction amongst them concerning their status and conditions. The number of civilian candidates for admission to the Army Schoolmasters' ranks had dropped from 34 in 1861 to only 3 in 1869. Not only were appointments so little sought after by civilians, there was scarcely greater attraction to those serving, in spite of the lowering of the military qualifications required from soldiers for admission to the Normal School. The number of military competitors had dropped from 32 in 1867 to 14 in 1869. It was feared that unless steps were taken to attract a larger number of applicants the supply of trained schoolmasters would, in the course of a few years, be inadequate to meet the vacancies. Whilst the Commission could not agree to Schoolmasters resuming their former Warrant Officer rank which placed them above the Regimental Serjeant-Major, nevertheless the Commission improved their conditions in a number of small ways. They were exempted from the punishment of reduction to the ranks and from having to show their kit for inspection.* They were relieved from Sunday School teaching. They were permitted again to engage in private tuition after the conclusion of regular school hours, subject to the sanction of the Commanding Officer. In consideration of their increased responsibilities the title of Superintending Schoolmaster was changed to that of Sub-Inspector of Army Schools with a pay increase.

For the lower ranks of schoolmasters the Commissioners felt that their pay on first entering the Service was insufficient to enable them to maintain their position and recommended an increase on first appointment and every third year thereafter (£88 to £114 pa.) In determining the rates of pay for Army schoolmasters the Commission was guided to some extent by the salaries offered to civilian schoolmasters in a comparable position, remembering that the Army schoolmasters received clothing, fuel and light and rations and had the prospect of a pension after 21 years, while on the other hand necessarily incurring expenses consequent upon moving station, which did not fall upon his civilian colleague.

---

* 'Because some bad fellow has made off with his kit, I don't see why the whole body of schoolmasters should have to show their kit every month,' Gleig protested to the Commissioners.

Schoolmistresses were appointed between the ages of 21 and 30 and had to be either persons holding certificates of proficiency under the Committee of the Council of Education, or to be employed as Assistant Teachers in Army schools. For their training, there was no normal school maintained at public expense. The former class of candidates were appointed without further examination; the latter class were examined before appointment as schoolmistresses with the object of proving that their education and skill in teaching were satisfactory. They were of three classes. Their first appointment was to Class 3 and they were promoted according to merit and service.

The Commission supported their representations that their pay, especially on first appointment, was inadequate and that the married schoolmistress was worse off than the unmarried because of lower lodging money and allowances. Their pay * was therefore increased and married and single were placed on the same footing for lodging and ration allowances. (£30 pa (3rd Class) to £44 pa (1st Class)).

To assist the 238 schoolmistresses in charge of the 172 infant and industrial schools 66 pupil-teachers and 336 monitresses were employed. Thus there was a total of 695 females (including 55 acting-schoolmistresses) engaged in conducting the Army's infant and industrial schools (1872–73 Inspector's Report). The latter were invariably selected from the girls attending the school and pupil-teachers generally from former monitresses. A monitress was authorised when the number of children exceeded twenty-five and a pupil-teacher when the number exceeded fifty. Monitresses had to be between the ages of 13 and 17 and pupil-teachers between 17 and 21. Because of the difficulty of finding candidates, the Commission reduced the appointment of monitresses to 12 and pupil-teachers to 15 and raised the monitresses' pay.

Normal School, Chelsea, 1870. The Commission next turned its attention to the Royal Military Asylum, Chelsea, which had the normal school for training Army schoolmasters and the model school for the orphan sons of soldiers. The general management of both was vested in a body of Commissioners, some ex-officio by virtue of their official Army appointments, while others were specially appointed. The Secretary of State for War and the Com-

* 'Our pay of £24 p.a. is less than that of a drummer of Infantry. We have to rely on the generosity of our friends and deprive ourselves of food to keep up respectable clothing,' a schoolmistress testified to the Commission.

mander-in-Chief were ex-officio President and Vice-President respectively of the Board of Commissioners which controlled finances and discipline and the appointment and dismissal of most of the school's staff. A Commandant was the military head, responsible for discipline and interior administration of both schools, which for instructional purposes were separately organised, each with its own staff of teachers under its own headmaster. On the Commandant's staff were a Quarter-Master (whose duties also included pay), Chaplain, Medical Officer and an Adjutant, who acted as Secretary of the Board of Commissioners. Admission to the normal school was by half-yearly competitive examination, open to both civilians and soldiers between the ages of 20 and 25. Candidates from civil life had to be certificated schoolmasters or pupil-teachers who had completed their apprenticeship. Originally, military candidates had to be of the rank of Serjeant but gradually this had been waived and even privates in possession of a good conduct badge were accepted as competitors. The majority of candidates were military and included pupil-teachers from the model school, Chelsea, and monitors from the Hibernian School, Dublin who, on attaining the age of 20, were admitted to the competitive examination. The entrance examination consisted of reading, writing and spelling, English grammar, scripture history, English history, geography, arithmetic and Euclid for a course lasting two years.

During the first year students were instructed in the Normal School and during the second year employed as teachers in the Model School where they were trained in the art of teaching. During the first year at the normal school they studied arithmetic, mensuration, algebra, geometry, trigonometry and logarithms, industrial mechanics, English and Indian history and the history of the British colonies, English grammar, geography, chemistry and physics, fortification, singing, drawing, reading, penmanship and scripture knowledge. Instruction was also given in the art of lecturing and in the performance of lecture experiments since, in addition to teaching their children, they taught the soldiers and NCOs themselves.

The authorised establishment of the school was forty students, under a Headmaster and an Assistant Master (whose services had been dispensed with because of the small number of candidates). Fortification was taught by the Adjutant, religious instruction by the Chaplain, singing and drawing by two non-resident masters, who also taught these subjects in the Model School. At the time of the Commission there were only sixteen students of whom thirteen were soldiers and three civilians. During their period of residence civilian students were provided with their food and uniform at public expense and soldier students with the same clothing and pay and messing as if they were with their regiments. On completion of training and successfully passing an examination the students were appointed Army schoolmasters, the civilians being required to enlist for twelve years, and the soldiers discharged from their regiments and re-enlisted for a similar term of service.

The Headmaster of the Normal School, Mr W. J. Reynolds, MA, was asked by the Commissioner to give his views on the suitability of Chelsea as a site for teacher training. He replied,

'It is supposed by some that the inducements to immorality (using the word in its widest, as well as in its most specific sense,) which beset a student outside the walls of his school, are greater in a metropolitan establishment than in a provincial one. This seems to be a prevalent opinion; I believe it to be a mistaken one. For young, insufficiently-occupied or vacant-minded men, under no supervision and with means to a greater or less degree superfluous, there are indeed special allurements to evil in a metropolis like London. To an earnest man, whose time is sufficiently occupied by useful and improving work, and whose mind is capable of receiving and of valuing knowledge of any kind, it is far more correct to affirm that in London there are special inducements to morality. The adult students who in London are immoral, would be immoral any-where, and they are unfit to become schoolmasters.

'Induce eligible men to try to become army schoolmasters, give to them when students in the Normal School the same distinctive uniform, adapt the accommodation within the building at Chelsea to the habits and requirements of a selected body of well-conducted men, and then (with those exceptions from which no school or college can ever hope always to be free, and which under due supervision would soon be eliminated when they occurred,) the men will, in fact, conduct themselves well, and the tone of the school will at once become all that could be wished.' (Gleig, however, thought there were 'too many public houses round about for the good of the students'.)

It seemed to the Commissioners that the Normal School had of late not fulfilled the expectations of its founders. The numbers of students had fallen off considerably and few civilian candidates offered themselves for appointment. The Commissioners hoped that their recommendations to improve pay and status would attract more applicants, but although they gave full credit to the ability with which the system of instruction at the Normal School had been carried out, they felt it was no longer cost-effective and that, whilst the twelve months' training in the model school provided teaching practice with children, it was not the best method of training schoolmasters for their other duties with adults. This deficiency was not remedied by placing young schoolmasters, on first entering the Service, to work under an experienced teacher. The Commissioners considered an alternative method of using civilian institutions for training schoolmasters but rejected it because it would exclude soldiers from attaining the position of Army schoolmasters who, because of their military training and habits of discipline, were considered better than civilians for teaching adult soldiers.

The Commissioners, therefore, recommended that appointments to the situation of Army schoolmaster should be thrown open to public competition among civilians who had passed a period of not less than twelve months in some recognised training institution, and soldiers who had either been employed as school assistants for a similar period in an Army school or had passed six months in the latter capacity and six months at a civil training school. The pupil teachers at the Model School at Chelsea and monitors at the Hibernian School should, as under the existing arrangements, be admitted to the competition on attaining the age of 20 under the same conditions of character and educational qualifications as other candidates. Instead of entering a normal school, successful candidates should be appointed on probation for a period of six months and should serve during that period under a schoolmaster of not less than five years' standing, during which period they would acquire practical experience in the art of teaching adults. The schoolmaster was to receive a gratuity of £10 for this instruction, provided the candidate successfully completed his six months' probationary service.

The Commissioners concluded this part of their report with self-congratulation on achieving

'a saving on expenditure not only by the abolition of the staff of the Normal School but also by the diminution of the ordinary period of training during which candidates are maintained at public expense. They will, moreover, during their course of training be utilised as instructors in Army schools thereby affording some return to the State. At the same time, as the competition with civilians, combined with the opportunity of taking advantage of civil training institutions, will secure a high educational standard on the part of the successful soldier candidates, we believe that the plan we propose will supply the Army with a staff of teachers, at least as efficient as at present, and in the art of teaching adults possessed of greater experience than under the existing system.'

Model School, Chelsea, 1870. The Model School had been established for 500 pupils which, on sanitary grounds of affording increased space in the dormitories, had been reduced during the previous two years to 458. In addition to the general staff of the asylum there was a Headmaster, four resident Assistant Masters, the two non-resident masters for singing and drawing, students from the Normal School and thirteen pupil teachers. Additionally, there were some NCOs (pensioners of the Army) and female nurses, employed in the superintendence and care of the pupils, admitted formerly between 5 and 10 and presently between 7 and 12. The school was organised on military lines, the boys being divided for purposes of interior economy and discipline into six companies, superintended by the Serjeant-Major and six Serjeants under the direction of the Adjutant. In awarding punishment and in the treatment of offenders a military system was followed. For purposes of instruction the pupils were divided into five classes or 'schools', one of them being an infants' school. Each class was under the charge of a Master, the Headmaster having overall control. Instruction comprised religious knowledge, reading, writing and composition, arithmetic, Euclid and mensuration, geography, English grammar, English history, Object Lessons,* singing, drawing and natural history. The elder boys were additionally either trained as musicians in the band or taught the trades of tailoring and shoemaking. Normally, boys were not kept at school after the age of 14, except for those in the band who were permitted to remain until 15 or 16. Leavers who were physically fit and who volunteered for military service were enlisted into the Army. The remainder were either delivered to their friends or apprenticed to trades. Although no restriction was put upon the pupils in the choice of a future career the fact that they were all the sons of soldiers and the military spirit of the institution naturally gave a military tone to their ideas and the great majority of those who were not physically disqualified volunteered for the Army.

'It is unnecessary for us to dilate upon the great advantages which such an institution as the Model School must, if properly conducted, confer upon Your Majesty's Service. Not only are a gratuitous education and maintenance afforded to the orphan children of soldiers, who would otherwise often be thrown helpless and destitute upon the world, but a body of young recruits is diffused through the ranks of the Army and carry with them into the Service the

* A Pestalozzian lesson about an object (rabbit or loaf etc.) examined in the classroom to establish its main characteristics.

groundworks of a sound and useful education, and a military spirit instilled into them from early childhood. The returns with which we have been supplied, and the evidence furnished both by Regimental Officers and from other sources, afford proof of the excellent character, almost invariably borne throughout their future career, by soldiers who have been brought up at the school.'

The Headmaster, Mr Walter McLeod, was questioned by the Commission and gave some very interesting answers, which reveal something of the character of the man and of the conditions of his Model School.

Q. In school if a boy misbehaves himself do you punish him or do you report him to the military?

A. I punish him; the boys in the school are under my control; the corporal punishment is by a cane, and the greatest amount of strokes is 6 upon the hand, and on no other part of the body.

Q. The time-honoured* instrument of punishment in this country, namely the birch, has not been made use of?

A. No, we have not made use of it for some years.

Q. By your answer I understand you to be of opinion that the birch should be altogether suspended?

A. I should like to discard it from school altogether.

Q. I suppose you have no difficulty in maintaining discipline in school?

A. Very little.

Q. Would you remove the school from its present situation into the country?

A. Most decidedly.

Q. Have the children not entire liberty for recreation in the afternoon?

A. They are supposed to have it from 12–2, but there are so many duties which come in to interfere in the hours set apart for play. A Board recommended 18 months ago that children should go to Battersea Park for the purpose of play, but not as they do now, merely making a parade march of it. They leave at 11.30 am, carrying their big drums and blowing their instruments, they march out for half an hour, and then back again at 12.30. There is no recreation; the boys do not enjoy it.

Q. Are the nurses the kind of women who are fit to be trusted with looking after the boys?

---

* An advertisement in the Church Guardian (1871) supports this view. 'Barrister's daughter (35), healthy, good-tempered, vigorous, desires a matronship. Is experienced in applying the birch rod.'

A. In many cases they are not. There has been a great deal of drunkenness.

Q. Each boy has a bed to himself, has he not?

A. All the elder boys have beds to themselves; for the younger boys there are double beds.

Q. If we abolish the Normal School, as you suggest, how are we to provide teachers for the Army?

A. The plan which I propose is this. I would first of all admit civilians who have been a twelve month in one of the Government Training Colleges and had passed the examination by the Committee of Council of Education. Secondly, soldiers not under the rank of Serjeants, and thirdly, pupil teachers from the Model School when they had attained the age of 20 or 21 years. The civilians should come to the Model School for six months in order more fully to acquire the art of teaching. The Serjeants and the pupil teachers, if it was considered desirable to give them such a training, should be sent at the cost of the Government to some establishment for six months, and they should then return to me for another six months; and on appointment as Army Schoolmasters, each man should be attached for 6 months either to a Garrison or to a Camp.

Q. Are you satisfied with the industrial education?

A. They used once to make their own clothes and shoes; now they are taught to mend their shoes and to make their own clothes. I would close the shoemaker's shop, give more tailoring and add carpentry and telegraphy.

Q. What changes would you make in the instruction at the school?

A. I do not recommend any change either in the course or the method of instruction in the Model School. The system, which was introduced by me, has been in operation for 23 years, and has worked satisfactorily, as the various reports on the state of education in the schools testify. I may state that the schools are organised according to the plans adopted in Holland; and the methods of teaching in the galleries and in the classes are based upon those of Pestalozzi,* Wood and Stow. (See illustration 8.)

The Commissioners paid their tribute to him, praising the 'excellence of the system of teaching originally introduced and still pursued by the present Headmaster, of whose abilities and qualifications for his post everyone acquainted with the school has spoken

* Dr Andrew Bell visited Pestalozzi's schools in Switzerland, whilst advising the Army on his monitorial system.

in the highest terms.' But having praised the excellent educational state of the school, the Commissioners commented adversely on, and advocated improvements in, its mode of government, organisation and discipline, and its general sanitary state. For example, the supervision of the instruction was the responsibility of the Director General of Military Education who had no control over the discipline and administration of the Institution which was the responsibility of the Board of Commissioners. Similarly the military staff was distinct from the teachers. The Commandant was responsible to the Commissioners for discipline and the children out of school and had no responsibility for instruction, whilst the Headmaster was responsible to the Director General of Military Education for instruction with no responsibility outside his school. This had naturally given rise to conflict and at least one instance had occurred in which the Headmaster 'has not been treated with the respect to which his position entitles him'. The Commissioners recommended that the Board of Commissioners should cease to have any connection with the discipline or internal administration of the Institution, their duties being confined to the consideration of the claims of candidates for admission. Instead, the Director-General of Military Education should assume these responsibilities, including the appointment and removal of the school staff. The Commissioners strongly condemned the system whereby the Commandant was responsible for discipline and the Headmaster for instruction. Authority for both should be placed squarely in the hands of the Headmaster.

'A purely military system of discipline and an organisation by which the general supervision and the instruction of the pupils are placed in separate hands, are ill adapted to the management of boys of the age of the pupils at the school. We consider that in an establishment of this sort it is desirable to make the connection between teacher and child as close as possible and to afford every opportunity for the former to exercise his influence over the latter. We therefore recommend that the duties of imparting instruction and of maintaining discipline should be combined in the same hands, and that the authority at present divided between the Commandant and the Headmaster should be combined in a single individual, directly responsible for the well being of the establishment in all its departments.'

(In spite of these recommendations this dichotomy was to last for the next 100 years and was not finally resolved until 1967, when the appointment of Commandant was abolished and overall control given to a professional headmaster of the Royal Army Educational Corps.)

The Commission was seriously concerned about the poorness in physique of the boys compared with that of the boys at the Hibernian School, particularly as this led to a higher proportion of rejects for the Army. They felt the quality of food was good but that more attention should be paid to the sufficiency, suitability, and frequent variation of the diet. They attributed the higher tone at the Hibernian School to the better site and to the better arrangements for healthy recreation and exercise. They found the every day school life of the pupils at Chelsea confined and monotonous.

> 'It is mainly for this reason that we decidedly recommend the removal of the school into the country for, although there is nothing to prove that the present site is actually unhealthy, we do not consider that a situation in the Metropolis is well adapted for a school for young boys, entailing as it does, a deprivation of the facilities for recreation so essential both to their happiness and to their health.'

When the school was built in 1801, Chelsea was recognised as being in the country. Well-known places like Belgrave Square and Eaton Square were not begun until 1825 and 1827 and Chelsea could be reached by a daily service of coaches from the various hostelries in the City, Strand and Charing Cross. In 1801 King's Road was a rural hamlet, but the nearby Jew's Row (Pimlico Road) was a centre of depravity, thriving on the out-patients of the Chelsea Hospital. In spite of the Royal Commission's recommendation, there was much opposition to the removal of the school from Chelsea. Finally, the increasingly cramped site and the need to improve the health and physique of the boys dictated the move in 1909 to the present beautiful and extensive home on the top of the cliffs of Dover.

Royal Hibernian School, Dublin, 1870. The Royal Hibernian Military School in Dublin was designed on the same lines as the model school at Chelsea 'to afford a gratuitous education to the sons of soldiers, orphans having a prior claim over others to admission.' Originally founded in 1769, like its sister establishment at Chelsea, it had been entirely re-organised in 1846. Its staffing, both military and educational, and its general lines of organisation and administration were similar to those of the Royal Military Asylum and it also had a Board of Governors. Its 410 pupils were, for the purposes of military training and discipline, distributed in six companies each under the charge of a Serjeant-Assistant. For the purposes of education the pupils were arranged in four divisions, each having its own master with a Headmaster exercising general supervision over the education of the whole school. Its subjects and trades were similar to those at Chelsea. Since the constitution and organisation of the two schools were so similar, the recommendations made by the Commission for the Model School at Chelsea equally applied to those at the Hibernian School.

The Commandant summarised the School for the Commissioners as follows:

'I cannot suggest any alteration either in the course or method of instruction. They both seem to me exactly suited for soldiers' sons intending, as almost all of them do, to join the Army. Of 983 now in the Army, and formerly in the RHM School, 251, or more than one-quarter, have been promoted from the ranks, and yet about 276 of the 983 are still under 18 years of age; another large proportion are detained as musicians in the regiments, and thus cannot (but with few exceptions) be non-commissioned officers.

'These results alone would deter me from proposing alterations of the course and method of instruction, more particularly as they seem quite to bear out the opinion of the examiners for the "Crimean" prizes in 1866,[4] when those gentlemen, thus expressed themselves – "Whilst a degree of proficiency considerably above the average has been realized in the several subjects of the school course, we were particularly gratified to observe that marked excellence had been attained in those most important points of primary education – reading and arithmetic – indeed, we had ample evidence that the instruction imparted in the Royal Hibernian Military School is of a thoroughly practical nature, and in our opinion well adapted to the course of life which the boys are likely to adopt.'

REFERENCES

1. Lord Granville in the House of Lords (1862).
   Quoted by Dawson and Wall in *Society and Industry in the 19th Century.*
2. Quoted by Dawson and Wall.
3. Report of the Royal Commission on Army Schools, HMSO, 1870.
4. 'The Crimean Banquet Fund Exhibitions originated in 1856 as a mark of esteem by the people of Ireland for the valour of the British Forces in the campaign against the Russians before Sebastopol.' They received 'the triumphant Army in Ireland at a public banquet' on 22 October 1856, in Dublin at which 'upwards of 4000 NCOs and soldiers were entertained sumptuously'. After payment of the expenses, the residue was invested and dividends applied to boys of the school who competed annually for the prizes. 'The examinations to be viva voce and by written questions, and will be as public as possible (with outside examiners) and comprise every branch of science, art, handicraft or matter of discipline taught or inculcated in the establishment.'

1 BN. GRENADIER GUARDS
Beggar's Bush Barracks, DUBLIN.

CHILDREN'S MORNING SCHOOL TIME-TABLE

FIRST CLASS

Time	Monday	Tuesday	Wednesday	Thursday	Friday	Saturday
9–9.30	Bible lesson (NT)	Geography	Bible lesson (OT)	Bible lesson (NT)	Bible lesson (OT)	Bible lesson (NT)
9.30–10	English history	Writing in copies / Euclid	Slate arithmetic / Euclid	English history	English history	Dictation
10–10.30	Slate arithmetic to Standard B / Algebra	English history	English history	Dictation	Dictation	Geography
10.30–11	Geography, British Islands	Slate arithmetic / Mensuration	Writing in copies	Geography in Palestine	Arithmetic / Mensuration	English composition
11–11.30	English composition	Religious instruction	English grammar	Writing in copies / Algebra	Geography	Slate arithmetic / Euclid
11.30–12	English grammar	Religious instruction	Singing	Slate arithmetic	English grammar	Singing

SECOND CLASS

Time	Monday	Tuesday	Wednesday	Thursday	Friday	Saturday
9–9.30	Bible lesson (NT)	English history	Bible lesson (OT)	Bible lesson (NT)	Bible lesson (OT)	Bible lesson (NT)
9.30–10	Geography (child's geography the whole book)	Dictation	Jones's Advanced Reading Book	Writing in copies	Writing in copies	Geography
10–10.30	Mental arithmetic	English grammar	Geography	English grammar	English history	Dictation
10.30–11	Reading 4th book	Slate arithmetic	Dictation	Slate arithmetic	Slate arithmetic	English history
11–11.30	Slate arithmetic	Religious instruction	Slate arithmetic compound rules	Reading 1st poetical book	Geography	Slate arithmetic
11.30–12	Writing in copies	Religious instruction	Singing	Dictation	Dictation	Singing

THIRD CLASS

Time	Monday	Tuesday	Wednesday	Thursday	Friday	Saturday
9–9.30 9.30–10	Bible lesson (NT) English history	Slate arithmetic Geography	Bible lesson (OT) Reading sequel 2nd book	Bible lesson (NT) Dictation	Bible lesson (OT) Reading sequel	Bible lesson (NT) English history
10–10.30 10.30–11	Sequel to 2nd book Child's geography, to page 53	Writing in copies Reading sequel 2nd book	Slate arithmetic Geography	Reading sequel Slate arithmetic	Slate arithmetic Writing in copies	Geography Writing in copies
11–11.30	Writing in copies	Religious instruction	Writing in copies	Writing in copies	English history	Reading sequel
11.30–12	Slate arithmetic	Religious instruction	Singing	English history	Dictation	Singing

FOURTH CLASS

Time	Monday	Tuesday	Wednesday	Thursday	Friday	Saturday
9–9.30	Bible lesson (NT)	English history Pt. 1	Bible lesson (OT)	Bible lesson (NT)	Bible lesson (OT)	Bible lesson (NT)
9.30–10	Adult reading book	Clock face	English history	English history	English history	My second school book
10–10.30	Writing in copies	My second school book	Transcribing	Writing in copies	Transcribing	Transcribing
10.30–11	My second school book	Writing in copies	My second school book	My second school book	Adult reading book	English history
11–11.30	Slate arithmetic*	Religious instruction	Slate arithmetic	Mental arithmetic	Writing in copies	Slate arithmetic
11.30–12	Simple truths	Religious instruction	Singing	Adult reading book	Slate arithmetic	Singing

* Multiplication

96

FIFTH CLASS

Time	Monday	Tuesday	Wednesday	Thursday	Friday	Saturday
9–9.30 9.30–10 10–10.30	Simple truths (OT) Transcribing My first school book	Simple truths (NT) Transcribing Reading sheets	Writing in copies Reading sheets Slate arithmetic	Simple truths (OT) Clock face Reading sheets	Reading sheets Mental arithmetic Secular E.L. book	Simple truths (N.T.) Writing in copies My first school book
10.30–11 11–11.30 11.30–12	Writing in copies Reading sheets Clock face	Slate arithmetic † Secular E.L. book Writing	Secular E.L. book Transcribing Singing	Transcribing Secular E.L. book My first school book	Writing in copies Transcribing My first school book	Slate arithmetic Reading sheets Singing

SIXTH CLASS

Time	Monday	Tuesday	Wednesday	Thursday	Friday	Saturday
9–9.30 9.30–10	Writing Reading cards	Writing My first reading book	Transcribing Reading cards	Writing My first reading book	Transcribing Reading cards	Transcribing My first reading book
10–10.30 10.30–11	Arithmetic My first reading book	Arithmetic Reading cards	Arithmetic My first reading book	Clock face Reading cards	Arithmetic My first reading book	Mental arithmetic Reading cards
11–11.30 11.30–12	Transcribing Reading cards	Clock face My first reading book	Reading cards Singing	Arithmetic My first reading book	Clock face Reading cards	Writing Singing

† Addition, subtraction, and multiplication by one figure

AFTERNOON SCHOOL TIME-TABLE

Class	Time	Monday	Tuesday	Wednesday	Thursday	Friday
I	2.30–3 3–3.30	Reading and Spelling Writing in copies	Dictation English grammar	Geography Slate arithmetic	English grammar Dictation	Writing in copies Reading and Spelling
II	2.30–3 3–3.30	Dictation English history	Writing in copies Geography	English grammar Writing in copies	Slate arithmetic English grammar	Writing in copies Slate arithmetic
III	2.30–3 3–3.30	Reading and Spelling Dictation	Slate arithmetic Reading and Spelling	Reading Writing in copies	Slate arithmetic Reading and Spelling	Reading and Spelling Writing in copies
IV	2.30–3 3–3.30	Writing in copies Reading and Spelling	Reading and Spelling Transcribing on slates	Reading and Spelling Writing in copies	Transcribing on slates Reading and Spelling	Writing in copies Reading and Spelling
V	2.30–3 3–3.30	Reading and Spelling Writing in copies	Reading and Spelling Transcribing on slates	Writing in copies Reading and Spelling	Transcribing on slates Reading and Spelling	Reading and Spelling Writing in copies
VI	2.30–3 3–3.30	Transcribing on slates Reading and Spelling	Writing in copies Reading and Spelling	Reading and Spelling Transcribing on slates	Reading and Spelling Writing in copies	Transcribing on slates Reading and Spelling

INFANT SCHOOL, DEPOT BRIGADE, RA. WOOLWICH.

9 till 9.30
Prayers and Bible lesson

9.30 to 10

I. Class	—	Arithmetic
II. „	—	„
III. „	—	Reading
IV. „	—	Ball frame
V. „	—	Reading (alphabet)

10 till 10.30

I. Class	—	Reading
II. „	—	„
III. „	—	Ball frame
IV. „	—	Reading
V. „	—	Cubes

10.30 to 11

I. Class	—	Spelling
II. „	—	„
III. „	—	„
IV. „	—	Ball frame or cubes
V. „	—	Reading (alphabet)

11 to 11.10
Playground for all

11.10 to 11.35

I. Class	—	Reading
II. „	—	„
III. „	—	„
IV. „	—	„
V. „	—	Cubes or alphabet

11.35 to 11.55

Monday	—	Clock face
Tuesday	—	Natural history
Wednesday	—	Poetry and singing
Thursday	—	Object lesson
Friday	—	Marching and singing
Saturday	—	Poetry and singing

11.55 to 12 noon
Dismissal

N.B.—In changing classes and in marching to and from the playground singing is practised.

99

CHAPTER 7

The End of an Era (1875–1914)

Educational and Military Reforms. The last quarter of the nine-teenth century saw great changes in the political, social and educa-tional structure of the country, many of which were to be reflected in the Army. Britain's period of isolation was ending and the clouds of war were on the horizon. There were reforms to combat social misery, crime and drunkenness and another Education Act (1902), which provided public aid for secondary education and took the denominational schools into the public system by making them eligible for rate aid. The military reforms of Cardwell and Childers between 1870–82 and the introduction of new automatic weapons marked the end of the Old Army, which had endured from Stuart times, and the emergence of the New Army, which would fight the South African and Great Wars.[1] The abolition of the purchase system (1871) produced a new and better class of officer, who began to pay closer attention to the education and training of his men. The days had passed when a General could write:

'There is not a man in the Army that cares one farthing whether his Commanding Officer, his Brigadier, or the Commander-in-Chief himself approves his conduct or not. His promotion depends not on their smiles or frowns – his friends can give him £1,000 with which he goes to the auction room in Charles Street and in a fortnight he becomes a Captain. Out of the 15 regiments of cavalry and 26 of Infantry, which we have here in Holland, 21 are literally com-manded by boys or idiots.'[2]

Other changes for the better were—the introduction in 1870 of the short-service system (six years with the Colours and six with the Reserve), instead of the previous system of enlistment for life; there were changes in the Barrack Room conditions, in food and recrea-tion facilities, and the once floggable, expendable British soldier now began to appear as 'humorous, human, and sometimes as an heroic being', instead of the drunken sot that the Duke of Welling-

100

ton had portrayed.[3] 'Gone to be a soldier' was no longer synonymous with 'gone to the bad'. It is not surprising, therefore, that the better conditions of the Service attracted better types of recruits, with corresponding improvements in family life and the capabilities of their children.[4]

But these were times of economic stringency and gradually the recommendations of the Royal Commission were to be undermined. The Report of a Parliamentary Committee in 1887[5] showed how children's education was to be dictated by financial restrictions. Instead of small regimental schools averaging twenty-five children, garrison schools were to be substituted to give the benefits of a better classification, which could only be attained by the assembly of larger numbers than were to be found in a regimental school. Teachers were expensive and economies had to be made.

'There are 277 trained schoolmasters in the Service and 23 students at the Normal School, Chelsea. When garrison schools are established it will be possible to get rid of the greater part of school assistants, whose extra duty pay at present amounts to £4036 per annum. The reduction will be possible when compulsory education for soldiers ceases and their education becomes voluntary.

'There are 258 schoolmistresses, whose average salary with allowances is £66 p.a. with a retiring pension of £36.10.0d p.a. at the age of 50 after 24 years' service. These schoolmistresses only instruct the infants up to the 1st standard, or 7 years of age, when they pass into the Master's school. In some cases acting schoolmistresses are employed: they are generally the wives of NCOs and are glad to increase their incomes by taking charge of the infant school. It has not been found that the children in their charge are neglected, either educationally or otherwise, and their respectability is guaranteed by the recommendations of the Officers Commanding of the corps to which their husbands belong.

'It seems to us quite unnecessary to continue employing trained schoolmistresses for such very elementary work and we recommend that in future acting schoolmistresses be employed at an annual salary of £25, without allowances or pension. To pass such an examination in needlework and elementary teaching as the Director General of Military Education may consider necessary.

'We strongly recommend the abolition of the Normal School, Chelsea, as previously recommended by the Royal Commission of 1870 and Lord Morley's Committee in 1882. (This time the Committee succeeded. It was abolished in December 1887 and the training of probationers transferred to Aldershot.)

'Pupil teachers from the Royal Military Asylum, Chelsea, and from the Hibernian School, Dublin, at the age of 19$\frac{1}{2}$ to be examined as to educational fitness, and if successful to be sent to a garrison school as assistant schoolmaster for 1$\frac{1}{2}$ years.

'Soldiers to be allowed to enter, up to 23 years, as assistant school-masters on probation for one year. If confirmed in the appointment of Army Schoolmaster to be allowed to count any previous service up to 5 years.

'Civilian candidates for the post of Army Schoolmaster to hold the parchment certificate,* to be recruited not under 20 and to pass a probationary year as assistant schoolmaster at a garrison school.

'The Army school districts to be rearranged and the number of inspectors to be reduced.'

There had also been a decline in the standards of school management since 1881. In that year Colonel A. C. Gleig, a nephew of the former Chaplain-General, had retired after being an Assistant Inspector and Inspector of Army Schools for twenty-five years. He had been a permanent official, responsible for superintending the work of his sub-inspectors; for inspecting all Army schools and for testing the capacity as teachers of all Army schoolmasters and mistresses. His long tenure of office gave him a detailed knowledge of every aspect of school administration and of the relative merits of the staff, so that promotions could be made on the principle of merit and not of seniority alone. Consequently, the Army schools were reported to have been in a high state of efficiency in 1881.

In that year the appointment of Inspector was abolished and an Assistant Director of Military Education appointed, a staff officer on the usual four-year tenure of appointment. For the next eleven years the schools were managed by a succession of staff officers, a change which, according to the Director-General of Military Education,[6] caused a decline in efficiency. They lacked the necessary intimate and technical knowledge of personnel and of school inspection and administration. Some lacked interest, and all lacked time to learn the job. A more permanent tenure of office was required and in 1892 a new post of Director of Army Schools was created with a tenure in the first instance of five years, the second and third periods of office, 'depending on continued zeal and efficiency'. To help this officer 'of long standing in the service' there were to be twenty-one 'inspectors' (the former post of sub-inspector being abolished), ten at home, four in the colonies and seven in India.

Not surprisingly, it proved necessary in 1889 to reverse the 1887 recommendations to employ the wives of NCOs and soldiers as acting-schoolmistresses in Infant Schools in the place of trained

* Of the Education Department.

102

Army schoolmistresses. But as these proved difficult to recruit,* a circular letter was sent to the Principals of the larger women's training colleges seeking the reason. The replies listed several causes, the chief being the low salary offered. Compared with the Army schoolmistress's average salary of £76.11.9d., irrespective of rent free accommodation, the students in one college were able to command salaries averaging £70 to £75; in another they were paid a starting salary of £85 under the London School Board and nearly as much by other boards and by some church schools. Their prospects of promotion were also better, since in civil schools schoolmistresses could aspire to posts offering up to £140 a year, with residence.

But the Principals gave other reasons to explain the lack of enthusiasm for Army appointments. Army schoolmistresses were required to serve away from their homes and relations for frequent long periods of foreign service in India and the colonies. Mothers, who felt concern for their daughters' morals, often objected strongly when the daughter wished to join a regiment as a schoolmistress. In any case better employment was readily to be had in the civil schools near their homes.

The years 1890–91 had seen the introduction of a number of changes in the Civil Code governing the education provided in the civil schools, whose managers were allowed a wider choice of subjects in the curriculum of their schools. Since 1886 the curriculum in Army schools had been assimilated to that of the public elementary schools, but the flexibility of this new system posed problems for the Army's migratory population.

'The curriculum in all Army Schools at home, in India and in the Colonies must be uniform, so as to enable the education of the children to continue on the same lines and in one progressive course, no matter which Army School they may for a time attend.'[6]

The Army schools, therefore, selected and made compulsory certain subjects: reading, writing, arithmetic, singing, recitation. physical exercise drill, English Grammar, Geography and English History and, for the higher standards, a choice of either Algebra, Euclid or Mensuration. Most of the other subjects authorised in the Code, e.g. Chemistry, Physics, Animal Physiology, Botany, French,

*On 31 December 1892 there were 251 Army Schoolmistresses – 138 at home, 32 in the Colonies and 81 in India – supported by 19 Acting Schoolmistresses, 30 pupil teachers and 217 monitresses.

Latin, etc., 'cannot be conveniently taught in Army Schools'. One other reason for this inflexibility was that the civil system of 'Payment by Results' did not apply to Army schools. Instead, the Army judged each school's efficiency by periodical and 'surprise' visits and by an annual examination, by age, of every child on the register. In civil schools the tests were made largely by 'sample', so that a child might be examined in one subject only. The Army school had to satisfy the inspector on the standards achieved by each child appropriate to its age. Furthermore, Army schoolmasters depended also on a satisfactory report on the tone, discipline, organisation and administration of their schools for the granting of their periodical increases of pay.

On 26 May 1888 the Royal Military Asylum, Chelsea, held a bazaar and military fête, opened by HRH the Princess Louise, to provide the money for a new chapel organ. *The Graphic*, reporting the occasion, described the school and its life.

'The façade is not unimposing. A fine stone portico of four Roman Doric columns is its most noticeable feature. On the broad gravel walk in front of the principal entrance stands a row of small field guns, with which the boys amuse themselves; the walk nearest to the roadway is reserved for the pupil teachers. The fine lawn before the building is devoted to cricket. Late in May the grass is thrown open to the exultant youngsters and the occasion becomes almost an annual ceremony. The boys assemble in crowds at the chain. When the word is given they raise a cheer, rush forward, and spread themselves eagerly over the grass.' (See illustration 6 and 10.)

The food had obviously improved, since the days of the 1870 Royal Commission.

'For breakfast they have cocoa, and bread-and-butter; for the evening meal tea, and bread-and-butter. Dinner is an ample and satisfying meal. The food supply is carefully calculated, not only on hygienic, but on economical grounds; for sixpence half-penny per day is the limit allowed by Government for the dietary of each boy. For this exceedingly moderate sum, however, the boys can be given such dinners as these: roast leg of mutton, potatoes, currant-pudding, and bread; or cold mutton, potatoes, pickles, bread and cheese.

'Each day has its allotted bill of fare; but other dinners may be substituted if the boys show themselves tired of particular dishes. Fish, for example, is not as a rule beloved by boys, and the dinner on the fish-day is then sometimes varied by "rice-pudding, bread and cheese;" or "apple-pudding, bread, and cheese", of which little is ever left. On certain red-letter days, such as the Queen's birthday, the Prince of Wales's birthday, the annual fête day, and so on, the ordinary dietary is increased by extras, such as oranges, buns, or

104

half a pound of cake. Eggs, too, are frequently allowed. In winter a change is made in the diet; soup and more heating foods being supplied. Ill-health is practically unknown among the boys. They are particularly free from those diseases of the eyes and head which so constantly afflict young children of the lower classes.'

In 1889 the Royal Military Asylum, Chelsea, decided to abolish the 'half-time' system, which it had instituted in 1875 and which had proved a failure. In spite of raising the age of admission to 10–12 years (instead of 7–12 as had previously been the case) there had been no corresponding rise in the level of attainment.

'The low educational state on admission of so many boys points to inexcusable neglect in these days of universal and free education. The fact that the boys come from all parts of the country indicates the existing state of elementary education in the country and shows that the results of the working of the Education Acts are not so thorough or so complete as they are generally supposed to be.'[6]

The 'full-time' system (which was also adopted by the Royal Hibernian School, Dublin, in 1890) permitted the hours af academic instruction to be increased from three hours a day to four hours for the three upper classes and four-and-a-half for the two lower. Not only could the subjects in the curriculum be better taught but the boys no longer had to spend several hours a week in bootmaking and tailoring 'under conditions most adverse to their health and physique'. The shoe-maker's shop was abolished and industrial training was reduced to two hours every other day, giving more time for recreation. The boys were also relieved from their heavy and laborious duties of scrubbing halls and floors, which interfered with their school instruction, reduced their time for recreation and caused much sickness, especially in winter. It was thus found possible to add another half-hour's instruction to the three upper classes, to teach English History to the whole school and Algebra to the first form. (See illustration 19.)

The 1896 Report[7] considered the garrison school system to be working satisfactorily, especially at Chatham and Woolwich and in Gibraltar, where the larger numbers had enabled the formation of separate and distinct schools for each sex, the older girls being taught by schoolmistresses, instead of by schoolmasters as hitherto. This permitted some divergence in the curriculum for boys and girls, owing to the necessity of having to teach needlework to the latter. It was planned that other stations should follow suit, when new schools were constructed under the Barracks Act. Meanwhile, strong criticism was made against the slow progress in bringing existing school premises up to the minimum standards required by the Education Department for public elementary schools. It was hoped that the new generation of Army schools being built would increase efficiency and the children's health. It was found that too many younger children were risking permanent deformity by sitting at desks constructed for adult soldiers and elder children. 'A new type of desk, with an adjustable rest to render it suitable for men and children, has now been designed and will be fitted in the new schools', was the solution proposed—a typical Army compromise dictated by financial, not educational, reasons.

The introduction of 'a modified system of kindergarten instruction' had proved successful and all new entrants to the Corps of Army Schoolmistresses had to undergo a course of training in the new methods at the Model School at Aldershot.

> 'Kindergarten occupations (i.e. bead-threading, stick-laying, pricking and embroidery, mat-plaiting, paper-folding, drawing and building with cubes) counteract the weariness produced by the ordinary routine work of books, slates and pencils, during a school day of five hours. It is found by experience that these occupations cultivate the intelligence of children, and enable them to obtain correct notions of form, size and colour, and clear perceptions of the nature of substances. They also tend to inculcate habits of thought, study and discipline.'[6]

There were two possible dangers. They might curtail the reading lessons and injure the children when they passed into the senior classes (Standards) or 'in the hands of an inferior mistress degenerate into mere play, a method of keeping them amused without deriving any real benefit.' The Army's School Regulations would prevent the former, and the new teacher training courses the latter.

Drawing had not been introduced as an obligatory subject for boys, in spite of its usefulness to them in after life, 'owing to the expense'. Physical exercises, 'a quarter of an hour every day', were highly commended, and special attention was drawn to handwriting, orthography and elementary arithmetic for boys of 14, who could compete for careers as 'Boy Copyists' in the Civil Service. During the previous six years attention had been given in Army schools to teaching a uniform style of writing because children were constantly moving from one Army school to another and because of the large number of clerical appointments now open to lads and young women, who could write a clear legible hand, not

106

only in the Post Office but in business firms generally. For girls trained in Army schools, there were appointments as monitress in an infant school, leading to the career of Army schoolmistress at no cost to themselves. 'These solid advantages are specially offered to the daughters of soldiers, and considering the comparative shortness of the daily hours of employment, the superior class of work and the position, the career of a mistress is one of considerable value.'

The 1896 report noted with great concern the fact that the annual wastage in the Corps of Army Schoolmasters could not be entirely filled by pupil teachers from the two military schools. The deficiency was made up by advertising for trained civilian schoolmasters, qualified under the Education Department. Not enough of these were forthcoming. The hindrances were stated to be:

1. Service abroad in all climates.
2. Liability to move from station to station, and the expense each move entailed.
3. Ignorance of military life.
4. Dislike of discipline.
5. The few prizes to be gained in the service, as compared with the large staff of assistant inspectors, and the very high salaries with houses given to headmasters of large civil schools.

On the other hand, the great inducement to the candidates who had come forward was the prospect of a good pension at the end of their service. But there was a general expectation that before long pensions would be given to schoolmasters of public elementary schools. If this occurred the special inducement offered in the Service would cease to operate, and it would be necessary to devise some other means for filling up the ranks.[7]

Many years later an Army schoolmaster[8] recollecting those days, wrote that in 1897 he had been recognised by the Education Department as a fully-trained teacher and on leaving college he had answered an advertisement in the *Schoolmaster* and obtained a job at a denominational school at Tooting with a salary of £85 p.a. He discovered that the pay and allowances of an Army schoolmaster were £120 p.a., with a pension at the end of twenty-one years of service, so he applied to the Military Asylum, Chelsea, one Saturday morning to become one. He was asked to read and sing 'for the information and amusement' of a number of gentlemen and was eventually informed that the Secretary of State for War had been pleased to appoint him an Army Assistant Schoolmaster from 3 January 1898. He should report for duty at the Aldershot Garrison School.

He well remembered his first day in the Army School.

'After being introduced to the members of the School Staff, I heard a small bell tinkling from a window and the boys assembled by classes, in the asphalted playground. Hands, hair and boots were inspected and the scholars then marched into a large classroom where staff and boys joined in singing one of the well known hymns for the young from the "Ancient and Modern" Hymn Book. The opening note was provided by means of a "C" tuning fork, supplied for the public service, the harmony was ad lib and the result quite pleasing and suitable. Morning prayers were then read by the schoolmaster in charge and this was followed by certain prescribed verses from the Bible, which had to be learned by heart and repeated all round the class at the half yearly inspections. Then came the Scripture Lesson proper, and at 9.30am the boys dispersed to various rooms for instruction in their class work. Let me say that the school of between 70 and 80 boys in which I found myself was well staffed: in addition to the Schoolmaster in Charge and two masters on probation, there were four Army schoolmasters of warrant rank, three very useful NCOs attached as School Assistants, and an invaluable School Orderly. The morning session ended at 12.30pm and I was introduced to the Sergeants' Mess of the regiment.

'One hundred up at billiards cost twopence and by the time I had made fifty the hands of the clock were approaching 1.50pm and the afternoon session commenced at 2pm. Children's School finished at 3.15pm and from the surrounding Guard Rooms came the buglers to rend the air with high pitched notes of the "School Call".

'At 3.25pm the men were marched to school by the Battalion Orderly Sergeant who brought the Attendance Rolls for each of the eight companies and one for the band and drums, duly marked by the Company Orderly Sergeants, and reported to the schoolmaster in charge that all the men were present. This done, the men were marched into school and went to class rooms for instruction in First, Second and Third Class Certificates of Education.

'I thought I had done a very good day's work at 4.45pm and in my polite civilian way I bade "Good-day" to the Schoolmaster in charge, only to be informed that he would see me after tea, as the Second Attendance for men who had been prevented from being present at the First, was due at 6pm and lasted until 7.15pm. I was immensely surprised but I learned on further explanation that this was the ordinary routine on every night except Wednesday, when there was no Second Attendance. I pondered this deeply and very nearly concluded that one such day in the Army was enough for me.

I had not enlisted and was quite at liberty to leave, but the prospect of returning to my little back room in Tooting and my nightly wanderings to Brixton or Balham, finally made me decide to continue where I was, for a little longer – and for how long I scarcely dreamed.'

RMA Chelsea's Centenary Celebrations. On 10 and 11 July 1902, the Duke of York's Military School* celebrated the centenary of its foundation 'with every manifestation of military pomp, as suited the occasion.'[9] Grand Day was held on Wednesday, 10 July, before many distinguished civilian and military visitors, headed by Earl Roberts, the Commander-in-Chief, who took the salute. The 545 boys of the school were drawn up in line facing the terrace, their band in the rear and presented 'a striking picture of youthful soldiery, erect, smart and alert, that indicated powerfully the fine stock from which they sprang.' Earl Roberts made a close inspection of the parade. beginning with the smart battery of three-pounders on the right and then the boys marched past to the stirring strains of the 'British Grenadiers', proudly carrying the new Colours presented to them in 1897 on behalf of Queen Victoria by their Royal Highnesses the Duke and Duchess of Cornwall and York.

> 'The infantry went through a series of parade movements with a precision that would not have shamed a Regular battalion of infantry. Then, the gunners manipulated their guns with astonishing celerity and accuracy to be followed by the gymnastic class, in flannels, who gave a pleasing exhibition of free gymnastics, vaulting horse and parallel bars exercises.'[9]

Lord Roberts began his speech:

> 'My Lords, – It affords me the greatest pleasure to be able for the 8th year in succession to present to your lordships and his Majesty's Commissioners a most favourable report, which cannot fail to gratify all who are interested in the welfare of the British Army, and more especially of the sons of our soldiers, who alone are eligible to become pupils in this old military institution.'

He reminded his audience of the laying of the foundation stone almost exactly 100 years previously by HRH Frederick Duke of York, and that 'formerly girls were admitted, but had been banished', and continued

> 'Very soon indeed did the school begin to repeat in the persons of its inmates the example of devotion to duty set by their fathers, for

---

*The Royal Military Asylum became the Duke of York's Military School by a Royal Warrant of 1892.

in 1808 occurred the first recorded death of an old boy on active service in the Peninsular War, his name being Crooks of the 14th Light Dragoons, and in every subsequent war up to the present the traditions of the school have been worthily upheld by its old boys in the Army all the world over. Thus has the school given back to the State a splendid return for its care of soldiers' orphans.'

He then concluded favourably on the scholastic and sporting achievements of the school and on their smart, well mannered and cheerful appearance. He spoke of the good record of the school's 1673 'old boys' serving in the Army on 1 January 1902, which included 28 commissioned officers, 64 Warrant Officers, 600 NCOs and 981 other ranks.

After presenting the prizes and complimenting the staff on the very fine state of the school, he finished on a high note.

'Always endeavour to maintain that high reputation, which over so many years, in so many distant places, the Sons of the Brave (the school motto) have so well earned for themselves, exemplified by that old Dukie, Corporal J. Shaul of the 1st Highland Light Infantry, of whom we are all so proud and who has just been awarded the v c for conspicuous bravery at Magersfontein in South Africa.'

The same year, 1902, the third and last of the Army's military boarding schools in the United Kingdom was established—The Queen Victoria School, Dunblane. The idea of establishing in Scotland a school of the same nature as the military schools at Chelsea and Dublin 'in commemoration of the Scottish sailors and soldiers who fell in the South Africa War' was that of a General Officer Commanding-in-Chief in Scotland in 1901. The National Memorial would take the form of a boarding school for the sons of Scottish servicemen, with priority of admission to boys who had lost their fathers in that war. Queen Victoria gave the proposal her warm support but died before the project was far advanced. It was, therefore, decided that the school should also form Scotland's Memorial to the Queen and be named after her. A Committee was formed, under the patronage of the Dukes of Connaught and Cambridge, both Field-Marshals, and of Princess Louise, Duchess of Argyll, to launch a national appeal. Sufficient funds were raised to build and found the school, but not to endow and maintain it, so the War Office agreed under the Royal Warrant of 1905 to support the school 'in perpetuity'. On 28 September 1908, HM King Edward VII formally opened the school and laid the foundation stone of the Memorial Chapel. The first of the 270 boys arrived the following summer.

3 Military Committees. Yet another Committee[10] sat in 1904 and made detailed proposals about the reorganisation of children's schools. In spite of the care and thoroughness of the Inspectors, the Bowles Committee considered the schools generally were still over-examined and over-inspected, the schoolmasters' hours of work were excessive and should be reduced, even though more masters would be required; there should be a library maintenance grant of 1*d.* per head per annum for the elder children's schools; and classes of girls should perform their physical exercises in a drill shed or in a walled-in playground, since 'on two occasions, they saw the girls performing their exercises in the open, overlooked by the men in the neighbouring barracks.' They recommended one or two mistresses should attend a course of lessons at some London school of music, since the model school at Aldershot could not provide this form of training and that all mistresses 'should receive thorough instruction in school hygiene, a subject which is now receiving great attention from educationalists.' Too much time was given to the instruction in temperance but not enough to manual employment, but they hesitated to recommend its general introduction 'because the expense would be considerable'. Because whole careers of most of the inspectors had been spent 'within the four walls of an Army School, first as children in an Army School, then at a students' class at Chelsea or Dublin and subsequently for 20 or 25 years as teachers in Army Schools', they recommended the Board of Education be asked to permit Army inspectors to accompany one of the Board's inspectors on his inspections of civil schools and that trainee Army inspectors should attend suitable civil courses on the latest developments in education and methods of teaching.

This echoed the most important recommendation of the Cross Commission of 1888, which considered that the training colleges suffered from in-breeding. Most of their staff consisted of men and women who had come from the elementary school, served their apprenticeship as pupil teachers and taught in the elementary school, without any opportunity of mixing with those training for other professions.[11] It recommended the establishment of day training colleges in association with the universities and university colleges. These were reorganised in 1890 by the Education Department and became the forerunners of the present University Institutes of Education.

The recommendations of the Bowles Committee were submitted

to the Army Council and were approved 'with the exception of those involving additional expense'.

The most important question, however, was whether or not greater use could be made of the civil elementary schools by soldiers' children and in 1906 an Interdepartmental committee under the chairmanship of Lord Portsmouth submitted its report on this problem. The Army schools fulfilled a double purpose—the education of the adult soldier and the education of his children. As the soldier was available for school only in the late afternoon, the instruction of the elder children was for the most part carried out by the same staff as for these adults; infant children were taught by a separate staff of schoolmistresses, who also instructed the elder girls in needlework.

> 'Since the education of the adult soldier is more important than that of the child from a military point of view, was there sufficient justification for maintaining schools for adults alone?' 'Yes,' said all the evidence, 'since the soldier on entering the Service is not sufficiently educated to receive profitably instruction on such subjects as musketry, gunnery, tactics, map reading etc, it would be nearly impossible to get on without the schools.'

The Committee argued that one reason for retaining the present system was that soldiers' children were often located in isolated places where there was no civil school available, or in districts where there was no accommodation in the local school. But a more important reason, perhaps, was that

> 'the military population is constantly migratory, so that the frequent removals of the children from one public elementary school to another would hamper their educational progress, and distort the organisation of the civil schools to which they are transferred.'

The Committee noted that another Committee under Lord Harris in 1887 and the Inspection Report of 1896 had also considered this problem and had given additional reasons for the Army retaining its own schools. Since there were no civil schools in India or in most of the colonial stations, which Army children could attend, schoolmasters had to be posted to stations abroad for the education of these children, and as schoolmasters could not be expatriated for the whole of their service, the necessary reliefs had to be maintained at home.

> 'Army children move with their corps and civil teachers look upon them as birds of passage who will bring no credit to themselves or to their schools, for before the annual examination of the school

comes round the children may have left the station. Consequently, they are apt to be neglected, especially if they join in the middle of term and perhaps shortly before the annual inspection.'

Curricula and textbooks differed from school to school, but the scheme of work in Army schools, although based on the Civil Educational Code, was specially framed to meet the peculiar conditions under which Army children were placed. Children could continue the same course in every subject, in spite of frequent moves from station to station, for the courses were identical throughout all Army schools, whether at home, in India or in the colonies, and the same books were used. The course prescribed was generally more extended and liberal than in most civil schools, and the instruction more thorough and more closely supervised, so that Army children on leaving school were, on the whole, better educated than most of the children in the country.

Finally, the Harris Committee had reported:

'We are convinced that the existence of Army Schools is appreciated by the married men as a reward for their long and good service, by the children as tending to encourage in their minds the feeling that the Army is their home, and by the Service in general as in many ways raising its tone. Again, the influx of children from the Army would probably in some cases necessitate the enlargement of existing school rooms at the expense of the rate payers and to their dissatisfaction.'

We shall note later the outcry that was raised in 1968–69, when local authorities had to find school places to meet the influx of Service children from East of Suez.

The Portsmouth Committee, having weighed the arguments, recommended that the Army should aim at abolishing infant schools at home and that the children should go to civil schools, except where it was necessary to retain teachers for the adult school, who would thus be available for children's education.

This recommendation was approved in principle; it was left to the Adjutant-General's department to decide particular cases. As a result twenty-two schools in England and Scotland were closed in 1907, Ireland not being affected. By November 1909 the number had risen to forty-eight, but the process of closing Army children's schools was then arrested, because the Board of Education strongly deprecated their further suppression. In 1912 Treasury sanction was obtained to reopen the elder girls' and infants' schools at Windsor, Regent's Park, Chelsea and Caterham on the grounds that the especially frequent changes of stations peculiar to the Guards created a need for special educational arrangements to be made for their children.

Board of Education Report 1904. The Board of Education was invited in 1904 to survey Army children's schools. Its terms of reference were limited to making 'recommendations which should not involve any but slight expenditure'. Its report, published in 1906, showed the most pressing need was to modernise the old-fashioned curriculum which every soldier's child followed. There were too many facts to be memorised in such subjects as religious instruction, history and geography. Music was taught, but no Army school possessed a musical instrument. Drawing and science had not yet been introduced, but each school had three 'copious' text-books on temperance to be mastered. (Thus were the sins of the fathers visited on the children!)[12] The 1902 Education Act allowed local authorities to create new secondary schools and to link these with the elementary schools. No such provision was being made for Army children, whose schools, still largely linked with the regiment, were not offering the same facilities as were becoming increasingly available to their civilian counterparts. Furthermore, the financial support was often lacking, since to secure pianos for Army children's schools was considered an increase on the Army's military spending. The cumulative effect of years of deciding what was financially expedient rather than educationally necessary was having its effect. The Army's schools were beginning to fall behind the level of provision found in the country at large.

What helped to mitigate the effects of these deficiencies and to keep the standards higher than would otherwise have been the case was undoubtedly the training and character of the Army school teachers. HMIs who visited and reported on the training centres at the Duke of York's School, the Royal Hibernian School and the garrison schools at Aldershot were somewhat dismayed at the system. The syllabuses were out of balance, nearly half the time being spent on mathematics, whilst drawing and science were entirely omitted. There were too few good modern books, whilst the teaching was too inflexible. The gymnasium and playing field featured prominently. Had not the students been made of 'such good physical and intellectual stuff', they declared, the results would certainly have been disastrous. The students were excessively over-worked. A Hibernian student described his training as – 'a Monastic

114

life, in which the worst crime was to be seen with a member of the opposite sex. That meant instant dismissal.' What impressed the HMIs, however, was the force, dignity and self-reliance of the students, whom they described as a corps d'élite, contrasting their moral earnestness with the less vigorous climate of some training colleges. The training staff was excellent. The HMIs concluded: 'We set a very high value on the type of teacher produced here, whom we class with the best in the country.'[12]

On the advice of the HMIs, the Board of Education announced in 1909 that they would accept the Army schoolmaster as 'ipso facto' certificated, if a more balanced syllabus were introduced, and if more time were allowed for relaxation and private pursuits, including private study, during training. The War Office accepted these conditions and, although arrangements over the Teacher's Certificate were not concluded until 1918, Army schoolmasters could, henceforth, on leaving the Army, take up civil appointments, counting Army service for increments on the recognised scale of salaries. This proved of immense value at the end of the First World War, when many discharged Army schoolmasters took posts as Headmasters and Assistants in civil schools.

1902 Education Act. In 1891 parents were given the national right to demand free education for their children and in 1893 the school leaving age was fixed at 11 and increased to 12 in 1899. For children who stayed on later at school a Standard 7 was instituted and it became convenient to group the older pupils in one central school or, in rural districts, to add 'higher tops' to elementary schools. Additional subjects were included in the curriculum, such as history, geography, cookery, laundry, dairy work and cottage gardening, so that by the end of the century the concept of elementary education had changed radically.

'The purpose of the Public Elementary School is to form and strengthen the character and to develop the intelligence of the children entrusted to it, ... to train the children carefully in habits of observation and clear reasoning ... to gain an intelligent acquaintance with some of the facts and laws of nature; ... a living interest in the ideals and achievements of mankind ... some familiarity with the literature and history of their own country; ... some power over language as an instrument of thought and expression ... a taste for good reading and thoughtful study. ...

'The School must at the same time encourage to the utmost the children's natural activities of hand and eye by ... practical work and manual instruction. ...

115

'And, though their opportunities are but brief, the teachers can yet do much to lay the foundations of conduct. They can endeavour, by example and influence, aided by a sense of discipline, which should pervade the school, to implant in the children habits of industry, self-control, and courageous perseverance in the face of difficulties; they can teach them to reverence what is noble, to be ready for self-sacrifice, and to strive their utmost after purity and truth. . . .'[13]

The Forster Education Act of 1870 had been concerned with elementary education only. The Education Act 1902 linked elementary and higher education together for the first time in our history. It empowered the new education authorities (LEAs) to provide for both types of education. They were given power to provide for education 'other than elementary', an elastic term which covered not only secondary schools but technical schools and institutions, training colleges for teachers and even adult education. Before 1902 secondary education was mainly the privilege of children whose parents could afford to pay school fees. Now public opinion was demanding that secondary schools ought to be open to elementary school pupils who showed they could benefit from secondary education. This was a step towards the view that secondary education was a stage which should be available to every boy and girl.

The 1902 Act ended the era of the 2559 school boards whose powers were taken over by the new LEAs run by County and County Borough Councils. Under the new system Board Schools became *provided* Council schools (i.e. the money needed to maintain them was *provided* by the LEAs). The old voluntary schools became known as *non-provided* schools which were entitled to assistance from the rates to meet running costs, while school managers remained responsible for the provision and up-keep of school buildings. The following report on a board school in the East End of London shows what progress was being made, even if there were still no grounds for complacency:

'*A Headmaster's Notes on changes in his Board School 1882–1900*

'The boy of 1900 as compared with the boy of 1880: Much more docile; insubordination, then endemic, now almost unknown, and if it occurs very likely to be the fault of the teacher. Cheerful and eager now, then often sullen and morose. Relations with teachers generally friendly, often affectionate – no streetcalling after them or stone throwing as there used to be. All this, the result of discipline and control at school, reacts beneficially at home. Truancy almost extinct and when occurring there is usually something in the blood to explain it. Theft rather common but perhaps more often detected owing to better supervision.

'Personal cleanliness: Greatly improved; verminous cases among boys rare, but among girls almost universal, due to their long hair. Out of thirty examined, twenty-eight required attention. As to dirt, it is necessary to distinguish between recent dirt got at play and the ancient kind that gives the strong smell. Swimming is taught and has a good effect. The really dirty seen when stripped, would not be allowed to bathe, but would be sent home to wash there first. This now seldom happens. The vermin referred to are lice; bugs are rarely seen; but fleas are common, especially on children coming from homes where there is a baby.

'Obscene Language: Common both in the street and in the home, but not common in the school where, if disagreeable words are heard, they are checked.

'Obscene conduct: Very rare. As to boys and girls, the latter are the aggressors.'[14]

Most children still went to an elementary school until they started work at 13, although from 1907 they could compete for 'scholarships' to grammar schools under the Free Place system. Children who failed to win a scholarship might go to a central school, which developed after 1911 and provided a four-year course from 11+ with a more practical bias than grammar schools. Even the Education Act of 1918 did not provide free secondary education for all, though it did raise the school leaving age to 14. Secondary education for all had to wait until the Butler Act of 1944 with its radical change of educational philosophy.

Army Achievements. The Army's School Regulations for the period 1910–13 show that many of the recommendations discussed in this chapter were turned into administrative instructions. Candidates for the position of Army schoolmaster had to be

'unmarried: in good health and of a good constitution: free from any defect of vision, hearing or voice and from any physical deformity: between 20–24 years of age on the 1st of the month in which the examination was held: of unmixed European blood and of pure British or Irish parentage. They had to be at least 5ft 4 inches in height, 8 stone 3 lbs in weight and 33 inches chest measurement, taken naked.'

After selection for the position of Army schoolmaster they had to undergo a probationary period of about a year in the rank of

Quartermaster Serjeant, during which they had to perfect themselves in the art of teaching, physical drill, the Army system of singing and of handwriting, in Army school regulations and in the keeping of regimental accounts, and pass an examination in the same. Their seniority depended on the place they obtained on the pass list: failure meant dismissal or discharge. They enlisted for twelve years into the Corps of Army Schoolmasters, ranking next to the Master Gunner, 3rd Class; after eight years they were granted the rank of Warrant Officers, a limited number being promoted to first class rank. They could marry after three years' enlisted service or after reaching the age of 23. A very few were selected for commissioning, as inspectors, with the honorary rank of lieutenant, rising to captain after ten years in the inspectorate.

Candidates for the situation of Army Schoolmistress, who had to be between 20–22 years of age, had to satisfy appropriate physical and educational standards and during their probation undergo a course of twelve months' training at the Model School, Aldershot. A schoolmistress was not permitted to marry a soldier below the rank of serjeant and became liable to retirement on marriage, though this was not necessarily enforced.

Qualified schoolmasters and mistresses were no longer tied to the regiment, but could be moved around a Command as circumstances dictated, and from home to a station overseas in their turn.

There were changes for the better in the schools. The list of books and materials was improved; drawing was extended to all children attending Army schools, and authority was given for occasional short excursions in the country and for visits to museums and places of educational interest. Infant schools or classes had to be held in a separate building or room from the elder children. A school could close on the Saturday if it had been open for five hours daily, making twenty-five hours attendance each week.

The step-children and adopted children of serving soldiers, the children of barrack labourers and the children of pensioners and of ex-soldiers, occupying with authority government quarters, were added to the list of those entitled to free tuition in Army schools.

Where there were Army schools within a mile of their residences, NCOs and soldiers were required to send their children to such schools. But officers in charge of the Army school could authorise attendance at a certified efficient civil school, if a soldier applied in writing, but at no expense to the public:

a. if in the medical officer's opinion the distance of one mile from an Army school was considered too far;
b. if the soldier had a conscientious objection to his children attending an Army school;
c. if children, who had passed Standard V, needed higher (secondary) education.

Where no Army school was available, children were required to attend an efficient civil school and LEAs were requested to arrange that soldiers' children continued to attend school until their fourteenth birthday, or passed Standard VII, local bye-laws notwithstanding.

At the beginning of the war in 1914, civil and Army schools were requisitioned as billets for the new armies which were being raised. The boys of DYRMS, who had moved from Chelsea to Dover in 1909, were evacuated in September to Tonbridge School for a few days and thence to the Poplar Board of Guardians' School at Hutton in Essex, where they remained throughout the War. Classes became larger and schools were chiefly staffed by women. Married women and retired teachers came forward to fill the ranks depleted by conscription and voluntary enlistments into the male combatant and female auxiliary services. 'The Army decided that its schoolmasters were wanted most where they were; if they had been allowed to go abroad with fighting units, the Garrison Schools must in large numbers have been closed.'[15]

Regimental officers spoke in the highest terms of the Army schoolmasters and mistresses as individuals, but for some years past they had lacked recognition collectively. Education at the close of the Victorian era did not stand very high in public esteem, nor schoolmastering as a profession, and both had to wait until after the War to gain that recognition they deserved.

What had the Army achieved in the education of its children? It had given an early lead to the country by providing education for its children, first by voluntary effort and then by public grants, in an age when few civilian children received any education at all, and none at public expense. It pioneered a system of education in one of its schools, adopted later in all of them, which was followed by many English and continental schools. It sent trained monitors to help to establish the monitorial system in England and overseas. The Army was among the first organisations to provide schoolmasters and schoolmistresses for its schools, to establish them as

119

professional corps and to set up normal schools for their professional training. If towards the end of the period it had ceased to pioneer and was obliged by financial limitations to follow the national pattern and its curriculum to lag behind, it could nevertheless proudly boast that the education of all its children was soundly based, professionally directed and able to stand comparison with its civil counterpart, at least in the field of elementary education.

REFERENCES

1. Fortescue, *History of the Army*, Vol. xiii.
2. Biddulph, *Lord Cardwell at the War Office*, Murray, 1904. (Major-General Graig to Sir Hew Dalrymple on 12 October 1794, before the Battle of Nimeguen. Seven days later it was captured by the French and the British driven out of Holland.)
3. Notes on Conversations with the Duke of Wellington (1831–1851), 1889.
4. The Royal Commission on Military Education, 1870.
5. Committee on Army Schools and Schoolmasters, Chairman, Lord Harris, 1887.
6. Director General of Military Education, 4th Report on Army Schools, 1889–93, HMSO. Froebel's kindergarten ideas were introduced into England in 1851 by the Baroness von Marenholtz-Bülow, but were slow to gain recognition. The Froebel Society, formed in 1874, provided training for teachers in Froebel's principles and methods.
7. Director General of Military Education, 6th Report on Army Schools, 1896, HMSO.
8. W. Blackman, 'Reminiscences of the Retired'. *Army Education*, September 1946.
9. *Military Mail*, 12 July 1902.
10. Committee on Army Schools, Chairman Col. H. Bowles, War Office Paper, 1904.
11. Code of Public Elementary Schools, 1904. HMSO.
12. White, *The Story of Army Education*, Harrap.
13. Elementary Code 1904. Quoted in *Society and Industry*, Dawson & Wall. OUP.
14. Quoted in *Society and Industry*. Dawson & Wall, OUP.
15. Gorell, *Education and the Army*, OUP, 1921.

PART 2:

MODERN TIMES

George R.I.

ROYAL WARRANT.

Army Educational Corps.

WHEREAS WE deem it expedient to authorize the formation of a Corps to be entitled "Army Educational Corps";

20

Gen. No.

4829

OUR WILL AND PLEASURE IS that the Army Educational Corps shall be deemed to be a Corps for the purposes of the Army Act, and that the words "Army Educational Corps" shall be _substituted_ for "Corps of Army Schoolmasters" in the Schedule to Our Warrant of 7th July, 1916,* defining the expression "Corps."

OUR FURTHER WILL AND PLEASURE IS that Our Corps of Army Schoolmasters shall be disbanded forthwith.

IT IS OUR FURTHER WILL AND PLEASURE that the ranks and rates of pay and non-effective pay and the classification for allowances of officers, warrant officers and non-commissioned officers of Our Army Educational Corps and the general conditions of service shall be as laid down in the Schedule appended to this Our Warrant.

LASTLY, IT IS OUR WILL AND PLEASURE that Our Army Schoolmistresses shall bear the same relation to Our Army Educational Corps as they bore to Our Corps of Army Schoolmasters. The rates of pay and pension and the conditions of service shall be as laid down in Our Warrant of 29th March, 1920.†

Given at Our Court at St. James's, this _11th_

day of _June_ , 1920, in the 11th year

of Our Reign.

By His Majesty's Command,

W. Churchill

---

* Army Order 250 of 1916.   † Army Order 136 of 1920.

CHAPTER 8

Between the Wars

Army Educational Corps. The end of the fighting in 1918 was by
no means the end of the war-time tasks of the British Army.
There was a zone of occupation around Cologne on the Rhine to
be garrisoned under the terms of the Armistice with Germany,
and the Peace Treaty signed at Versailles in June 1919 prolonged
the period of this occupation until 1925. Strong forces had to be
retained in Egypt, Palestine, Mesopotamia and in India, whose
troops were soon to be engaged in a large scale conflict with
Afghanistan, a series of arduous frontier expeditions and a period
of prolonged internal unrest. A large proportion of the great
armies of 1918 thus remained unaffected by the demobilisation
which began in December 1918. It was not until September 1920
that the last of the war-time soldiers could be returned to civil life
and compulsory military service replaced by the pre-war voluntary system. As was to be expected, military retrenchment and
economy soon followed and these were to affect education in the
Army.

Towards the end of the War demands for social and educational
reform had increased. H. A. L. Fisher, introducing his Education
Bill to the House of Commons in 1917, claimed that 'the industrial workers of the country are entitled to be considered primarily
as citizens and as fit subjects for any form of education from which
they are capable of profiteering.' [*sic!*][1] Although his Act of 1918
did not provide secondary education for all, it did raise the age of
compulsory school attendance to 14, abolished the half-time system
and required provision to be made for practical and advanced instruction in elementary schools. Thus the elementary system began
to overlap and run parallel with the secondary system and the
Board of Education adopted the Consultative Committee's recommendation in 1926 to reorganise elementary schools into

123

Royal Warrant forming the Army Educational Corps, 11 June 1920.
Presented by Rt Hon. Winston Churchill and signed by King George V.

primary and senior or 'modern' schools with a break at 11.[2] This need to provide secondary education for its school children was to be a new concept for the Army, as it was for the country at large, and was to prove especially difficult to satisfy in stations overseas, until after the Second World War when Army secondary day and boarding schools were authorised.

In 1919 the Corps of Army Schoolmasters numbered 323 Warrant Officers and 27 Commissioned Inspectors of Army schools who, together with the Army schoolmistresses, were continuing their war-time duties of educating the Army's children at home and abroad. As the post-war scheme of adult education and resettlement training got under way, increasingly many of these schoolmasters were needed at home and abroad for duties in connection with these schemes. Lord Gorell, who, as Deputy Director of Staff Duties* was in charge of educational planning at the War Office, was convinced that a completely new organisation for Army schoolmasters and mistresses, with enhanced pay and status, was necessary to meet the Army's future educational needs. In this he was supported by the National Union of Teachers.[3] He felt that it was necessary to

'improve and broaden the training of Army schoolmasters by ending the narrow system of a few students at each of the Military Schools – that is to say, in the same atmosphere all their lives – and by creating a proper Training College on the lines similar to those of the Board of Education; and to provide a plan whereby every Army schoolmaster would, after 5 years' service, attain automatically to commissioned rank.'

Equally he wanted to improve the training and conditions of service for Army schoolmistresses. These proposals were not accepted, but on 15 June 1920 a Royal Warrant was published, authorising the formation of the Army Educational Corps and the disbandment of the Corps of Army Schoolmasters, whose members could transfer to the new Corps. It ended the system of entry through the student departments of the military schools (Duke of York's, The Royal Hibernian and the Queen Victoria School at Dunblane), limited new entries of NCOs to certificated or recognised teachers and to soldiers with a Special Certificate of Educa-

* Children's education was now the responsibility of the General Staff: from 1902–14 it had been the responsibility of the Adjutant-General and would become so again in 1940, when the appointment of Director of Army Education was established.[4]

tion.† Officers in future were to be Graduates of Universities or others 'with special qualifications' who would undergo a one-year training course, while the NCOs would complete a two-term course at the Army's School of Education. By December 1920 a large proportion of the Corps had joined and were at work, including the 70 Army schoolmasters who, out of a total of 300, were ultimately transferred as officers.[4]*

The proposals for the Army schoolmistresses were considered separately since, although administered with the Army Corps of Schoolmasters, they had an independent existence as far as questions of pay and conditions of service were concerned.

> 'Neither civilian nor military, they suffered under the disabilities of both. They were governed by War Office Regulations, liable to be sent each in their turn to Garrison schools in India and abroad, but still women and therefore no official part of an Army of men, not so much even as the personnel of Queen Mary's Auxiliary Corps had been, for these had uniforms and the Army schoolmistresses had none.'[3]

When the pay of the Army was raised theirs was left unchanged and at the end of 1919 they were paid about the same as a Lance Corporal. The first Burnham Report (1919) had laid down provisional minimum scales of salaries for civilian certificated and uncertificated teachers. It was only reasonable that there should be some correlation of pay and status, if Army children were not to be at a disadvantage. It was equally certain that the gradings of Army schoolmistresses should be based primarily on educational qualifications and that as many as possible should be given the opportunity of gaining the Board of Education's certificate. Their changes in pay and conditions were announced in the Royal Warrant of 7 April 1920 and being worse than those offered to civilian teachers were to cause grievances among the 289 serving Army schoolmistresses and adversely to affect recruiting, as the following letter shows.

> 'The principles introduced into the new system of payment of Mistresses are sound and therefore make pleasant reading for the impartial. The method of small but frequent increments of pay is in accordance with modern usage and is a good innovation; the revised scale of pensions is more just than the old; the recognition of the Board of Education certificate as a qualification for special early

† The Army's highest educational certificate.
* The Corps now numbered 482 Officers and 595 Warrant Officers and Sergeants, later reduced under the 'Geddes Axe' to 162 and 474 respectively.

promotion is as it should be; and the fact that the new rates of pay may be taken up at option prevents cases of immediate loss of pay. All this is excellent, and if all Mistresses were philosophers there would be nothing more to add on the subject.

'As, however, all Mistresses are women, the immediate effect of the new order of things has been to separate them into groups according to as it affects them individually. There is a happy band – ten per cent of the whole, maybe – who have been placed on the higher scale. About forty per cent, who feel they have opportunity, time and energy after the normal day's work to obtain the Board of Education certificate, welcome the change, bringing, as it does, new chances of accelerated promotion. A further forty per cent, failing to perceive how the certificate is to be gained, have to balance a present increase of pay against future cessation of increments and promotion. The remainder are malcontents.

'These last are they who for a decade have been journeying as Second Class Mistresses towards a portal through which they thought to pass as a matter of course to become First Class. It would seem that this portal is now closed for all time. The road towards the happy land has been wearisome; it is bitterly disappointing to reach the threshold only to have the door slammed in one's face.'

(The Army Schoolmistress, July 1920)

The newly-formed Army Educational Corps took over from the Corps of Army Schoolmasters responsibility for the 190 Army children's schools, the majority of which were overseas. For example, there were some 60 schools in India, 20 on the Rhine, 4 in Gibraltar, 8 in Malta, 13 in Egypt, 2 in Palestine, 7 in the West Indies and 9 in the Far East, including China. In the United Kingdom the 66 Army children's schools were centred around garrison towns, such as those in Aldershot (19) and Southern Commands (14). The 5000 children came largely from the families of other ranks, since officers generally preferred the continuity of UK civilian boarding schools.

Army Schools 1920. What were these schools like immediately after the War? Let the Army schoolmistresses who taught in them answer.

'Tidworth, Salisbury Plain, where many are ordered but few report, appears to have a bad reputation as a station. One of the greatest disadvantages is a lack of "digs". Mistresses have to do one of three things; exist in Quarters – since losing lodging, fuel and light allowance it can be called nothing else – depend on the kindness of friends, or travel to and from Andover daily. We hope, however, the time is not far distant when Quarters will be provided and furnished on the lines of those of the Queen Alexandra's Imperial Nursing Service and an adequate allowance made for the upkeep of the same.'

(*The Army Schoolmistress*, October 1919)

'I sailed from Southampton with glowing accounts from many friends of the glorious time they had spent in India and of the delightful social gatherings which spell life in that country. On my arrival at Bombay, orders were given to me to proceed to X. You may imagine how important was this station when I say that only two of my fellow passengers had ever heard of it, and they were experienced Indian travellers. One said it was near Bombay, the other informed me it was a few miles from Calcutta, while in reality it is nearer the North West Frontier. Perusal of the pamphlet issued led me to expect a male escort to my destination, but, like Micawber, I might to this day be hopeful of something (in my case, a male) turning up. I had to do my little trip of three days and two nights in the train, left to my own resources. . . . The day following my arrival on remarking to my hostess that I would like to see something of my new station she replied "You can see it all from my verandah"; and so it proved. My school was a perfect barn in which for 18 months I taught five children, three of whom were black, though the number rose to about 12 later on. My own house, which consisted of four huge rooms, was in the same block as the Guard Room, a men's Barrack Room in front and the nearest woman 200 yards away. Two years later my worries ended by my committing matrimony.'

(*The Army Schoolmistress*, July 1920)

'The Garrison School is situated in Tanglin Barracks, $3\frac{1}{2}$ miles from the town of Singapore, and occupies a good position adjoining a large recreation ground. The married quarters are within a short distance of the school, consequently children are seldom late and very rarely absent. One building, formerly a church, and still used as a chapel on Sundays, accommodates infants and elder children, a wooden partition, not quite reaching to the roof, separating one school from the other. The attendance of infants in normal times ranges from 20 to 25; sewing school totals about 35 and, as a rule, the mistress has to manage without assistance.

'Another Schoolmistress is usually employed with the Royal Garrison Artillery on the island of Blakang Mati, which is about 7 miles from Tanglin, and reached by riksha – the ordinary land conveyance – and either sampan or government launch. Usually the Mistress, if single, lodges with one of the married families living in quarters, but Tanglin is an ideal station for a Mistress married to an Army Schoolmaster.'

(*The Army Schoolmistress*, October 1919)

Simultaneously, with the 1920 Royal Warrant, the Army published *Army Educational Training, Part I,*[5] which reflected the new spirit in educational thought and set out the general principles which

127

were to govern its children's schools – principles which echoed the aims of the elementary school as set out in the Board of Education's Code from 1904 to 1926 and reproduced unaltered in the 1927 *Handbook of Suggestions for Teachers*.

'They are established for the purpose of affording to the children of officers, warrant officers, NCOs and men, an opportunity of acquiring a sound primary education.'

'The minds of little children are as delicate and unstable as their bodies, and the business of their teacher is the removal of obstacles to free growth, the encouragement – by example rather than by deliberate instruction – of an interest in common things, such as animals, flowers, and plants; and the cultivation of cheerfulness and good temper. These ends are secured by the provision of as much space as can be afforded for play, by the supply of material for the spontaneous creative instincts of the child, the telling of simple stories, and by the encouragement of the children themselves to talk, to sing together, and to practise amongst themselves little courtesies and kindnesses.

'Life in the infant school should be considered as an enlargement and continuation of the education which in favoured circumstances is always in operation in a well-conducted "nursery".

'The teacher will bear in mind that, as the Education Act of 1918 comes into full operation, the Primary School will be a first stage only; and that, in the case of the more favoured pupils, the Secondary, or Technical or Senior School, and in the case of others, the Continuation School, will carry on the work of instruction and discipline begun in the Primary School. If the teacher does his duty, by the time his boys and girls have left his school at fourteen he will have laid a solid preparatory foundation for any superstructure; and he can do little more. But he will render a service of great value both to the pupil and the community if he can contrive to make his pupils aware that he is, in fact, preparing them for another stage of work which will be more interesting and valuable to them than anything they have yet done, and that they must make up their minds what they can do best, and do it in the best way they can.'

Later training manuals extended the educational provisions and laid down instructions for school administration. Schools could be maintained at stations where no suitable civil school was accessible; but Commanding Officers could authorise the attendance of children at a civil school, provided no expenditure from Army funds was involved, if an efficient civil school existed nearer than the Army school and if the distance to the Army school put a strain upon the children. Parents were also permitted to send their children to a civil school for secondary education at their own expense.

'The GOC is responsible for the efficiency and administration of the schools, delegating to his command education officer responsibility for the standards of education in them and for assisting the head teachers in the arrangement of the syllabus, the drawing up of the time-table and the introduction of progressive and modern methods of instruction.'

The Commanding Officer was given responsibility for regular and punctual attendance, the maintenance of school premises and the accounting for stores. The school had to be formally inspected each year by an Officer of the Army Educational Corps, but more frequent informal visits were encouraged.

'Without any warning a school door opened with a bang and a stalwart Guardsman, standing rigidly to attention, announced "Orderly Officer". Immaculately attired, the sash worn over the left shoulder, Lt. X or Lord Y walked across to the desk and signed the Visitors' Book. Sometimes spotlessly white kid gloves would be taken off before the Officer accepted the pen; more often the gloves were not removed. As a rule the children carried on with their lessons, unless it happened to be a collective period, when they, too, would stand to attention. Morning calls are no longer made, for it is years since Orderly Officers were required to visit schools.'[6]

Every child had to be thoroughly examined by an Officer of the Royal Army Medical Corps on first admission and when finally leaving the school, parents being encouraged to be present. The results of each medical examination were recorded and filed in the child's documents.

But not everyone profited from such enlightened regulations.

'One young lady, who began her school career at the Infants' School in Khanspur, India in 1930, was an Amalgamated child in the Punjab in 1932, a Mixed Infant in Norwich in 1933, who left her Record Book behind in Kowloon and her tonsils in Ambala and who attended 3 different schools in 1935, is credited in her Record Book and Medical History Sheet (now arrived from China) with being somewhat backward, but a pleasure to teach in Sabathu; weak in Mathematics, but good at skipping. At the age of twelve, after 13 schools in 6 and a bit years, she can read with tolerable fluency, but weeps over sums a child of nine at home would call "money for jam", can sing a little, sew a little, skip magnificently, has a few words of alleged Chinese, rather less Hindustani, and a disarming smile.'[7]

The Auditor-General, in his report for the year 1923–24, drew attention to the fact that, contrary to regulations, certain Army schools were being maintained at places where adequate civil educational facilities appeared to exist. Investigation confirmed that there were thirty-five Army schools in UK, whose children were within a reasonable distance of a civil school (i.e. one mile for infants, two for elder children). A Committee was appointed in 1926, under the chairmanship of the Under Secretary of State for War, the Earl of Onslow, to examine this question and to make recommendations as to the future of Army children's schools. It weighed the evidence – the danger of Army children, potential future soldiers, coming into contact with people in other walks of life who might hold seditious views; the risk of infection 'being spread in barracks as a result of contact with civilian children, whose domestic circumstances are not subject to the same supervision as are the conditions in barracks and lodgings'; the difference in curricula between the two systems; distances involved; the extra burden of Army children on local rates and the capital and maintenance costs. There were two problems of paramount importance. The Army needed its eighty schools at home to maintain a rotation system for its schoolmistresses abroad (in December 1925 there were 137 overseas and 202 at home).[8] On the other hand, even with the advantage of smaller classes, the Army could not provide the more comprehensive facilities for gardening, handicraft, cookery, etc. enjoyed by the civil schools. Faced with strong reasons for the Army to retain its own schools, but well aware that civil provision should not be duplicated, it came to the compromise that

'if there were not a large number of children and there were civilian schools convenient to the purpose, it would be desirable that Army children should attend these schools, instead of having special schools built for them; but in general the Committee were strongly of the opinion that no change should be made in the present procedure.'[9]

Schools in India 1920. About the same time (13–18 July 1925) a Committee of District and Area Education Officers met at Army HQ, Simla, to report on British Army Children's Schools in India. They considered, and made recommendations on, a number of issues – the poor reception arrangements made for Army schoolmistresses on their arrival at Indian ports and the inadequacy of some of the quarters allotted to them, especially in Hill Stations: the need for more generous equipment grants; the need to prune the multiplicity of Army forms used in school administration and the need for more realistic school fees for civilian children attending Army

Schools and for more frequent dental inspections and free dental treatment. In addition, the Warrant Officer Instructor (Education) should assist the overtaxed schoolmistress, by instructing in the elder children's school for a period of not less than two hours daily. He should assist also in the teaching of children over 14 years of age, as far as possible 'without undue interference with other duties or his legitimate leisure'.

This problem of the education of children over compulsory school age was beginning to worry the education staff since such children were often compelled to stay in India, thus being at a disadvantage with their fellows at home. The answer lay in the provision of some form of secondary education. Though the warrant officer might do a certain amount, there was a growing need for some schools to be organised in special departments or classes where adequate secondary education could be given. But an even bigger problem (and one with a modern flavour) was the problem of 'turbulence', leading to recommendations for standardisation of curricula, of syllabuses in all compulsory subjects and in school text books. The Committee took into consideration the following special features:

a. The primary object of the Army school was to ensure a thorough elementary education.
b. In a large number of schools in India, children spent six months of each year on the plains and six months in hill-stations, with no guarantee that children would be taught by the same teacher in both.
c. The staff of each school did not consist entirely of fully qualified, experienced teachers.
d. The Schoolmistress was frequently in charge of a school containing children varying in age from 6–14 years, with the assistance of a warrant officer or regimental sergeant-instructor for a limited period each day.

As a result, later the same year, a 'syllabus of instruction for Army Children's schools in India' was produced and issued for use in all schools. The preface stated:

'It is realised that the tendency in modern educational methods is towards complete freedom to the teacher with a choice of syllabus, yet it has been found by experience that the conditions in India are such that, unless a certain definite scheme is provided for all British Army Children's Schools, the education of the child will suffer.

Continuity both in subject and method is desirable and it is obvious that under the conditions of turbulence prevailing, unless a definite scheme, with definite stages of work and with a system of recording is laid down, there will be breaks in continuity in some cases and overlapping in others. It is not the intention to repress initiative on the part of the teachers, but, on the contrary, within the scope of the syllabus they should be allowed, both in schemes of work and in teaching method, as much latitude as possible.'

To meet the case of schools which closed in the plains and opened in the hills, the work in all schools was to be organised in two half-yearly periods, the first from 1 April to 1 October and the second from 1 October to 1 April.

Queen's Army Schoolmistresses 1930. What were conditions of service like for a QAS? In India, where on 8 May 1930 there were serving 89 QAS and 17 Acting QAS on loan from LEAs,[11] a QAS might have worked in a hill station like Dalhousie, Murree or in the Biddulph Summer Home, Mussoorie.

'Situated in the heart of the Himalayas, Dalhousie is very beautiful. After the flatness, barrenness and heat of the plains it seems a land of enchantment. On leaving the train at Pathanket it is reached by a car ride of 52 miles. Dalhousie lies on the top of a hill. Here is the residential part, and the principal shops, but the Barracks are situated much lower down – first Ticca, lower still Balun and half an hour's walk round one of the spurs, Mankote. As Balun is the most central, the children's school is there. It is built in the compound of the RC Church, the largest level space in Barracks, except the football field and tennis courts.

'The situation is apparently ideal, till monsoons begin, when the compound becomes like a sponge, from the drainage down the khuds at the back. In front of the school are swings and a see-saw, greatly appreciated by the children. The edge of the playground is protected by a light wooden railing, and from here is a splendid view of rolling hills and valleys. From this vantage spot, while the girls are at needlework, the elder boys study physical geography and nature under a Sgt-Instructor AEC who is a keen naturalist.

'The compound is so big that in the shadow of the church or under the trees, shady spots can always be found for physical training – and three squads can be working at once without disturbing each other.

'The school building itself is a long bungalow, divided into one large and one smaller room, this latter devoted to the Infants' use. The long room, when the number of teachers permits, is divided into two by a tent wall. The Infants' room is very light, having glass doors or windows on three sides. The long room is not so light, but for all that it is a pleasant room and the walls, covered with the children's drawings and paper cutting pictures, look quite bright and attractive. Altogether a very pleasant school.

'The two school quarters lie in a bungalow next to the school, and across the compound is a group of about four married quarters.

'If any Mistress, after a tour in Northern India, is not an adept at packing and unpacking books, she never will be. I was just out from Home and had no idea what this yearly exodus to the Hills meant to school people. Imagine my consternation, then, at viewing a school, clean certainly, but with desks, forms, blackboards, piled one on the other. Presently ten cases of books, etc. were dumped on the floor, keys and lists handed to me, and I was asked "to please check contents and have school ready to open on Tuesday". This was Friday. However, my husband came to my rescue, and all was ready by Tuesday morning.

'It takes over a month for all the families to be safely shepherded to the Hills, so that the school opens with comparatively few children and is added to daily. In the height of the season there are between fifty and sixty children ranging in ages from six to fourteen, mixed boys and girls. Owing to the constant moving and consequent change of teachers, the average child in Northern India is generally backward, therefore teaching is much more trying than in England. Also for half the season we were one Mistress short, but when we had our full staff work was pleasant and successful. Here the larger Hill Schools score over the small Plain Schools, as, having a larger staff the children can be grouped more easily and subjects can figure on the curriculum which a Mistress, singlehanded, could not attempt.

'The children come from all over Northern India, from Karachi to as far south as Nagpur; some from Army schools, others from convents; some had had private tuition, and yet others had been attached to no school for months. One group of children had had six or seven different teachers in the previous twelve months.'

(*The Army Schoolmistress*, July 1925)

'From the spur of the Murray Hills may be seen on a clear day the Hill Stations of Upper Topa, Murree, Juldana, Barian, Kyra Gali and Kahanspur. Others also visible are Lower Topa, Cliffden, Kalabagh and Bara Gali. At these places are Army schools varying in the numbers of children attending from 7–70, so that one can see that quite a large proportion of the teachers in Northern Command* are quartered up here for the summer months, leading a more or less camp-like existence. The annual migration to the hills takes place every April and the return to the plains in October. Education under these conditions must suffer since schools and teachers are continually changing. The only remedy would be one large central boarding school in the hills for the whole Command with all Army children of school age compelled to live there the whole year round.

* India was divided into 4 Commands and 13 Districts.

The present system is wasteful and expensive and the results must be out of all proportion to the money expended.'

(The Army Schoolmistress, 1927)

Mussoorie had a purpose-built school (with the teachers' quarters adjoining), commanding a wonderful view into a Himalayan valley.

'This "pioneer of hill refuges" was founded in 1876 by Major-General Biddulph, RA, as there was no hill accommodation to escape the summer heat for the wives and children of soldiers in India. He had noticed the high mortality and pallid faces of the children. Army teachers have been supplied since 1901. Nowadays, hill accommodation is available for most married families from the really hot plain stations. Far removed from barrack life, the children can enjoy a happy, healthy life in ideal surroundings.'

(The Army Schoolmistress, 1927)

QAS posted to Egypt in 1923 could obtain this advice.

'The main garrisons are in Cairo and Alexandria. Cairo is no place for invalids nor for ladies in summer, who, if liable to internal chills, should wear a cholera belt. Alexandria is pleasanter and is not so plagued with tourists. Officers are advised to leave behind their frock and morning coats and tall hats and to order their polo breeches (30 shillings a pair) from local tailors of Indian origin. Dog carts and pianos are in short supply: the former being superseded by the motor car and the latter bought and sold so often that a youthful tune is not in them. Bicycles are useful in Cairo, less so in Alexandria, as the streets are nearly all paved. Servants are available, except in the tourist season, when they disappear without notice and return if jobless. Abandon English ideas of cleanliness. You may find a good cook, but he will only cook well when guests are expected. He will feed himself and his family at your expense and make his commission on every market purchase. The *fellah* is hard working, but very unreliable and does not understand the meaning of the word gratitude. He is the true Egyptian!'

(RE Booklet)

But garrisons in other parts of the world had their attractions, too. A QAS might have been stationed in Cologne, Mulheim or Solingen with the British Army of Occupation.

'This will probably be our last term in Cologne (December 1925), as the Army is soon to evacuate the town. Our next station is Wiesbaden, a famous beauty spot. Our School Entertainments, staged in the theatre, are dressed throughout by the Cologne Opera House, the Director of which last Christmas lent us 85 costumes. The only disadvantage in Cologne is that an afternoon session is out of the question, because most of the children have to travel long distances – by tram!'[12]

Or she might have served in Malta at the Tigne or Valletta schools.

'There are now 18 mistresses stationed in Malta. There are two available quarters, pleasantly situated at St Andrews and Imtarfa. The other mistresses all have houses or flats in Sliema and Floriana, two generally living together and sharing housekeeping expenses and a maid. Furnished flats or small houses can be had from £5 per month but rents are rapidly soaring and houses are difficult to get, owing to the very large Fleet in the Harbours at present, with its attendant quota of women-folk from England.'[12]

In the UK, the schoolmistress 'soldiered on', beset with worries, which have a topical ring.

'Rumour is always rife in our Department. Yes, our Army Schools at Colchester, Belfast, Chelsea Barracks (London), York and Windsor have been closed. We hear it is because it is more economical for the children to be taught in the Elementary Schools nearby. We regret their passing but it does not signify that all Army schools are doomed, as some of our members overseas think.'[12]

The Military Schools. Other changes were taking place at home. In 1922 the Royal Hibernian Military School left Ireland, at the same time as the withdrawal of the British forces, to find a temporary home at Shorncliffe; but since there were no more admissions it was accommodated within the Duke of York's School, Dover, in 1924, until its students wasted away. So ended a school with a great military tradition. In the First World War, 1250 'Hibs' served in the Armed Forces, fifty-one being commissioned and one gaining the Victoria Cross. Its military bands were famous, performing at many public occasions, and the School produced thirty-three Army Bandmasters or Directors of Music. It fostered a great race of athletes, especially hockey players, ten of whom in the decade from 1911 gained International honours. Its motto 'Fear God and Honour the King' was proudly kept, not least among the large number of schoolmasters the school produced for the Army, through the Training Centre it established in 1889, when the Normal School at Chelsea was closed.[4]

Changes were taking place at the Duke of York's School, Dover. An Upper School was formed in 1923 to replace the Students Training School, made obsolete by the new entry qualifications for the AEC. The Preface to the 1924 Standing Orders claimed it had been

'transformed into a Military Public School, at which the sons of soldiers can obtain a complete secondary education and receive an elementary military training up to the age of 19 years, and are

135

thus prepared for service in the Army with enhanced prospects of promotion.'

In 1931 its aim was broadened and described as

'a recognised secondary boarding school for the sons of soldiers and ex-soldiers, who can enter the junior school when they are 9 years old and can, if they show sufficient promise, remain at the school until they reach the age of 18+. All boys receive a sound secondary education to the age of 15, and boys who are kept on until they are 18+ have the advantage of higher and more specialised education in preparation for scholarships for the Royal Military College and Royal Military Academy, for the ultimate career as bandmaster, instructor AEC and other senior WO and NCO posts in the Army.'[13]

Hadow – the Army Schools Reorganise. The Hadow Report of October 1926 is recognised as one of the milestones of English education, but while it added some benefits to Army schools, it also brought considerable problems to them. It set out its new philosophy and school organisation in the often quoted terms:

'There is a tide which begins to rise in the veins of youth at the age of eleven or twelve. It is called by the name of adolescence. If that tide can be taken at the flood and a new voyage begun in the strength and along the flow of its current, we think that it will "move on to fortune". We therefore propose that all children should be transferred, at the age of eleven or twelve, from the junior or primary school either to schools of the type now called secondary, or to schools (whether selective or non-selective) of the type which is now called central, or to senior and separate departments of existing elementary schools. . . .

'The scheme which we advocate can be simply stated. It is that between the age of eleven and (if possible) that of fifteen, all the children of the country, who do not go forward to the traditional "secondary education" (i.e. to the grammar school), should go forward nonetheless to what is, in our view, a form of secondary education in the broader and truer sense of the word . . . should spend the last three or four years in a well-equipped and well-staffed modern school (or science department), under the stimulus of practical work and realistic studies, and yet, at the same time, in the free and broad air of a general and humane education. . . .'[14]

The Army reorganised its schools on these lines. 'Schools consist of infants, junior mixed and senior schools, and all warrant officers, NCOs and men, married on the strength, will normally be required to send their children to them', states the 1931 *Manual of Educational Training*. It continued to delegate to Commanding Officers the power to authorise attendance at a civil school on account of distance and for secondary education, since its garrison secondary population was usually too small to provide secondary education, except in 'tops' at primary schools, with all their limitations. In this respect, Army provision began to fall behind that of civil education and would not catch up again, until after the Second World War. The effects of these proposals can be seen through the eyes of the Army schoolmistresses of the time, who in 1927 had been collectively honoured by the title Queen's Army Schoolmistresses, in recognition of their services. Her Majesty Queen Mary became patron of a Corps, whose records show them to have been the Army's first women workers.

'It was decided to reorganise certain children's schools in the Aldershot Command so as to bring them into line with the civilian educational progress. The main objects were to provide more suitable instruction for elder children and to secure accommodation for the increased numbers that will present themselves, when the school leaving age is raised.* The existing classification into infants and elder children's schools was abandoned and a new division into Infants, Junior Mixed and Elder Children substituted.

'The affected schools were reorganised as follows:

1. The Model School was re-named "The Stanhope Infants School" (below Standard 1).
2. Maida Infants School became the "Maida Junior Mixed School" (Standards 1 and 2).
3. Barrosa Elder Girls remained an Elder Girls School (Standards 3 and above) and took over the Centre for Queen's Army Schoolmistresses on probation.
4. The RE and RASC Elder Boys' School (for Standards 3 and above) was re-named "The Haig Elder Boys School".
5. The Cavalry Elder Children's School was closed and these pupils distributed between Maida, Barrosa and Haig Schools.'[15]

'The name "Model" brings to the minds of many of us visions of busy hard working hours, when time was yet found to forge links of friendships which have never been broken. Each year a new class assembled with numbers varying from 2–30. Most of the new students knew the preceding class and also those who followed. We met again often – in India, in Egypt, or at our yearly reunion. The Model was one of the biggest links and as such we regret its ending. The casket presented by HM Queen Mary, the pictures presented by students of the past, the Library and the remains of the

* In 1929 the Labour Party returned to power and Sir Charles Trevelyan introduced a Bill to raise the school leaving age to 15. The Bill was defeated in the House of Lords.

Museum, are now in Barrosa Elder Children's School and will be jealously guarded. Only two pictures have been kept in Stanhope Infants, as a reminder of the former use of the school.'[15]

'The New Road Infants School, Woolwich – the last to remain open – closed on October 29th, the children being sent to civil schools where there were vacancies. The Elder Children's School, which closed on 5 January 1929, is now being used for men's education and the infants school will probably be used for the same purpose. Thus another station with its many associations and happy memories passes from us. We leave it with regret.'[15]

Reorganisation did not come speedily nor uniformly in the Army Schools.† Chatham reorganised its schools in January 1935 into a garrison infant school and a junior mixed school and sent all its 11+ children to civil schools, and Portsmouth followed suit later in the Jubilee Year of King George V. Catterick had reorganised its schools in 1930 with infant, junior mixed and a new secondary school in the centre of the Garrison. In India as late as 1935 schools were reorganising into garrison children's central schools, or amalgamated infants and elder children's schools, because stations varied so much in size and because the Hadow proposals demanded new buildings and more expensive equipment.

Trumpets of War. Other events were taking place at the time, which were not caused by the Hadow recommendations. The schoolmistresses reported:

'In Malta, the 1932 Annual combined Sports Meeting was held on the King's Birthday for the Infants and Elder Children from the Tigne, Floriana, St. Andrews and Imtarfa schools. The Royal Artillery turned up trumps as usual and surrendered their holiday to prepare the square.'

'Aden is by no means as black as it is painted. School conditions in 1933 are very pleasant. The QAS are responsible for the Infants' Department only and there is an average attendance of about 25. The School is under RAF administration, but modelled on Army routine and governed by our own Army Educational Training Manual. Children of both Services attend and, considering the climate, and the fact that the majority are only here for one year – their standard of work compares favourably with the standard of children at home stations. Only morning work is done throughout the year.'

'Tientsin, where our school numbers 24 children (1934), is divided into "Concessions", each preserving its national characteristics. In

† Neither did it in civil schools in UK, since by 1939 only about half had been reorganised.

the Japanese concession you may eat Sukiyaki squatting shoeless on the floor, tended by Geisha girls, and soon become proficient with chop sticks. In the ex-Russian concessions you may eat Zabouska, a Russian hors d'oeuvre but a meal in itself. The Italians hold an Annual Ball. Go if you are lucky to be invited, for the Italians are marvellous dancers. In the British concession you will find plenty of sport!'

Gibraltar had two infants' schools at Line Wall and Buena Vista and two elder children's schools at Montague Bastion and Buena Vista for the children of its garrison of 2100 military and 400 Naval personnel. In 1933, one of Buena Vista's younger children was presented by Sir Robert Baden-Powell, on a visit to the 'Rock' at the time, with a silver cross for saving the life of a 3-year-old girl.

'This boy had been most difficult to teach to swim, because of his extreme timidity in water, and his appeals to be spared the ordeal of a lesson were heart-rending. At last he could manage a few strokes by the summer holidays, when he bravely jumped into deep water in Rosia Bay to the rescue of this small girl.'

'In Hong Kong it is Coronation Day, 1937. The service from Westminster Abbey came through very clearly, and one could almost imagine oneself back in England. All the ships in harbour, both battleships and liners, were illuminated. The whole water-front blazed with lights, while across the dark hillside "God Save the King" stood out in letters forty feet high and visible for miles. The Chinese procession was miles in length, with resplendent floats depicting scenes from ancient Chinese history, dragon dancers and acrobats, and crowds of coolies, fantastically garbed. The Japanese residents provided the magnificent display of fireworks which closed a memorable day.'

But two QAS sounded a more sombre note.

'After the great earthquake (1935), Quetta is no more. I am at Karachi and, although it is many miles away, the injured and the refugees are pouring in by the thousand. It's really dreadful to think it all happened in a few seconds. Thank goodness all our schoolmistresses and children are safe, but our lovely Infants' School is down. I spent three very happy years there and left only after the 1931 earthquake.'

'In Singapore we are feeling the first repercussions of the European situation, though we have not been so alarmed as those at home. The new school at Alexandra is almost complete (1938). It is in a most delightful spot, being high enough to catch the sea breezes and having a splendid view of the whole island and the sea. School hours have been extended in Singapore from 20 hours to $23\frac{1}{2}$ per week, but it means a very long morning for those who have to travel by boat and bus to and from school. The Gillman School has 80 children and 3 staff while the Blakang Mati Garrison Infant and Elder Children's School celebrated its Annual Prize Giving and Display of Handwork before a distinguished group of visitors and parents.'

But events were moving quickly. The schoolmistresses, who continued to record their experiences in their journal, the *Link*, did not know that the edition published in July 1939 would be the last for many years.[16]

MALTA

'Owing to the departure of the Navy and consequent flight of many Navy families, we at Tigne suffered considerable reduction in our number of scholars. Whether they will return in the near future it would be difficult to forecast, but we are beginning to fear the worst.'

HONG KONG

'Not only has the colony become a news centre on account of the Sino-Japanese hostilities, which have brought the war to our doorstep during recent months, but also many interesting and exciting events have occurred amongst our members. During the September 1938 crisis, Hong Kong got excited about the possibility of a lightning Japanese swoop on the Colony, had war broken out in Europe. An Army Children's School was opened at Stanley in 1938 and orders have been received for a QAS from Gun Club Hill School to be sent to Shanhaikuan, in North China, to teach at the Summer Camp there for three months. Shanhaikuan is close to the Great Wall of China, is a train journey from Tientsin, and has a lovely bathing beach. The Colony has added economic and social problems thrown upon it, as a result of the war in China, but somehow it manages to maintain the placid complacency which is so essentially British, and which makes it almost impossible to believe that Japanese artillery and bombing planes have been appearing a few miles away. The constant influx of helpless refugees is a vivid reminder that death and destruction are not far removed from this British Colony.'

SINGAPORE

'Our new school at Alexandra was opened on 5th January, 1939 by Mrs Dobbie, wife of the GOC, Malaya. We are all anxiously awaiting the publication of the 1939–40 trooping list and anyone who is posted to Singapore will receive "a right royal welcome".'

This final edition included the trooping list. Starting on 1 September 1939 twenty-one QAS were due to sail for India, six for Egypt, two for Gibraltar, three for Hong Kong, three for Malaya and one for Tientsin. There were twelve on the Waiting List – 'destination unknown'. The Editor wished them 'a very happy tour', not knowing that few would ever set sail!

Here we must bid farewell to India and its schools, home to so many generations of the Army's children and their teachers. What a wealth of British Army history, educational as well as military, is conjured up by such names at Agra, Bombay, Barrackpore, Rawalpindi, Jhansi, Belgaum, Fort William, Bangalore, Lucknow, Karachi, Peshawar, Cawnpore, Calcutta, Meerut, Chaklala, Allahabad, Benares, Mhow and Secunderabad. Each station had its Irish, Scots, Welsh or English unit of artillery, cavalry, infantry or corps. Each had its small regimental school of one mistress and half-a-dozen children or 'amalgamated' larger schools with Army schoolmaster and QAS. Some stations were rich in historical and social interest, with a round of gaiety and European shops – Quetta, Delhi, Poona, for example – some were isolated, far from town or railway, dependent on the contractor's canteen or the tiny counterless shops of the native bazaar.

It was goodbye, also, to China Command – the most distant and extensive military command in the Empire, embracing Hong Kong, Shanghai and Tientsin. It took 8 days (with luck) to travel from HQ in Hong Kong, wearing solar topee to avoid sunstroke, to reach Peking, where one needed the War Department issued fur cap to keep out the intense cold.

Both Commands added a chapter to the continuing story of the education of Tommy Atkins and his children.

REFERENCES

1. *Hansard*, 10 August 1917.
2. Hadow Report, 'Education of the Adolescent', 1926.
3. Lord Gorell, *Education and the Army*, OUP, 1921.
4. Colonel White, *The Story of Army Education*, Harrap.
5. Issued with Army Orders, June 1920.
6. Dorothy Bottle, *Reminiscences of a Queen's Army Schoolmistress*.
7. Quoted from the magazine of the co-educational Lawrence Royal Military School, Sanawar, June 1937, and reproduced in the *Journal of the Army Educational Corps*. [The school had 520 Army fee-paying pupils.]
8. Précis for Army Council, No. 1235.
9. Report of the Army Children's Schools Committee, 18 March 1926.
10. Copy in RAEC Museum.
11. AG Branch, Simla, Army HQ, India.
12. *Army Schoolmistress*, editions 1924, 1925, 1930.
13. *Educational Training*, 1931.
14. Quoted in *Society and Industry in the 19th Century*, Dawson & Wall.
15. *The Army Schoolmistress*, December 1929.
16. The next issue would be December 1943.

CHAPTER 9

The Second World War and the

1944 Education Act

Wartime Education. Dispersal, evacuation or closure was the fate of many schools, civilian and military alike, in the United Kingdom during the Second World War. 1 September 1939 was to have been the day for the raising of the school leaving age from 14 to 15; it saw all the military schools in Aldershot Command closed. The QAS reported daily at Maida School to hear lectures on Gas and First Aid. They did voluntary work with the Post and Food Offices or with the WVS. On 18 October 1939 Stanhope School re-opened as an 'all-age school', to be quickly followed by Marlborough Lines, Cavalry and Blackdown schools. QAS left surplus by the evacuation of their pupils were posted to other stations; some were loaned to civil schools in the area. Salisbury Plain District schools managed to remain open without a break throughout the war years: many of the children of the garrison school, Portsmouth, were evacuated and 'those who remained continued to attend the Infant School, until it was burnt out during the Blitz, and then carried on in Married Quarters nearby'.[1]

The Government's evacuation plans divided the country into reception areas, whose schools soon reopened after the outbreak of war, and neutral areas, where schools had to delay their re-opening until the regulation trench shelters had been provided. A Queen's Army Schoolmistress described her 'war' in a neutral area in the following words:

'School life started smoothly, if a little uneasily. Soon came the call to join the ARP and I enrolled at a First Aid Post in a Red Cross Detachment. One day, London schoolchildren with several of their teachers arrived to share our building for a while. In due course shelters replaced the trenches and we scampered into them fairly

142

often as the bombs began to fall – 61 hours in the first 8 weeks. No damage was sustained at school beyond cracks and small breakages and we joined in the bonfires and celebrations with all and sundry when victory finally came. We were fortunate for during the bombing 34 persons were killed, 22 houses wrecked and over 3000 damaged. Alerts exceeded 1000 and over 400 patients were treated at our First Aid Post.'[2]

DYRMS was evacuated from Dover to Devon, some boys going to QVS Dunblane. But let a 'Dukie', the Chief School Prefect at the time, tell his own story:

'I joined the Duke of York's Royal Military School when I was ten years old; that was in April 1939. After a preparatory term I went to my new Company house in the Upper School on 3 September 1939. As I entered, I was curtly ordered to be silent. I had arrived at the moment of the Prime Minister's speech, declaring war on Germany.

'For the first month or two we were busy filling sandbags and digging trenches in preparation for air-raids and later for an invasion, which all but came. Even the smallest was doing his bit.

'I remember the continuous rumble of gunfire across the Channel. Due to the collapse of the French and the nearness of the enemy, we were evacuated at short notice. We left Dover on 1 June 1940, travelling by train to London. We saw many trainloads of troops, returning from Dunkirk, and we cheered them madly. To our utter amazement, we also came in for cheers along the line; it was probably the sight of our khaki school uniform. At every stop we were showered with cakes, cups of tea and even cigarettes.

'For 3 months we stayed at home, then spent 2 months at Cheltenham; not long enough to appreciate the town but long enough to discover the orchards, which surrounded the school, and then another 3 months at home before I was sent a ticket for Braunton in North Devon. On 4 January 1941 I arrived at Saunton Sands, my new school, a hotel beside the sea. As soon as everyone else arrived (3 weeks later), despite the cramped conditions, we settled down with classrooms in corridors and foyers and drill on the sands, tide permitting! For 5 years we carried on a hum-drum existence. We trooped the Colour four times at Saunton, much to the delight of the local residents.

'The war ended but it was not until a year later that we were allowed to return. After a month at home I returned to Dover for the first time for 6 years.* I couldn't help noticing the damage in the town, but that didn't interest me, as I was eager to see the school. I went through the Deal gate and saw the old familiar buildings.

*School re-started at Dover 6 May 1945, with 15 RAEC instructors and 3 QAS. It was fitting that at the first post-war Grand Day Parade (27 July 1946) Field-Marshal The Viscount Montgomery, CIGS should take the salute.

143

Only I had changed. I had left it a new boy and now I was a School Prefect, with the responsibility of helping to bridge the gap caused by seven long years of war.'[3]

It was the same for most Army children's schools overseas. Children were evacuated from Burma to India, from Singapore to Australia; in Ceylon, Hong Kong and Gibraltar the schools were closed. Because the Army Educational Corps at war had other duties to perform, the staffing and management of those wartime children's schools, which remained open, fell onerously on the QAS, who in July 1939 numbered 299 (plus thirty uncertificated).[4] Their devotion is exemplified in Malta, where under the ordeal of continuous bombardment fom June 1940 to September 1942,[1] short of food and sleep, they kept open the three Army children's schools so efficiently that the children 'maintained through the siege mental alertness and a confident bearing'.[5] An ex QAS (Mrs N. Carter) broadcasting in July 1947 to South African schools under the title of 'Malta under Fire' described her experiences, in which she was knocked unconscious and her home demolished over her head in March 1942.

'In September 1939 I went to a large Junior School in St. Andrew's, a barracks on rising ground five miles North West of Valetta. Nestling under the great guns of Fort Maddelena the school looked North and West over sloping ground to the sea and East over the roofs and domes of Sliema to the walls of Valletta. Here came the children of British soldiers from St. Andrew's and the neighbouring barracks of St George's. In those beautiful surroundings we spent several happy months, the children unconscious of the uncertainty which daily deepened over the island. This uncertainty as to Italy's probable entry into the War on the side of Germany filled the churches to overflowing with crowds of Maltese, praying that this calamity would be averted, little knowing that their faith was to be tried to the utmost in the fires of suffering and loss.

'As the weeks passed the children became aware of the strain under which their parents were living, for the time had come when the womenfolk had to decide whether to return to Britain leaving their men behind, or to stay and share in whatever the future held. One day on arriving at school I found that 75% of the children were missing – the long expected moment had arrived – they, with their mothers, were leaving the island that evening. This was a day made sad by partings. Those who remained saw along the coast the ugly spread of barbed wire and the growth of Beach Posts and Gun Positions. Now came the opening of rock shelters, the issue of gas masks, the visit of the Mobile Gas Chamber, the practice Air Raid Warnings and finally the Declaration of War by Italy in June, 1940.

'At dawn on that first morning, the wail of sirens and the drone

20. *School library. St David's Junior School, Rheindahlen.*

21.   *Tommy Atkin's children. Malta Primary School.*
22.   *RAEC Education Officer visits the Dhekelia Primary School.*

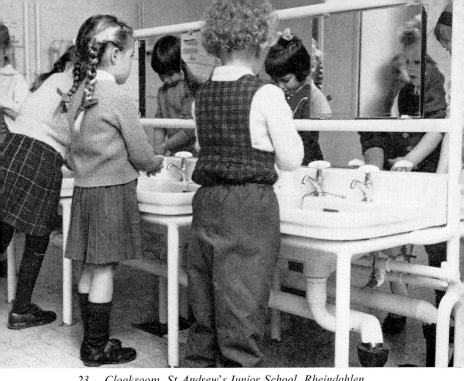

23. *Cloakroom. St Andrew's Junior School, Rheindahlen.*
24. *Gurkha Primary School, Slim Barracks, Singapore.*

25. *Agility apparatus. Dhekelia Primary School, Cyprus.*

26. *Batu Junior School near Kuala Lumpur.*

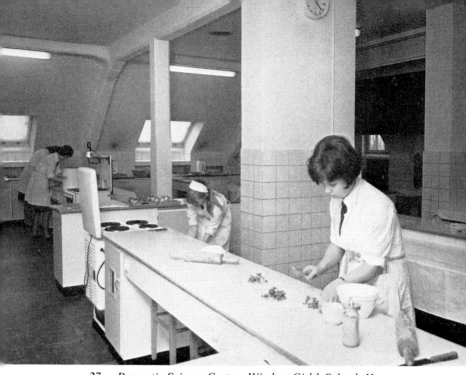

27. *Domestic Science Centre, Windsor Girls' School, Hamm.*
28. *Metal work in the smithy. Windsor Boys' School, Hamm.*

29. *Ladies' Mess, Hohne, Germany, 1964.*
30. *Music-making in the Far East.*

31. *St George's Infant School, Line Wall Road, Gibraltar.*
32. *RC Chapel, Windsor Girls' School, Hamm.*

of high-flying Italian bombers drove us to trenches dug in the rock close to the houses. During the successive raids of those first weeks the school closed and many houses in the Capital were damaged. To St. Andrew's and St. George's, now empty of their menfolk who had gone to help man the island's defences, came the women and children from the military areas of Valletta. After a while school re-opened in our barrack room, where nearby trenches could be used during raids.

'In January 1941, the RAF brought the news that the Luftwaffe were in Sicily. Those were dreadful days, followed by hideous nights. Valletta was in ruins, the dockyard areas devastated. As the children assembled for morning school we had to seek shelter and so throughout the mornings lessons were interrupted again and again. Now it was that the children showed the gallant spirit that was theirs; the attendance was regular, their bearing undismayed and their trust in the Staff touching. The trenches could be reached in three minutes and the children were divided into groups of fifteen to each of eight trenches. Here in the cold and damp many hours were spent. To the concussion of bombs, the crash of gunfire, the zip and hiss of falling shrapnel and the scream of diving planes, they passed the simple jokes of childhood. When raids permitted they gave their afternoons to rehearsals for a concert which was produced at Christmas time, attended by H.E. The Governor, and brought a substantial cheque to the Malta Relief Fund. In April, after a day of terrible raids, St Andrews and St George's lay in ruins. The people lived in the open and slept in the shelter. Our school had to be abandoned and we next opened a school in what had once been the Commanding Officer's house. This building, also damaged, was cleared and made ready for use by German Luftwaffe prisoners. Later in the year I occupied two rooms in this building, making them into a home until the time came in October 1942 to leave for home. I had come to work for 18 months and had stayed for three years.'[6]

There were 3 QAS in Burma when the Japanese attacked. One left Rangoon on 20 February 1942 on a hospital ship which took the few remaining women and children to Calcutta but the 2 QAS in Upper Burma were given only a few hours' notice to quit Maymyo, and join a civilian evacuation party going by the Chindwin route. Let QAS Mrs P. Mansfield tell her story:

'On 28 February we joined a train at Maymyo, crowded with women and children, fleeing from the bombs falling on Rangoon. We made our way through Mandalay to the River Chindwin and then by boat to Sittaung. Here we were met by elephants who led us through forest tracks over the mountain ridges, laden with our bed rolls and packs. The youngest of the children we had to carry, the others made their own way. At the Tamu River, which marked the border with India, the elephants had to return for the next party.

'The second half of the journey was the worst. The constant rise and fall of the ground and the fierce thunderstorms taxed us physically, while many laboured under the mental strain of not knowing the fate of relatives left behind in Burma. The comradeship helped us at last to reach the road at Imphal, when we were able to finish the rest of the journey to Calcutta by lorry and rail. Our escape had taken four days short of a month.'

Another QAS spent 3½ years in Japanese captivity in Sumatra. 'We tried to teach the children when and where we could, seated on rice sacks in a garage, in a store, under trees, with no books and no paper but with a few damaged slates', she modestly recalled.[7]

In India a few schools struggled on under pressures of shortages of accommodation, staff and materials, but in Singapore it was a different story.

'When the war with Japan began, I was in Singapore at the Alexandra School. This was situated on one of the highest points of Singapore and presented a fine target for bombers.

'To have the care of two-hundred children during air raids was no light responsibility for the staff, and in this case was doubly alarming as no shelters had been provided. When the alert sounded, we all had to climb over the railings that surrounded the School verandah, then scramble over very rough ground to some low bushes on the hillside, and creep under these for shelter. Here we were either scorched by the tropical sun or drenched by pouring rain.

'Later, shallow trenches were dug in the School playing field. These were hopeless as there was no drainage, and after heavy rain the trenches were flooded. On several occasions the children and staff had to bale the water out of them before they could be occupied. Why we were not all stricken down with divers diseases was a miracle. Conditions became so alarming, that, after representation of the plight of the children, it was decided to evacuate the School.

'Many families were at this time (end of December and early January) leaving Singapore for England, Australia or India, and so there were numbers of vacant quarters. Some of these were taken over for schools, where we worked until the last.

'Books and equipment had to be packed and transported by the children and staff – no light task – and often we had to leave what we were doing and fly to the trenches. There was no road to the School and all equipment, including desks, had to be carried by a narrow path, down a hazardous hill to the lorry. Many such journeys were necessary and in this work W.O.1. Instructor Geary, A.E.C., was outstanding. He worked like a nigger and at times looked fit to drop. The children naturally thought all this great fun, and the boys particularly enjoyed watching a "dog-fight" from the trenches.

'By the middle of January, 1942, School numbers were greatly depleted. I was left with fifteen elder children and carried on in a

146

married quarter in Tanglin. All agreed to remain while we could carry on, and did so until January 30th. On that day we received urgent notice to be ready to leave immediately, with hand luggage only. Our feelings can be imagined as we hastily packed what we thought would be most useful and regretfully left most treasured possessions. There was no time or opportunity to get to the bank for money, having left my last dollars with a friend to cable to my daughters in England, and given all my small change to the taxi driver.

'Getting to the docks was a nightmare. I stood on the roadside for almost an hour before I got a taxi. There were many evidences of destruction by bombing on the way, and at the docks was chaos. Huge clouds of smoke came from burning ships and buildings, and we had to make a wide detour owing to an unexploded bomb in our path. We had to pick our way over masses of debris, hose-pipes, etc. to the ship's side. There it looked as if the whole of Singapore's women and children had congregated. After many weary hours of waiting, 1,500 passengers, mostly women and children, were accommodated on our boat.'[8]

More fortunate was the garrison school in Bermuda, where school life went on normally throughout the war years, although the children's thoughts were turned homewards as they worked for the War effort, held Red Cross Fêtes, saved for the War Savings Scheme and knitted socks, Balaclava helmets, scarves and mittens for the Services. QAS also served in South Africa where the evacuee children attended the European schools, either primary or high Schools.

'All Primary schools are free, and books are provided, but each school has its uniform, navy shorts and blazer for boys, and coloured dresses and blazer for girls; caps or hats with distinctive badges are worn. The school year commences in January and there are four terms. Some Secondary schools are free, but fees are payable at most. All children of serving soldiers and sailors attend all fee-paying schools free of charge, but they have to buy books. There are several very good Preparatory schools and many of our children attend them.

'Apart from Afrikaans – which all children have to learn – and a preponderance of S. African History and Geography, the syllabus is very similar to our own. Much formal grammar is taken and great stress laid on spelling, oral composition and letter-writing. Very little time can be given to General Knowledge and Literature. Singing and Physical Training specialists visit each school twice weekly; up-to-date science and woodwork laboratories adjoin the boys' school, whilst modern kitchens equipped with electric stoves and refrigerators make cookery lessons a joy. Cookery and needle-work are taught by Domestic Science Teachers.

'Most schools have delightful playgrounds and playing fields shaded by beautiful flowering trees. There are rugby or soccer pitches for the boys and tennis courts, and netball and hockey pitches for the girls. All sports are taken out of school hours. Our children are very happy there and the teachers take a great interest in them. Having taught in a primary school, which many of our children attend, and served for four years on the tennis, netball, and swimming Executive Committees, I speak from experience and I am sure that our children will leave S. Africa with many happy memories of their school days there, and regrets that they have to leave the school behind.'[8]

Butler and the 1944 Act. But as the War drew to a close in Europe and the Far East, the demands for social reform and change, of which the chief was perhaps for a brighter future in education, became more insistent and, if the war years reveal a break in continuity and development in Army children's schools, the years immediately following were to prove a period of rapid expansion, of challenge and success to the RAEC, unequalled in its history, as the story which follows will show.

It is strange but true that the biggest advances in English education during the past century have been associated with large-scale warfare. There are three likely reasons. 'Prolonged war serves as a national audit – exposing weaknesses and arousing a determination to make good deficiencies. It smites the public conscience, engendering a resolve to create a better world after the sacrifice of so many young lives: it serves as a reminder that education can be an important source of national strength.'[9] The period of the Crimean War produced the Newcastle Commission: the Franco-Prussian War the Education Act of 1870, for Germany's success was attributed as much to her schoolmasters as to her drill-sergeants. Forster's reply was 'we must make up the smallness of our numbers by increasing the intellectual force of the individual'.[10] Balfour's Bill of 1902 was introduced in the House of Commons on the very day the Boer War ended – a war which not only revealed shortcomings in the Army's tactics but also in the nation's physical fitness. As a result there was a Royal Commission on Physical Training which led eventually to the creation of School Health and School Meals Services and to systematic physical education and improved standards of school accommodation.

War created the opportunity for the Education Act of 1918. 'The war was my opportunity,' Fisher wrote later. 'I was sensible from the first that while the war lasted reforms could be obtained that would be impossible to realize in the critical atmosphere of peace.'⁹ It also created the Education Act of 1944, as Butler reminded the House of Commons when he introduced his Bill.

'Hammered on the anvil of war, our nation has been shaped to a new unity of purpose. We must preserve this after victory is won, if the fruits of victory are to be gathered: and that unity will, by this Bill, be founded, where it should be founded, in the education and training of youth.'⁹

It is a source of satisfaction and inspiration to the Royal Army Educational Corps, that Lord Butler drafted the Bill at Eltham Palace, since 1946 the Headquarters of the RAEC.¹¹ *The Times*, 8 April 1944 praised his achievement in the following terms:

'By dint of unwearying patience and immense resourcefulness in negotiation, Mr Butler produced a policy which provided for the complete recasting of the educational system, and yet at once commanded the widest measure of approval from Parliament and the Public. Circumstances favoured him, it is true. There was a general, keen desire for large-scale educational advance. ... Nevertheless, the unhappy history of educational legislation in this country served to throw into bold relief the greatness of his achievement.'

The 1944 Act was 'a courageous and ingenious attempt to create a single national system where previously there had been a variety of services, each with its own aims and methods, attempting to cover different parts of the educational field.'¹² By giving wide educational powers and duties to LEAs, by reorganising the structure of education in three progressive stages of primary, secondary and further, by legislating for religious education, handicapped children, for certain welfare services (free medical and dental treatment and school milk), for maintenance grants and teachers' salaries (Burnham scales and equal pay for men and women), by raising the compulsory leaving age to 15 and abolishing fees in maintained schools, the Act not only completely transformed the British educational system but also Army schools and children's education in the Services. The War Office, through its Directorate of Army Education, set itself the task of implementing these, or similar, provisions by regulation and practice in the post-war Army schools overseas, interpreting the spirit if not the letter of the Act, since the Act itself was confined to England and Wales.

REFERENCES

1. *The Queen's Army Schoolmistress*, February 1946.
2. *The Queen's Army Schoolmistress*, July 1947.
3. P. Cartwright in DYRMS Magazine, *The Chronicle*, September 1946.
4. War Office Seniority List.
5. *Times Educational Supplement*, 15 June 1945.
6. Mrs Carter and another Headmistress in Malta were decorated for gallantry.

   Compare this account with that of Mrs Norman, *For Gallantry: Malta's Story by a Naval Wife*. Quoted by Stewart Perowne in *The Siege within the Walls,* Hodder and Stoughton, 1970.

   'Army wives were told that they would be sent home at six hours' notice. You must understand that Army wives are part of the regiment; they have rations and quarters, their journeys are paid for and arranged and they come very much under War Office orders. As far as the Admiralty is concerned Naval wives are just indiscretions and we are accustomed to fend for ourselves, to turn up when needed or vanish when we are in the way.' Naval wives whose husbands were in seagoing ships were the first to be ordered home in a liner, dubbed *The Slave Ship*, which reached port without incident. Wives whose husbands held shore appointments could do as they wished. They all stayed—accommodated in St George's barracks with the other Service wives.
7. *Army Education*, The Journal of the Royal Army Educational Corps, June 1946.
8. *The Queen's Army Schoolmistress*, December 1944.
9. *Government of Education*, Lester Smith, Penguin Books.
10. Verbatim Report of the Debate of the Elementary Education Act 1870, National Education Union.
11. See letter to the author 1949 (in the RAEC Museum).
12. *The New Law of Education*, Wells & Taylor. Butterworth.

CHAPTER 10

The Children Return

The Schools Reopen. In June 1944 children began to return to Gibraltar; in July there were 400 boys and girls at their desks. From December 1945 and into 1946 the trickle of families joining their husbands at overseas stations began in earnest, a trickle which was to become a flood during the following three years. In March 1946 small schools opened in Rome, Naples and Graz and in May one at Tripoli for 18 children 'several of whom make the journey to school daily from Castel Benito, 17 miles away. It is a long, slow business obtaining books and stationery, as everything comes by road convoy from Egypt. We share the school building with St George's British School for Maltese children: next week we move to an Education Centre, complete with gymnasium, woodwork and needlework rooms, library and tennis courts with AEC Instructors at hand when needed and a District Education Officer in the same building.'[1] Quite exceptional was the Garrison School, Bermuda.

'Since Xmas 1945 our school numbers have decreased, for most of our scholars during the war years were the children of soldiers of the Local Forces and their fathers have been demobilised.'[2]

In October a small Primary school was started at Mingaladon, North of Rangoon in Burma and in November 1946 the first post-war school opened in Singapore. These were rapidly followed by others in Hong Kong, Malaya, Cyrenaica and Egypt. In spite of warnings to all officers and other ranks who proposed to bring out their families that it would be difficult, perhaps impossible, to make official provision for the education of their children, owing to shortages of teachers, accommodation and equipment, requests for authority to open schools began to reach the War Office in volume from all parts of the world. The War Office had agreed in December 1945 to send abroad such few Army schoolmistresses as could be made available but warned it would be some months before they could arrive overseas and they would then be insufficient in numbers for the rapidly increasing population of children, which by 1947 had reached 3000 of school age, excluding the British Army of the Rhine. Commands were permitted to open schools for a minimum of 10 children of Service parents, instead of the historic 15. Education in the Army schools was to be free for the children of all ranks or, where no school existed, civil school fees refunded. Additional teachers were sought from Service wives, and local British and native sources were tapped.

There are few difficulties, however, which resource and improvisation cannot overcome and this fact is well exemplified in the history of the Army Children's Schools in Italy and Austria – a pattern repeated frequently in other Commands. By October 1946 there were 12 schools for 500 children in Italy and Austria. Of the 28 teachers, 11 were QAS, 6 qualified and 5 unqualified teachers of British origin, and 6 Italians and Austrians. Textbooks, materials and equipment were desperately short: local purchase was almost impossible and only a few of the textbooks supplied to the troops under the Release Schemes of Education were suitable: there was an extreme shortage in UK and the War Office supplies were therefore always small and too late for the growing demand. Teachers had to adjust their syllabuses, and curricula were framed to suit the qualifications of the staff. Italian teachers, for example, could not be expected to teach British history, British weights and measures nor Citizenship as effectively as British teachers.

Everywhere, school accommodation had to be hurriedly requisitioned or improvised, until adaptations or new buildings could be supplied. In Singapore, there was one large, modern pre-war school building, Gillman School, Alexandra (opened on 5 January 1939). Elsewhere in the Far East, schools started in tents and attap huts, in barrack blocks and private houses. In Trieste, the Army school opened in a villa, overlooking the Adriatic. In Tripoli, the school shared a fine building with the Education Centre in Mussolini's show place of the African coast-line.

'I was posted from Sarafand to El Ballah two weeks ago,' wrote a QAS in July 1947. 'After Palestine it is very dreary, being just a tented camp in the desert, but there are some compensations. The camp is run by POWs and we have nothing to do for ourselves. They make our beds, "do" our tents, clean our shoes – everything in fact, and the food is quite good. Inside the camp there is a cinema, two halls where they hold concerts and dances, three shops, a washing and ironing room and a NAAFI. There are only two drawbacks – the Ghibli wind and the Arabs!'[1]

The CEO, Middle East, writing in the Spring term 1949, summed up the position in his Command as follows:

'At the end of last term there were 2000 children on roll; 2400 are forecast for 1 April. Every month sees an increase in the number of families, necessitating frequent and considerable increases in teachers, books and equipment. Other than in Mauritius and Malta, there are no pre-war school buildings available. Our present provision varies in standard and suitability from the top floor of the railway station at Benghazi, private houses in Greece and Cyprus, to newly built schools in the Canal Zone. Two well-constructed and equipped secondary schools at Fayid and Moascar cater for the 11 + population. A new secondary school has been opened recently in Athens, where the number of American children considerably exceeds that of British Services' children and creates administrative and financial problems of a high degree in their complexity.'[3] He gave instances of the ever present Army problem of floating military populations and children's turbulence. For example, at Moascar, a school with 170 places, there were over 400 names on the roll in one term, so frequent were the moves. He described how RAEC,* including many National Service officers and sergeants, were employed in the secondary field to supplement the excellent work of the QAS, who bore the brunt of the initial burdens, and of locally engaged teachers, and noted the close cooperation with the other two Services. In Egypt the RAF ran their own primary schools but sent their secondary aged children to the Army's Secondary schools: in Malta, the Army's secondary aged children attended the Royal Navy School. In E. Africa, the lack of accommodation in Government and private schools compelled the Army to open its own schools in Mombasa, Nanyuki and Mackinnon Road (which a QAS described as 'a large stores dump miles away from anywhere, but the new school is about the best building in the place').

'One major point must be remembered – namely, that but for the English school at Heliopolis (Cairo) and the Government and private schools in East Africa, there are no schools, other than our Service schools, which can be attended by British children. Our responsibility is therefore very heavy if children are not to suffer "from following the drum",' the CEO concluded.

Far East. At the same time the CEO, FARELF, was reporting that his schools 'were overflowing'.

* By a special Army Order of 28 November 1946, King George VI had conferred the title 'Royal' on the Corps in recognition of its wartime services. At that time it consisted of 633 commissioned officers and 956 Other Ranks.

'Despite the bandit operations and terrorism in Malaya, progress has been steady. 15 schools exist now in the Command and more are projected. In Hong Kong secondary children attend local schools; in Singapore we intend opening our own (Alexandra Secondary School) to replace civilian secondary schools. In Malaya, because children are scattered, we shall set up our own secondary boarding school in the hill-station Cameron Highlands. In Ceylon, schools (which had closed 1941/1942) were opened at Colombo, Diyatalawa (Army), Trincomalee (RN) and Negombo (RAF) in October 1946. The problem is to provide, instead of the primary provision of the pre-war school, an education scheme for children on something near the UK scale. Owing to climate, afternoon school is impossible, except in Hong Kong. Many children travel up to 10 miles in buses to reach school each day. The only answer is a long morning session, beginning for the children who live farthest from school, when they board the school bus after 7 a.m. and continuing until 1330 hrs when they reach home. We ensure adequate "breaks" and the parents an afternoon rest for the younger children. The first seconded teacher disembarked on 9 June 1946 intended for the Singapore schools, whose attendance figures have doubled in twelve months. We are also providing schools for Gurkha children.'[3]

This problem of educating the children of non-UK troops was to occupy FARELF in particular and other Commands in general for years to come!

In July 1947 a QAS wrote home to a still austerely rationed England of living conditions in Singapore.

'The cost of living is high and most commodities are still scarce, but your eyes would pop out if you could see the amount of tinned food in the shops – all the Heinz 57 varieties and then some. There is a fair amount of textiles about (at a price!) and in Singapore itself there is plenty of English china and glassware but prices are undoubtedly too high for everything. As a matter of interest (the dollar being 2s. 4d.), I pay the cook sixty and amah forty dollars a month – and tea is three dollars a pound.'

Japan. Another example of splendid improvisation can be seen from Japan where the British Commonwealth Occupation Force (BCOF), originally a composite force of British, Australian, Indian and New Zealand Army and Air Forces, occupied the Western portion of the central Island of Honshu. The main part of the Australian Army contingent, together with a British Army force, was located in the neighbourhood of the Japanese naval base at Kure, some 10 miles from atom-bombed Hiroshima. Twenty miles south-west of Hiroshima was the main RAF base at Iwakuni, a former Japanese Air Force station, with a small contingent at Miho on the north coast. Headquarters BCOF occupied the former Japanese Naval Academy at Eta Jima, an island off Kure.

Families started arriving early in 1947: to accommodate them houses were constructed and furnished in selected areas near the military camps. It was first intended to open four schools, solely for British children, to be staffed by QAS, since the Australian Government had not authorised its families to go to Japan. When permission was given in the summer of 1947, large numbers of Australian children began to arrive but without their own teachers or equipment. A Joint Plan was quickly made, under which the Service with the largest number of children would provide a qualified Education Officer responsible for each school, while administration throughout BCOF would be centralised under one Director of Education. Temporary school accommodation had to be used, until permanent construction could be built by Japanese contractors working under a British Chief Engineer. In order to eliminate problems of transport or school meals, schools were opened in family lines. At Miho the entire staff was British (QAS, later supplemented by RAEC Sergeants): at Iwakuni, Hiro and Eta Jima the schools would be predominantly Australian. A proposed Central Secondary Boarding School at Hiro for the 146 children between 11 and 15 did not materialise so each school became an 'all age' school, supplemented for Australian children by correspondence courses, supplied by their State Education Departments. At the beginning of 1948 there were 423 children between 5 and 15 of whom 337 were Australian, 76 British and 10 American, for whom the various curricula and syllabus demands of their national or State systems of education provided many problems. Tables, chairs and desks were requisitioned from Japanese sources and adapted for size, until new American designed equipment arrived from the Japanese contractors. Australia supplied all the school books, stationery and materials.

The withdrawal of British Forces early in 1948 closed these schools, just when the results of this joint experiment were beginning to be seen. As only a sixth of the children had been British but over half the teaching force qualified RAEC and QAS, one can imagine the problems which faced the Australians, when they were left to fend for themselves.

'There had been close cooperation between the staff over syllabus and method; parents had helped with clubs and activities; the children had derived both profit and pleasure from their experiences;

155

there had been many fruitful contacts with the Japanese people. Finally, in view of the professed objects of the occupation, the interest shown by Japanese teachers and educationalists in this exposition of the democratic principles of education is very encouraging.'[3]

Army Schools handed over to LEAs. While the RAEC's responsibilities for the education of Army children were growing rapidly overseas, the War Office invited the Ministry of Education to ask each LEA to accept responsibility for the education of Army children in its area. All the LEAs concerned accepted; consequently, the War Office instructed home commands to complete the handover by the end of the financial year 1947/1948.[4] As a temporary measure suitable Army school buildings and playgrounds, land and unfurnished quarters for teachers in isolated areas could be leased to any LEA, which was unable to provide for these Army children the necessary accommodation itself. Equipment, books, stationery, etc., used in the Army schools could also be transferred. Furthermore, the Army arranged for Queen's Army Schoolmistresses to be loaned to LEAs under a similar instruction.[5]

On 1 April 1948 the 24 Army children's schools in Southern Command were handed over, and it was agreed that 'in all cases the local Military Authority will continue to be closely associated with the administration of these schools on local Boards of Management, on which RAEC members will also sit.'[6] One of the QAS headmistresses reported, 'The Atomic Age has reached even the Marlborough Lines school and we are in the process of disintegration!' Other Commands reported similar arrangements, so that by the end of the year all Army Children's Schools in UK had been taken over by the appropriate LEAs, except for the two boys' boarding schools, DYRMS Dover and QVS Dunblane. Thus, after looking after its own schools in UK for over 200 years, the Army relinquished this direct responsibility, but it still retains to this day close links with LEAs over Service children's problems. Whereas once the Army could legislate for all its schools, at home and abroad, on matters of curriculum, syllabus and teaching method, now problems must be solved by consultation with the Department of Education and Science, the various LEAs and the Services.

There was one far reaching consequence of the handover of Army schools in UK, which should be noted. The QAS could no longer alternate duties at home and abroad and a life career in Army schools was no longer possible. Since no QAS had been recruited during the War, their numbers had halved to 154 in March 1946. Faced with the urgent demands for more and more teachers to go overseas as well as to staff the Army's schools at home, the War Office obtained Treasury approval in June 1946 to engage another thirty, and five more early in 1947. In 1948 the War Office decided on a new policy of short term contracts and, instead of recruiting more QAS, invited male and female qualified teachers to apply for three-year secondments from LEAs to serve as civilians in the Army's schools overseas. Consequently, the number of serving QAS declined to thirty in 1957 and by 1970 only one remained to represent the many thousands who had served the Army so well, since their establishment in 1840. On the other hand, the number of UK based teachers steadily rose to nearly 2200 in 1969, when they totalled over half the Army's civilian UK-based force of 3375 overseas.[7] These teachers were given officer status with conditions of service partly akin to any other civil servant temporarily serving overseas. To this teaching force must also be added those locally entered, selected by local Boards and paid for previous experience and qualifications at rates, negotiated by the Army Department with local governments.

British Families Education Service. In March 1946, the Director of Army Education was requested by the Overseas Reconstruction Committee, which was discussing all aspects of the possible move of families to the British Zone of Occupied Germany, to consider the means of setting up the equivalent of a Local Education Authority there, working under the Control Commission for Germany (CCG). A Working Party, consisting of representatives of the three Services, the Control Office for Germany and Austria, the Ministry of Education and the Scottish Education Department, was established to make provisional plans. The Cabinet decided on 20 June 1946 to permit families to join their husbands in the British Occupied Zone, at first largely of Control Commission personnel, later predominantly from the Services. Since the Ministry of Education's jurisdiction for education did not extend beyond the boundaries of England and Wales, educational responsibility was vested in the Foreign Office. The Director of Education, Westmorland, Mr John Trevelyan, became the first Director of Education for British Forces, Germany.[9]

The preliminary report to the Working Party estimated that 7000 children (3000 under 5, 3000 aged 5–11 and 1000 of secondary age) would be scattered over some 20,000 square miles of the British Zone, the British Sector in Berlin and the lines of communication in the Low Countries.

'The educational pattern was likely to be one of a large number of local nursery and primary groups, varying in size from ten to one hundred children, together with two or three larger primary groups of between one hundred and 300 children.'[8]

It was assumed that half the secondary aged children would be within daily travelling distance of school and the other half would need boarding provision. Teachers would be found from LEAs by public advertisement. The organisation would be known as the British Families Education Service. Its Director would be responsible to a Zonal Board of Education, chaired by the Chief Administrative Officer of CCG and sitting on which would be representatives from the three Services and the Ministry of Education.

The Director established his Headquarters at Herford on 24 September 1946 with a Deputy, six peripatetic specialists (two each for physical education, school meals and educational psychology) and an administrative officer for supplies, finance and general duties. He had Regional Education Officers at Berlin (for the British Sector), Hamburg (for the Hansestadt and Schleswig-Holstein region), Hanover (for Hanover region) and Dusseldorf (for Land North Rhine/Westphalia). Each (except the Officer in Berlin) controlled an area of 8000–10,000 square miles, with the help of two deputies and an administrative officer. All the HQ and Regional Staffs were in post by mid-November 1946, by which date the first two teachers had also arrived.

What were the conditions in Germany, which greeted these early arrivals? Mr Frank Buckley, for many years a Regional Director and one of the founder members of BFES, can best supply the answer.

'Their first impression must have been one of appalling destruction. Whole towns were in ruins, supplies of gas and electricity were limited, and water had to be boiled before use. The only transport seen on the roads belonged to the Control Commission or the Military Government. The German population was apathetic and bordering on starvation. There were few shops and those which remained had nothing to sell. Money had no value, barter replaced currency, and the black market was everywhere. Although the opening of German schools had been given high priority, the majority

158

had either been destroyed or damaged, and such few children as could attend school worked a shift system.

'The British families lived in requisitioned houses, among neighbours who were sometimes hostile and very rarely friendly, but life for them, after the austerity of war-time Britain, exceeded belief. They were provided officially with domestic help – cook, housekeeper, boilerman – and drink was cheap. Consequently, they could enjoy the social round. Anything of value could be purchased for the price of a few cigarettes. The fathers held responsible and well paid positions in Occupied Germany: their children were intelligent and rapidly matured socially. A 9-year old could mix a gin and tonic, as expertly as his parents. He could sail, ride or engage in a host of other out-of-school activities. How could such children take their schooling seriously?

'As British Military Government officials had been appointed to every German Kreis (county, borough and rural councils), the British schools were widely spread and most were small, established in private houses, flats or barrack blocks. Classrooms were small and schools lacked at first the amenities of hall and workroom. Nevertheless, they had many of the advantages and the atmosphere of a good village school. The staffing scale was generous by UK standards and designed to cover small groups, with a wide age and ability range. Mid-day meals were prepared in the nearest Mess and conveyed to the school in insulated containers. The schools were furnished with whatever could be requisitioned, usually more suitable for domestic than school use. It was only later that Rhine Army was able to supply proper furniture and equipment, built by German contractors or UK manufacturers to BFES specifications.

'At first BFES could only buy such books as were readily available from publishers in the UK. "Old Lob" was the basis of the reading scheme. There were seldom complete sets of arithmetic, history and geography books to cover the whole school. For some teachers the lack of suitable books was a disaster, but for the majority it was a challenge. Without text books to inhibit them, teachers began to develop group work, not necessarily through a belief in its educational value, but because it was the only way to teach with such limited material. Personally, I never enjoyed my teaching more; we were using then discovery methods and projects, which now are hailed as progressive. In art and crafts we had to experiment and use what the environment offered. Since there were few exercise books, teachers improvised with ordinary paper, as many good infant teachers do today. They made their own equipment, which suited exactly their own children's needs. There is a moral to this story, for I am sure that many of our teachers today would do better, if they used fewer commercial products and relied more on their own initiative and experience.'

At the end of the summer term 1947 there were 220 teachers at work with about 4000 children in some 70 locations. The nursery, infant and junior groups were found to exist, as had been predicted, in teachable concentrations but the scatter of secondary children meant that there had to be 'senior tops' to primary schools, with Secondary Departments possible only at Hamburg and Berlin. However, this 'evil necessity' began to be removed by the first two boarding schools, which were opened on 1 July 1947 at Wilhelmshaven (Prince Rupert School) for 250 children in the former German Naval Barracks, and at Plön (King Alfred School), which received its first pupils on 7 May 1948, when a trainload of 350 of them arrived to occupy the former German U-Boat Training School. The school, under its first headmaster, Colonel Spencer Chapman, of *The Jungle is Neutral* fame, was officially opened five days later by the then Minister of Education, the Right Honourable George Tomlinson, MP.

Thus was the British Families Education Service born and soon began to prosper.

REFERENCES

1. *The Queen's Army Schoolmistress*, December 1946.
2. *The Queen's Army Schoolmistress*, July 1946.
3. *Army Education*. June 1949.
   CHIEF EDUCATION OFFICERS, FAR EAST:
   1946–47   Col. A.C.T. White, VC, MC, BA
   1947–50   Col. A.L. Gadd, MA
   1950–52   Col. W.S. Beddall, OBE
   1952–54   Col. G.T. Folkard
   1954–57   Col. J.H.H. Coombes, CBE, MA
   1957–59   Col. A. Nicholls, TD, MA
   1959–62   Brig. B.L. Rigby
   1962–65   Brig. E.C. Gould, OBE, MA
   1965   Brig. E.F. Foxton, OBE, BA
   1966–68   Brig. H. Thomas, OBE, BSC
   1968–70   Brig. W.S. Mullin, OBE, MA
   1970–71   Col. N.T. St John Williams, BA
4. Directorate of Army Education letter, dated August 1947.
5. War Office Letter dated 4 October 1946.
6. The Ministry of Education Circular appeared in December 1948.
7. 1969 figures.
8. *Army Education*, March 1946, F.J. Downs, Deputy Director, BFES.
9. *DIRECTORS, BFES:*
   1946–49   J. Trevelyan, OBE, BA
   1949–52   G.A.N. Lowndes, MC
   1952–54   J.A. Humphreys, BA
   1954–57   H. Priestley
   1957–66   H.E. Pacey, CBE, MA, MSc
   1966–   E.E. Lowe, CBE, MA (formerly Colonel RAEC).

CHAPTER 11

The Years of Improvisation

(1946–1956)

Educational Planning. By 1948 Britain's war-time force had been reduced to 700,000, which included 150,000 colonial and Gurkha troops. National military service provided about 100,000 recruits annually to the Army. The military commitments were widespread. The occupation of the British Zone of Germany was accepted as a long-term obligation and there were still small British forces in Austria, the Trieste area and Greece. British troops had withdrawn from Japan, while the transfer of power to the new Dominions of India and Ceylon, and to the independent nation of Burma, obviated the need for troops there. Outside Europe there were 115,000 men, mainly in the Middle East.[1] It was the children of the married men in these overseas garrisons, which provided the population for the Service schools.

The Army was quick to realise that, if its children overseas were to enjoy the opportunities and benefits of the 1944 Education Act, it would need to translate the provisions of the Act into a military context and obtain considerable financial support. Since the problem was not confined to the Army, the three Services, the Colonial Office, the Treasury and the Ministry of Education combined in 1947 to formulate plans for inter-Service schools overseas. The following year, this Inter-departmental Committee on Education of Service Children Overseas (ESCO) submitted its proposals to the Treasury and obtained the necessary approval. In type and scope, education was to conform as nearly as possible to that provided at home. Education was to be free for the children of all ranks in Service schools or, where none existed, civil school fees refunded. The need for boarding schools was recognised and approval given to special staffing ratios to offset the problems of wide-age groups in small schools and frequent moves of pupils. Treasury confirmed the teachers' secondment scheme and provided some ancillary services for schools, such as transport and school meals. A Standing Inter-Service Committee (SCESCO) was established in London under the permanent chairmanship of the Deputy-Director of Army Education to watch over the requirements of Service children's education overseas. Each Service was to be responsible for its own schools on the principle that the Service which provided the most children in a particular school should be responsible for that school. Commands were to establish co-ordinating committees to ensure a uniform policy on major issues and to make the best use of local resources, allowing for differences in Service requirements and for differing administrative procedures.[2]

By the end of the first decade, despite all the difficulties resulting from the aftermath of the war, the changing political picture both at home and in each country overseas and the economic shortages, all the major Commands had instituted the new pattern of children's education. In addition to their responsibility for adult education CEOs established an organisation for the professional control and administration of Army children's education, set up neighbourhood primary schools in garrisons and family areas and comprehensive day secondary schools in the major catchment areas, or boarding schools where circumstances were favourable. The schools were staffed mainly by UK-based teachers with some QAS and some locally enlisted teachers. Headmasters were given freedom to organise their own curricula, syllabuses and teaching methods and were provided with grants of money, equal to the best of the LEAs, to purchase books and educational equipment. By 1956 HMIs had visited every Command at least twice and in some cases more frequently and a pattern of regular visits and in-Service training courses had been inaugurated. Everywhere the number of children was increasing as more married quarters were built and more of the time of HQ staffs, as well as of the RAEC, was spent on establishing and administering this rapidly expanding service. In 1947 the Director of Army Education was responsible for 164 teachers and 2500 children: by 1960 there would be 1334 teachers and 27,000 children. The cost of salaries alone would rise from £113,000 to £2$\frac{1}{2}$ million in that period.

Each Command had educational problems peculiar to itself, often the result of political disturbance in the area. For instance, the Suez crisis (1956) and War (October–November 1956) and the troubles in Cyprus (1952–55), in Aden (1955) and the Mau-Mau revolt (1952–57) caused troop movements and family upsets in the Middle East area; in FARELF the terrorist warfare in the Malayan jungles (1948–60) and the Korean War (1950–53) made similar difficulties for the Command, while BAOR had to reorganise and redeploy following the end of the occupation in 1955 and the entry of West Germany into NATO.

But there were some educational problems which were common to all. Before the Second World War, Army children's education had been limited to the primary field. Post-war, the biggest problem was undoubtedly secondary education, especially in areas where there were insufficient numbers to merit a viable secondary school. Secondary teachers with the necessary specialist qualifications were difficult to find. The 1944 Act required the provision of secondary-modern, secondary-grammar and secondary-technical education. The bulk of Service children, as in the UK, were in the first or non-academic category. Selection procedures (using both Moray House and National Foundation for Educational Research tests) were employed to decide the type of education for each child at 11+, but again small numbers and the more expensive equipment and buildings for this type of education took time to provide. Where suitable civilian schools existed – in Nairobi, Malaya, Hong Kong, Jamaica and Paris – fees were refunded for Army children attending. In 1954 the Treasury accepted the principle of an education allowance being paid for each child of secondary school age kept in a boarding school at home, whether the parent was overseas or not, provided continuity was maintained.

The second problem common to all Commands was incessant change – of staff, children, and even the schools themselves, known to the Services as 'turbulence'. In his overseas tour of three years the soldier might move from station to station or from Command to Command, whilst his family might also move within a single station from temporary to permanent married quarters. Hence a child would attend many schools, both at home and abroad. Teachers changed on average every three to four years under their engagement terms, while curricula, syllabuses and methods varied naturally from school to school. Whilst 'travel may broaden the mind', for the Service child there was a need for constant adjustment. Turbulence might not be the cause of backwardness, but it

163

undoubtedly caused some under-functioning, even of the above average child, and called for only the best of instructional techniques from the teachers.

A third problem was supply – of educational stores, equipment, books and stationery. These had to be requested, purchased in UK in competition with LEA schools, or contracts placed overseas and transported at first by ship, later increasingly by air, to all parts of the world, assessed for priority with other badly needed military stores. By the time the supplies arrived, they would be inadequate to meet the demand caused by the increasing numbers of children. Scales of entitlement for equipment, accommodation stores and for school buildings were worked out and issued in appropriate Equipment or Barrack Schedules. Army transport had to be provided and adapted for children, until more suitable coaches could be supplied. These needed escorts – mothers volunteered, local labour was hired, in some cases military personnel were used. Buildings had to be planned and constructed or adapted.

The small school of Barce, in Cyrenaica, provided a good example of improvised education under difficult conditions. In 1954, it was a typical regimental school, belonging to the Royal Scots Greys – an all-age, mixed school of two classes for twenty-two children and two teachers. The Headmistress was a QAS and the other teacher UK-based. The infant class had thirteen children, of whom the CO, QM, SQMS, a Sergeant and a Corporal provided one each, the Padre two and Troopers three children. There were two children belonging to a Maltese doctor, working for the Cyrenaica Government, and the child of an American working with the Libyan American Technical Aid Service. As non-entitled children these paid school fees. The school was housed in the Regimental Education Centre and, although in an isolated area, the premises had been attractively laid out and were not ill-suited to the numbers on the Roll. There was a general shortage of suitable school furniture and equipment, including textbooks and reference books. The wide age range of the junior 'school' required individual and group work to meet the needs of children of differing ability. Some children lived more than a mile away from the school and improvised transport had been arranged by mule cart. The resources of the unit were put at its disposal. The Quartermaster supplied it; the padre took some of its children for religious instruction; the Medical Officer was responsible for the children's health and school hygiene. The Commanding Officer visited it and the families supported it. Professionally, it was controlled by the nearest Army Education Officer.

Middle East. In the Middle East, the events in the Canal Zone, after Egypt's abrogation of the 1936 Treaty on 15 October 1951, had their impact on the schools. In fact, the very first 'incident' was the stoning of a school bus taking children to a Moascar School and the attack by hooligans on the motor cyclist escort. The first 'operation' was the evacuation without incident of the 108 Army and RAF children attending the English School, Cairo, as boarders. The Army schools in Egypt had to be temporarily reorganised because of the difficulty of transferring children to Garrison Schools from their homes in civilian accommodation in the towns. The military plan was to reduce families in the Canal Zone and to redeploy the remainder into WD accommodation in the 'safe areas'. On the other hand, the reduction of the school population by half, because of the emergency, solved forthwith most of the earlier school problems of shortages of classroom accommodation and furniture and of manning the schools with fully qualified staff. In three months the numbers of children and teachers dropped from 1770 and 64 respectively to 920 and 51. Especially felt was the withdrawal of Egyptian labour from the schools, i.e. cooks, caretakers, bakers, drivers and labourers. A tribute should be paid to the loyalty, courage and devotion to duty of all those civilian teachers who carried on despite difficulties and often danger and who had in many cases to endure extremely hard-living conditions.

The troop movements caused by the events in Egypt affected Cyprus also and reminded one of a precedent for warriors leaving behind their families and children – Richard Coeur de Lion and his troops left behind in Cyprus Queen Berengaria and the other wives, while they soldiered in the Holy Land. In September 1951 Cyprus had two schools with 172 children: one year later it had five schools with 348 children, with a corresponding doubling of its teaching staff. The British Government School in Tripoli had to close because of these troop movements and because of the granting of independence to Libya. Since there was no other English school in the territory for civilian children, the Army Children's School in Tripoli was besieged by parents seeking admittance for their children. By admitting them, the Army earned the gratitude of the local British Community.

British Forces, Germany. In BAOR, by 1951, only 15 per cent of the school children were of CCG personnel and the Foreign Office resolved to relinquish control of BFES. The Cabinet decided on 25 January 1952 that the War Office, as the major user, should take over responsibility. It had long and relevant experience and had officers trained for the work. The logistic and much of the administrative support was already supplied by the Army and RAF; it was thus the cheapest solution.

The Director of Army Education became responsible for children's education in British Forces, Germany, on 1 April 1952. It was agreed that ultimate responsibility for the British Families Education Service would be assumed by the Commander-in-Chief, who would control it through his Chief Education Officer, under whom the Director, BFES, would serve: the Ministry of Education would continue to be represented on the Zonal Board, would select teachers and non-teaching staff (both responsibilities subsequently handed over to the War Office) and would continue to inspect the schools. No important non-teaching post would be abolished without prior consultation with the Ministry of Education. It was further agreed that inter-Departmental adjustments would be made to cover the pay of teachers, books and equipment, until these expenses could be included, as for all other Army schools overseas, in annual financial Votes; and that the War Office would offer teachers new terms of engagement, retaining the current ones until 31 December 1952, and make arrangements for their superannuation similar to those made for them by the Foreign Office.

Much of the organisation of children's education in Germany was the same as that established by the Army in other Commands overseas, but there were some differences, largely stemming from the fact that Germany was under occupation and that the support costs of the British Forces were borne largely by the Germans. Consequently, accommodation, equipment and staffing were on a more generous scale. School buildings were provided through the Royal Engineer and Quartering services: teachers were recruited and selected by the Director of Army Education (although officially employed, paid and disciplined by the Civil Establishment Branch of the War Office, operating through the Command Secretariat). Furniture and scaled items of equipment were supplied by Ordnance, books and stationery through HMSO, and special education equipment through UK firms – all sponsored by the Directorate of

Army Education. Children's health was the responsibility of the Royal Army Medical and Dental Corps.

The schools' organisation in West Germany was growing rapidly, in numbers of children and teachers, in building and equipping programmes and in the annual schools' budget. The provision of primary places generally kept pace with demand but secondary places continued to be insufficient. By December 1953 only one child in eleven between the ages of 11 and 12 years had been admitted to a secondary school. The opening of a new boarding school for 350 places at Hamm (Windsor School) in October 1953 helped, but by the end of the academic year four out of every five children aged 11–12 years were still being educated in primary schools and plans were in hand, even before Windsor School opened, to increase the number of boarders there to 520* (and eventually to 590) and to build a secondary day school for the new NATO HQ at Rheindahlen (Queen's School, opened 4 July 1956). Meanwhile the two secondary boarding schools, Prince Rupert School, Wilhelmshaven, and King Alfred School, Plön (650 and 620 children respectively), were full to capacity. There was also a Secondary Department at Hamburg for 96 children. Responsibility for secondary planning and direction was retained at HQ, BFES but primary education was the responsibility of the District Education Officers at Rhine Area, Lübbecke and Hamburg (the latter being also responsible for Hanover and Berlin). To help the administration of schools at District level four BFES District Committees were established, handling local administrative and building problems, the allocation of MQs, co-operation with the German authorities, etc. Membership consisted of Garrison Commanders, the chief administrative and quartering officers at District HQs and Military Education Officers.

Service tactical and strategic moves, following the decision to run down Hamburg District and to build up the Army and 2 Tactical Air Force, west of the Rhine, caused new adjustments to school building plans and increased the number of Married Quarters needed, often in entirely new areas. The build-up of the school population in Germany can be seen from these figures:

1948	5,201 children
1949	5,648 ,,

*Windsor Girls School, Hamm, opened in February 1961 for 500 boarders, having started its separate existence at King Alfred School, Plön, in September 1959.

1950	5,497 children
1951	6,398 „
1952	9,406 „
1953	10,400 „

It is only natural that teachers and children should wish to understand the country in which they are living and be interested in its people, culture and customs. This is especially true in European countries where mixed marriages introduce many bi-lingual children into the schools. The Services actively promoted good Anglo-German relations at all levels (especially later when Germany became a NATO ally) and such relationships were important to break down the British Army's tendency to isolate itself in self-sufficient garrisons. Teachers were encouraged to make use of the excellent facilities offered by die Brücke (Anglo-German centres under the aegis of the Cultural Relations Division of the High Commission) and new teachers were briefed on arrival by native speakers on the cultural and political background of modern Germany. Teachers were also encouraged to establish the maximum contact with neighbouring German schools, their staff and children, and through local studies to understand German social and economic life.

School visits were financed to places of interest and there were exchanges with German schools in English, music, art, physical training and sport and German children were invited to attend school concerts, carol services, nativity plays, etc., and local orphanages took part in BFES Christmas parties. BFES schools participated in German celebrations and festivals (Bunte Abende, Laterne Bummeln, tree planting, etc.) and organised Anglo-German club meetings in out-of-school hours for dancing, games and dramatics. Another opportunity to foster good relations was provided by the school camps opened in Winterberg in the Harz mountains during the summers of 1953–56, where British, German and displaced persons' children enjoyed the communal life and study in the open air. The mornings would be devoted to classroom sessions with mixed staff and children and the same policy was adopted for meals and the afternoon recreational activities and educational outings. Naturally, the German educational authorities and the Service Commanders took a great interest in these experiments in international living, of which over half of the 800 total places were allotted to non-British children and staff, the expenses of the thirty-nine displaced persons' children being met from BFES private funds.

The Director, Dr J. A. Humphreys, described life in BFES in those early days:

'A teacher after selection, documentation and a medical examination travels by train to Harwich, by boat to the Hook and military train to Cologne. She (or he) alights at the station, is carried away by car to attend a short residential course run for new British teachers and lodged in the hostel of the British Primary Boarding School. Most competently staffed by the Cultural Relations Division of the British High Commission, the course covers recent German political and social history, culture and education, with some talks on the organisation of the Education service she has joined.

'She may go to a British school serving some isolated garrison area where there are few German people and little German social life, as for example the little school (2 teachers and 28 children) at Wesendorf, North of Hanover and near the East Zone. She may go to a larger British school in one of the centres, Dusseldorf, Osnabruck, Cologne, Hamburg, Berlin, Bad Oeynhausen, where she will be in a position to see about as much of German life as her inclinations permit and to attend operas and concerts to the extent her pocket allows. She will learn that BFES comprises some 80 schools, including 3 large boarding secondary schools, some 9400 children and over 400 British qualified teachers. She will be assigned to one of these schools which conform to the general pattern of UK schools. Her accommodation, meals and transport are likely to be better than in UK. She may well be agreeably surprised by the physical conditions in which she will teach, in respect both of school accommodation and equipment. She may arrive at one of the 7 or 8 new primary schools built over the last year to the normal home specifications, spacious classrooms, an attractive hall and the other appurtenances necessary in an age where Hygiene is married to Education. More likely she will find her way into other schools, varying from the converted barrack block to the large private house (a standard modern German barrack can be converted at a cost of about DM 120,000 (£10,000) into a good primary school, well lighted, ventilated, easy enough on the eye and providing a generous scale of teaching space). The converted Fritz Thyssen house in Mulheim combines space with elegance – all paid for out of Occupation Funds, charged to the Federal Government. German schools are not requisitioned for obvious reasons. She will notice the large number of infants (numerically the 5–6 age group about equals the 7–11 group) and be pleased that her class will average 20–25 children with better equipment than UK. She will be pleased at the more comprehensive provision for nursery children and at the extensive school meals service. She will find the children rather rootless, changing schools frequently. She will certainly be disturbed at the instability of her class. She may be distressed at the low attainment in number in some of the junior children (number suffering more from change of school) though reasonably reassured about their attainment in reading and writing (which suffer less). She will certainly find herself more dependent on her own initiative and resource than she would at home.

'The normal British parent is probably more keenly interested in his child's education than at home – conscious of the problems caused by his own wanderings, interested in standards, even though this child could well keep up his end at a meeting of the Royal Geographical Society.

'The difficulties largely derive from the geographical changes in the child's domicile but also the thin spread of children over the Zone, often too few to make a viable school (both primary and secondary). These difficulties might be partly solved by universal boarding provision at all ages, and indeed there is a primary boarding school in Cologne for isolated children of 8 years and above. But it might have emotional problems for the younger child and would be grossly expensive. The problem of discontinuity is tackled by a fairly generous establishment of teachers. This enables more individual attention to be paid to each particular child. As a result, attainment in reading and writing appear comparable to that in most primary schools at home. Attainment in number is often lower than at home, since it suffers most from discontinuity. Unfortunately, it appears also superficially most easy to test by the critical and potentially irate parent.

'It has been contended that the bad effects of discontinuity would be neutralised by a high degree of standardisation – of schemes of teaching and books (as in the American Zone) but this would be against the British tradition of a teacher's freedom of matter and method. It does call for high standards of teaching and greater flexibility of approach to individual problems.'[3]

The advantages and desirability of standardisation of syllabus, method and equipment, especially in English and Arithmetic in the junior schools, would continue to be debated in the years ahead in the interests of providing continuity in children's education. Invariably the consensus of opinion was that so long as there was no uniformity among LEA schools, from which the Army children came and to which they mostly returned, it would be unwise to prescribe any such standardisation in Army schools. Not only would such a policy be opposed to the teacher's traditional freedom but the better teachers always sought to take full advantage of the local environment to enrich their teaching. What might have once been possible and advisable, when an Army child received all his education, both at home and abroad, in Army schools, was no longer possible nor desirable when he received his education under a variety of school authorities.

Far East. An interesting comparison can be made in the Far East Command between the conditions which existed in 1950 and the situation in 1954. The changes in the magnitude of the task can be seen from the following comparative figures.

| | March 1950 | | October 1954 | |
	No. of Schools	No. of Children	No. of Schools	No. of Children
Singapore	7	530	10	1690
Malaya	8	210	14	1210
Hong Kong	3	185	7	1275
TOTAL	18	925	31	4175

Some schools existing in 1950 had been enlarged, others housed in different buildings and a number of new schools had been opened. In Singapore two new primary schools had been built at Pasir Panjang and the Alexandra Bi-lateral Secondary School had been split into separate grammar and modern schools, with additional classrooms built for the grammar school. In Malaya there were new schools at Kluang, Sungei Patani and in the Cameron Highlands (Slim School). At Kuala Lumpur the all-age school had been split into three separate schools – infant, junior and secondary modern (the last in a new building). In Hong Kong a re-modelling of Victoria School and improved additions to Gun Club Hill had been completed, but the large increase in numbers of school children meant two new primary schools had had to be provided at Whitfield Barracks, a new secondary modern school (Minden Row) and an all-age school at Sek Kong.[4] Additional accommodation was planned in the New Territories and at Kowloon to relieve pressure on the Colony's other over-crowded schools. By measures such as these the Army had provided the school places; but what of the schools themselves?

Of the eight primary schools in Singapore, three were solely for infants, two for juniors and the rest were for the full primary age range. Most schools had three, four or five classes, but the two Alexandra schools had nearly 400 juniors and 250 infants respectively on roll. Senior pupils attended one of the Alexandra secondary schools, either the grammar or the modern, which admitted also the Royal Navy's senior pupils and some from the Royal Air Force. Thus there were centrally-sited secondary schools and scattered primary schools well placed to serve the chief groups of married quarters. The new Pasir Panjang extensions, when completed, would make it possible to create a single catchment area for the infants and juniors attending there, and another one for the Alexandra and Tanglin primary schools. Continuity between neighbouring infant and junior schools would thus be preserved, a development well suited to children whose education already suffered from too many changes and the short school working day in all areas in the Far East, except in Hong Kong during the winter months.

In Malaya there was only one large concentration of Army settlement, namely at Kuala Lumpur, where there were separate schools for infants, juniors and secondary modern pupils, together with a fairly large number of RAF children and a few from the RN. Mostly the schools in Malaya, however, were isolated and small, ranging from one to four classes, making it almost impossible to achieve suitable education for the few seniors in each of these 'rural' schools. Thus some secondary children had to remain in primary schools, but in general secondary education was now concentrated in Slim School (a bilateral boarding school) and the Kuala Lumpur secondary school for day pupils.

There was only one all-age school in Hong Kong – in a part of the New Territories rather remote from Kowloon; otherwise the schools were organised into separate primary and secondary schools, as was to be expected in a compact urban area. The primary school at Fort Stanley had about sixty children, but the rest had about two hundred each. Pupils selected for grammar school education still attended the civil King George V school, run by the Hong Kong Board of Education. A temporary secondary modern school at Minden Row had been established with a few pupils of grammar school calibre.

By adaptation and new buildings the Army had thus met the accommodation demands of the increasing school population. Some premises were aesthetically pleasing as well as being utilitarian in design. One unsatisfactory feature, however, of both extensions and new buildings was the space restriction laid down by the early Barrack Synopsis Scales, which authorised a classroom of 430 square feet for 30 children, small by comparison with UK standards, let alone in tropical heat. Conditions were not improved by the fact that most classrooms had to accommodate more than 30 places, because of the unrealistic statistical basis on which places were calculated. The Treasury insisted that, when building in permanent construction was planned to meet long term requirements, the figure of 1·2 children per family in married quarters had to be used; 34 per cent of the resultant total would be children of primary school age and 15 per cent secondary. The rest were under school age.

These figures had been taken from a 1955 Report of the Army Operational Research Group (AORG), and had been calculated on the demographic factors of the 1951 Census and based on the principle that marital conditions in the Services and civilian life were broadly similar. Such calculations had little relation to reality and did not produce the number of school places required to meet the number of children actually in the Commands. Operational moves prevented firm long-term plans being made and never quickly enough. Garrison location and strengths were constantly changing and the number of married quarters never equalled entitlements. There were, consequently, many families in private accommodation, the number of which varied by Commands, whose children had to be officially disregarded for school planning. Furthermore, each Service had a different basis of calculation, and cumbersome administrative procedures added to the delays in obtaining agreement to building proposals.

Eventually new Barrack Scales were negotiated authorising tropical increments and in 1966 a revised formula was produced to reflect the latest demographic and Service factors involved. Account was taken of all military and entitled civilian families in married quarters, hirings and private accommodation and of the actual numbers of schoolchildren in each Command. The forecast average number of school children per family was re-assessed for each year ahead and varied in 1966 from 0·63 to 0·72 in 1970 for primary children and from 0·23 to 0·27 respectively for secondary children. The result was a much more accurate and satisfactory basis for realistic school planning.

Equipment for primary schools was much more varied than it had been in 1950. Established schools were satisfactorily stocked with books and other teaching aids. But in the newer secondary schools apparatus for physical education was in short supply, both in quantity and variety, and some of the equipment and furniture, such as woodwork tools and benches, were the same as those provided for Army adult units and married quarters and were unsuitable, both in height and weight, for children. Part of the trouble lay in the fact that the capitation grants, while adequate for existing numbers, were insufficient for the rapidly increasing number of new schools and classes, for which setting-up grants, as well as annual maintenance grants, were needed.

There had been a steady improvement in the flow of teachers to the Far East from the United Kingdom, which now numbered 116 out of a total of 197. There was a greater stability in staffing and a better balance of men and women and of teachers trained for infants, juniors and seniors respectively than in the past. The quality of the staff was good, reflecting improved selection procedures. The greatest lack was in the secondary field – for teachers with the necessary experience and specialisation. No less than seven RAEC officers and NCOs had had to be employed in the Singapore grammar school. This made a strong argument for extending beyond the initial contract the periods of service of suitably qualified and satisfactory teachers, especially for posts of responsibility, and of headmasters.

The greater stability, the improvements in the teaching force and in the school facilities over the four years were reflected in the work of the schools. The primary schools were offering a better balanced curriculum and teachers were making more use of the local environment. Secondary education was still hampered by the physical conditions under which it was carried out. There were the shortages of equipment and of certain specialist teachers. Though a fair number of pupils were staying beyond their fifteenth birthday in the modern schools (some of which were aiming at external examinations), the age groups fell away in size towards the top of the grammar schools. There were three major secondary school problems to resolve – the removal of the Slim secondary school to Kuala Lumpur to form a single larger bilateral school, which would be more accessible, more economic to run and more attractive to teachers who felt isolated and insecure in the Cameron Highlands. There was the future of grammar school education in Hong Kong to be settled. Because of the great demand for places for Hong Kong's own children in the King George V School, the Army needed its own secondary school there. In Singapore, centralised secondary education for all three Services was being considered. This would permit a more varied and flexible curriculum and would allow for a bigger staff possessing a better range of qualifications.

The brunt of the organisation and administration of children's education fell on the RAEC officers in Districts and Commands. It was their task to plan schools, obtain supplies, and arrange for suitable staffs to be recruited, for apart from three officers in the War Office, no members of the Corps were then engaged on full-time school duties. They had their adult education responsibilities as their prime task. This economy of man-power persisted until 1956, when RAEC Staff Officers began to be appointed solely for duties connected with children's education.[2]

West Africa. In West Africa, in September 1951, size and distance dictated the pattern of educational provision. There were 330 children in four 'all age' schools at Accra (202), Kaduna (24), Lagos (36) and Freetown (68). The schools were reasonably well sited in relation to family quarters, and transport brought to school children who lived outside the main camps. Accommodation and equipment had been provided under conditions of extreme difficulty and consequently all schools lacked amenities and facilities normally provided elsewhere. For example, none of the schools had real assembly halls, nor the playing and shower facilities for a proper programme of physical education. Medical and dental inspections were more difficult to provide at UK standards; there was no provision of fresh milk and the substitutes were unsatisfactory.

Education in the basic subjects for primary children was thorough but teaching methods were inclined to be formal. What was needed in those early days was more imaginative teaching and a widening of the children's experience by projects and by more use of the environment. Nevertheless, the children and staff were contented and attendance was good. Parents made few complaints, largely because of the compensation of having their children with them.

All the primary schools had secondary-aged children—twenty-three in Accra, and nineteen shared by the other three schools. Only at Accra was it possible to organise a class; elsewhere individual programmes were attempted. The range of options was necessarily small and there was no provision for science, cookery or crafts. Under such circumstances secondary education by UK standards was obviously unavailable.

By 1956 the number of schools had risen to seven, with new schools at Kumasi and Takoradi in the Gold Coast and at Tamale in Nigeria, sharing fifty-seven children between them. There were now 579 children in the other schools. By this time the problem of secondary education was obvious. The Army medical authorities were agreed and adamant that the climate and conditions in West Africa were altogether unsuitable for children of secondary age; in fact, they advised against bringing children into the Command if

175

they were over 9 years of age. In spite of this advice, eighty-three children of secondary age were attending Army schools, spread out over this widely dispersed Command. This number was plainly insufficient to justify the establishment of a residential comprehensive secondary school, even if suitable accommodation could have been found for it. Furthermore, the school life of all children, whether primary or secondary, suffered from the interruptions caused by recuperative leave. All Europeans, including teachers, after eighteen months' continuous service in the Command, had to return to a temperate climate, usually in the United Kingdom. This three-months recuperative leave in the middle of a three-year tour, staggered as it was between children, disorganised classes and retarded children in their studies.

In such circumstances, it is not surprising that more than one Education Officer breathed a secret sigh of relief when Ghana gained her independence in 1957, Nigeria in 1960 and Sierra Leone in 1961, which resulted in the closing of the Army schools there.

Meanwhile other schools which had closed by the end of the first decade, but for different reasons, were the 'all age' school in Trieste (1953) and in Rangoon (1954), in 1954 the two schools at Ankara and Istanbul in Turkey, and in 1955 the schools in Austria – an 'all-age' school at Klagenfurt and primary schools at Graz, Spittal, Vienna and Villach.

We have seen that the problems of secondary education were exercising the minds of Command Education Officers everywhere: they were to exercise the minds of the members of the House of Commons as well.

REFERENCES

1. Sheppard, *History of the British Army*, Constable.
2. Col. A. C. T. White, VC, *The Story of Army Education*, Harrap, p. 211.
3. *Schoolmaster*, 4 December 1953.
4. Sek Kong, nestling under a mountain range in the New Territories, was in 1956 a village peopled and run entirely by British Army personnel, except for its shop-keepers and domestic staff. Housed in modern bungalows its 200 families enjoyed their own school, cinema, church, NAAFI, club and social centre with safe playgrounds for the children.

CHAPTER 12

Some Educational Problems

Secondary Education. In the House of Commons' debates during the early fifties, when children's education in the Army was discussed, interest and concern usually centred on the difficulties of providing satisfactory secondary education. It was realised that this problem was linked to good recruiting and to the general happiness and welfare of the soldier's family. For instance, in the House of Commons Defence review 1953, Brigadier O. L. Prior-Palmer (Worthing) said:

> 'I would emphasize strongly that most married personnel to-day, unlike the days before the war, demand – and intend to see that they get it – a really first-class education for their children, and if they find that they cannot get it in the Army, they will quit at the earliest moment. There is a good deal of inevitable disturbance of families in the Army to-day, and I ask the Secretary of State urgently to consider this matter, in consultation with local authorities at home and authorities abroad, in order to see that the children of the married personnel get the finest education that it is possible to give them and that they have every assistance in getting it.'[1]

Two alternatives were open to the Army. Overseas, they could continue to fulfil their obligations by maintaining their own secondary schools, day or boarding according to circumstances, and continue to solve the problems involved. At home responsibility belonged to the LEAs, but the Army could continue to advise Army parents on the various State and private facilities available, might offer some financial support through day or boarding allowances to provide continuity of education where the parents were likely to serve abroad, and could negotiate with LEAs to improve the facilities available for Army children and to resolve their many mutual problems. Ought the Army to re-establish its own schools in UK – it still had responsibility for the Duke of York's School,

Dover and Queen Victoria School, Dunblane* – or join with one or more LEAs to provide badly needed places, especially boarding, for Service children?

Mr A. Blenkinsop (Newcastle-on-Tyne), who had just paid a visit to the BAOR secondary boarding schools, co-educational, comprehensive, undenominational and inter-Service, said in 1954:

> 'Those of my hon. friends who are particularly interested in the provision of comprehensive schools might well go out to Germany and see something of what is being done under Army auspices. It is a very interesting experiment and considerable development is taking place.'[2]

All the Army's secondary schools overseas were organised on comprehensive lines. But its biggest problem was the constant movement of its children and the resulting effects on both primary and secondary education. Mr Nigel Nicolson (Bournemouth East) gave his views in 1955:

> 'In Germany', he said, 'where we have the very best conditions, less than 7 per cent of the children have spent more than two years in the same school: the average length of time spent by a child in a primary school is three terms and in a secondary school five terms. When I was in Germany last week I talked to a Service child of 13 years who had been to 14 schools. As I left him, he called me back to say he had just remembered a fifteenth!'[3]

Mr Nicolson, supporting the view that the difficulties of providing a proper education for their children was the biggest of all deterrents to long-service officers and men, considered there was a need for a greater degree of standardisation of syllabus and method in Service schools and pleaded for financial help for Service families who had to leave their children in the UK. 'The Education Act,' he said, 'places upon Local Authorities the power, but not the obligation, to help the children of parents who are serving overseas.' There were too few boarding places available in the UK, especially for secondary modern and senior primary children. His interim solution was that the Ministry of Education should form itself into a central authority to receive applications from Service and other parents overseas and for allotting them school places in this country. The Ministry of Education should also lay down a standard scale of financial assistance and the conditions under

* In September 1953 the Army also opened Welbeck Abbey as a residential college to prepare a number of 16–18-year-old boys, selected from secondary schools by examination and interview, for regular commissions in the technical Arms and Corps.

which it should be given. This would avoid soldiers in the same regiment obtaining different standards of treatment from different LEAs. In the long term, he thought the Ministry of Education should reserve boarding places or should build wings on to existing grammar and secondary modern schools or build special boarding schools for the children of Service parents, which would also be open to the children of the Foreign Office and colonial officials.

On the credit side, Nicolson thought that the Army child received many compensations – better school accommodation, smaller classes, hand-picked teachers and a broadening of the mind through travel.

'The children have an astonishing maturity and elasticity. They learn things with remarkable facility: to them geography is not a matter of books, but of places they have actually visited. These children know the world, but they do not know its sorry conflicts. To them the Mohne Dam is a place where one can sail on a Saturday afternoon, and Belsen is the name of a Primary school.'[3]

The Under Secretary of State for War (Mr Fitzroy Maclean), replying, said that the accommodation and equipment provided by the Army for secondary education abroad varied with conditions in the different countries. Facilities were naturally better in BAOR than elsewhere, because Britain, as an occupying power, could requisition what was needed and make Germany pay the bill. He contrasted Slim secondary school in the Cameron Highlands of Malaya where,

'instead of being in well-equipped barrack rooms, the classrooms are in straw huts. When the 138 boys and girls return from their holidays, they travel under armed escort in order to obtain protection from bandits, who infest the whole area. In spite of that the children carry on very much as they would if in England. At present £1 million a year is included in the Army estimates for the education of Army children. What is more it is an increasing commitment. (See appendix A.) Since 1950, the number of pupils in Army schools has risen from 14,000 to 20,000; the number of schools from 60 to 160 and teachers from 300 to 1000.'[3x]

This concern of the politicians had already been expressed by the Services themselves, and led to the establishment in May 1953 of an inter-departmental committee on secondary education and Service school children. Its terms of reference were 'to examine and report on present facilities for secondary education provided by the Services at home and overseas, to consider any lack of provision and to suggest practical improvements.' The committee recognised the difficulties which Service parents faced in educating their children, because of frequent moves between stations, both at home and overseas, the unpredictable length of stay at any one station, the often restricted range of secondary education available overseas, and the difficulty and cost to the parents of providing boarding school education at home. LEA boarding school vacancies were few and fees were high. In brief, most Service parents were unable to obtain for their children the full advantages provided under the 1944 Education Act, which the Services agreed might be one of the main reasons for the early retirement of regular officers and for the reluctance of high grade technical tradesmen to sign on for long engagements.

The committee concluded that a central agency might be able to find places for the 'academic' school children, but not for the 'non-academic' children, since such places were practically non-existent in the UK. It appeared, therefore, that there were three possibilities, which might together form a compromise solution to the problem:

1. 'The "all age" Day School which, although unsatisfactory in principle, must of necessity be maintained in a limited number of small stations abroad to cater for parents, who, within their rights, wish their children to live with them and to attend a local day school, where the number of such pupils does not warrant a separate secondary school.

2. 'A Command or District Secondary School with facilities for boarding children from distant stations, either weekly or by the term. This will provide continuity of education only so long as the parents remain within that Command or District.

3. 'Financial assistance to all ranks who wish to leave their children in the UK to obtain continuity of education whilst accepting the separation entailed.'

The Service Directors of Education had drawn up plans generally for the provision of secondary schools, both day and boarding, to cover proposals No. 1 and No. 2. These would satisfy the needs of Service children in a particular area overseas, bearing in mind future redeployments where these were known. (Particular difficulty was experienced in anticipating future redeployments in the Middle East.) They could not recommend to the Committee, however, a particular location for a school, nor the number of boarding or hostel places required in a particular area, since such detailed planning could only be done by the Commands concerned, in the light of local conditions. Command plans, already notified to them, provided for the two secondary boarding schools at Hamm, the Queen's Secondary Day School, Rheindahlen, in addition to those boarding schools already established in Germany; the provision of a new school in Hong Kong (since the local civilian King George V school was unlikely to be able to continue to provide secondary places for Service children much longer); for an extension of the Alexandra Secondary School in Singapore: while, in Malaya, it was thought the Slim School, Cameron Highlands, extended if necessary, would provide for Malaya's secondary population: it was considered that two day secondary schools in Cyprus would be sufficient for that island.

Left unresolved were a number of fringe areas, where the number of children was unlikely to be sufficient to support secondary schools or departments. For example, it was considered that secondary children in France and Belgium should go to one of the boarding schools in Germany, as should those in Austria, whose commitment was likely to decrease. The sixty children in Ceylon might board in Singapore, while those in Tripoli and Cyrenaica and similar extra Command areas might be accommodated in one of the major Command schools. In Malta increased accommodation would be necessary.

Education Allowances. The Committee's main recommendations concerned possibility No. 3 (i.e. financial help). The Committee pointed out that by the Education Act (1944) LEAs in England and Wales were empowered to place suitably qualified children at maintained and direct grant schools within their own areas, and also to place suitably qualified children at certain independent schools with which they had made special arrangements. Similar provision was made by the education authorities of Scotland and Northern Ireland under their own statutory powers. Tuition at maintained and direct grant schools under these circumstances was free, boarding charges being made according to an approved income scale. Each LEA had its own income scale, although guidance had been given in a Ministry of Education directive. In theory, therefore, a Service parent with certain county affiliations in England or Wales could expect to place his children at a suitable school controlled by his county LEA and to receive financial assistance according to that LEA's scale, dependent on his income. A parent without any clear county connection could be accepted by any LEA with suitable accommodation and the cost, including any assistance given to the parent, could be charged against a 'pool', centrally administered by the Ministry of Education. Unfortunately, in practice the system did not operate all that smoothly as far as Service parents were concerned. Every LEA applied its scheme differently and few LEAs, understandably, were more sympathetic towards Service children than to their own. Some LEAs did not use the pool system and were reluctant to assist children without specific county associations. There were not sufficient places available in the country generally, particularly for secondary modern and senior primary children, and in taking the gross emoluments of parents into account LEAs made no allowances for the extra expenses inherent in Service life and not encountered by civilians. Servicemen with children of secondary age were usually senior ranks, both officer and NCO, and so very little or no financial assistance was, in fact, available to the majority of potential Service users.

As a direct result of this committee's work a scheme of Education allowances for the Forces was authorised in 1955.[4] Recognising the fact that members of the Forces were subject to frequent changes of station and consequently might need to adopt special arrangements to ensure continuity of their children's education, the new allowances gave some financial assistance during the stage of secondary education to Service parents to send their children to boarding schools, or to leave them in the care of a guardian, in order to enable them to continue at a particular day school. The allowances were of two kinds, Overseas Education Allowance, and Home Education Allowance, the main difference being that the former was tax free. Boarding school allowances could be granted for each child up to a maximum of £75 a year and the day school allowance was £26 a year.* Boarding allowances were paid termly in advance and the day school allowance monthly in arrears, claims being made through the Army Paymaster.

In order to explain the working of these allowances and to list schools which offered special rates to Service children, the Director of Army Education published an annual pamphlet, available to all Service parents who wished to use these facilities. By 1960, 5000 Army children were benefiting from this provision.

---

* From September 1969 the new annual rates are: £282 for the first child; £336 for the second and £492 for the third and subsequent children. The Day School allowance is 4s. 1d. per day.

There is no simple answer to the Army's problem of providing satisfactory secondary education for all its children. Some Army parents choose to fulfil their statutory obligation to ensure their children receive 'efficient full-time education' by leaving them behind in the continuity of a UK day or boarding school. For these parents boarding or day school allowances are both right and necessary. Some, on the other hand, place a higher priority on family unity, preferring to take their children with them rather than face the emotional and social problems of separation. If these children are to be given equality of opportunity the Army must have the facilities to provide an efficient system of secondary education overseas, wherever this can be organised. From time to time the Army was asked to consider replacing this secondary system overseas, especially in BAOR, by Army (or Service) boarding schools in UK, chiefly in order to save foreign currency. There can be no justification for this on educational and social grounds, or even on grounds of financial economy. Can parents be compelled to leave their children behind? Should all military service overseas be unaccompanied? What will be the effects on recruiting? Are the Service boarding schools to be temporary 'transit' camps or, once admitted, should not the children continue their education there in the interests of continuity despite the increased number of places required? The first poses educational, administrative and social problems; the cost of the second would hardly be acceptable to the taxpayer. Since individual circumstances and conditions overseas vary so much, and since the Army has accumulated over many years so much experience in meeting the educational and social requirements of its families, surely the fairest and most practical solution is to offer Army parents a choice within the various possibilities of State and military overseas provision?

Troopship Education. School attendance by Service children everywhere abroad had always been excellent, in spite of the Army's lack of legal powers to enforce attendance (an LEA can use, if necessary, magisterial powers to make an Attendance Order under Section 39 of the 1944 Act), but school time was often lost between one school and the next on family moves. Of particular concern, before the advent of air trooping, were the lengthy voyages by troopships. Ships' Commandants were made responsible for arranging educational programmes and leisure activities for adults and children. There were study groups for languages and Army examinations, lectures and discussions, quizzes, etc., for adults, and films and libraries for adults and children. The average fifty or sixty schoolchildren on board were divided into three groups by age and received daily instruction during the mornings in dining halls or lounges, or in whatever space was not already occupied by troops doing PT or weapon training. Teachers were found from the RAEC, from seconded teachers, QAS or from wives (payment was authorised), and 'geography' or 'the ship' formed natural focal points of interest. Troopships such as the *Dunera*, *Dilwara* and the *Empire Hallidale* (to name but three) played their part in the story of the Army's education of its children.

Troopship education of adults and children dated back, in fact, for over 100 years and modern troopships were but a continuation of the *Holmesdale*, *Victor Emmanual* and *Bucephalus* of the 1850s. The fourth report by the Council of Military Education, for the year ending 31 March 1866, contained the following:

> 'I have the honour to enclose, for the information of His Royal Highness the Commander-in-Chief, school diary of the detachment 49th Regiment, proceeding to Bombay in the screw ship Melbourne, and beg to state that the school was carried on with great success, and if I had more space on board ship, I should have had a larger attendance each day. In the morning I had school for the children, and after the men's dinners I had the NCOs and all the men on board ship by turns (except the cooks). Each place the ship touched, an account of the countries which she passed, beside the latitude and longitude, was explained and shown on the map to those attending school. A library of books "judiciously selected, being instructive and interesting, suitable for soldiers of all ranks, and for children of various ages" was available and once a week "performances in the 'Christy Minstrel' style on the banjo, tambourine, bones, fife and drum, varied with negro songs and dances, riddles, melodies and conundrums helped to dispel the gloom and monotony of evenings on board ship during long and tedious voyages".'[6]

Conditions were not always so favourable however – the OC Troops on board the *Cospatrick* writing from Belgaum 24 November 1865, in compliance with the regulations for troops 'proceeding to Saint Helena, the Cape of Good Hope and to stations to the eastward thereof' could not carry out trade training and gymnastics 'because the decks were crowded with women and children' and 'the heat between-decks, for a large proportion of the voyage, was so intense that I could never allow the school to be kept open longer than an hour at a time, and on many occasions it had to be closed in less time.'[6]

184

Schoolchildren of Non-UK Troops. The Army had always been interested in the education of the children of non-UK troops because it had often recruited in overseas territories 'Boys', who later graduated as adult soldiers, NCOs and officers of the native forces. Education was crucial to successful advancement – where better to start than in the schools? Often without official recognition, either by the Service or civil authorities, schools appeared and prospered. In West Africa, for example, between 1953 and 1954, there were twenty-two unit schools with approximately 1300 pupils. In Far East the education of the children of Imperial Malays and Hong Kong other ranks was accepted as the responsibility of the local Governments but the shortage of places was so acute that 1 Singapore Regiment RA opened a school at Blakang Mati for its own regimental children, the Singapore Ministry of Education providing two Malay teachers, textbooks and materials and used one of the British Army Children's Schools in Singapore in the afternoons, until their own three-storey school for 600 children (or 1200 in two shifts) was completed in 1958. Help from territorial governments was limited, but CEOs set about obtaining recognition for their school arrangements in the full knowledge that to obtain such recognition and any financial assistance would often require long and tortuous negotiations.

In East Africa Command the King's African Rifles had provided education for the children of their Askaris. Although such education was not officially recognised, the practice of employing East African Army Education Corps instructors to teach children during those periods when they were not engaged with troops had grown steadily, with the result that in 1954 there were few units with attached families which did not make provision. Being unofficial, the schools depended for their existence largely upon the charity of the unit, which was understandably inadequate when it became a question of purchasing textbooks, equipment and materials. Requests to the territorial governments for financial assistance met with little success and other offers made by governments were so beset with conditions that the practical results were negligible. The task of instructors, therefore, was one of improvisation, and this they did remarkably well. Subjects taught invariably included English, Ki-Swahili, Kaffir, counting and singing. The scheme proved of considerable benefit to recruiting, morale and to the children themselves, the majority of whom were potential recruits.

The best example of education for the children of the Army's non-UK troops was that arranged for the Gurkha school children in the Far East which by July 1954 numbered 636 between 5 and 15 years of age. All but thirty-eight (twenty-one were in British Army Schools and seventeen in civilian schools) of these were being educated in 11 unit schools, with two in India, under the control of HQ Brigade of Gurkhas and the RAEC. Each school was authorised to provide education of an elementary type on the same lines as that provided in Nepal. The thirty-four teachers employed had been mostly recruited in the Darjeeling district of India and sent at regimental expense by the Gurkha recruiting organisation in India. The first classrooms were in tents; later, permanent accommodation was built and since suitable textbooks were difficult to obtain from Calcutta or from UK the Education Staff at GHQ, FARELF, settled down and wrote their own.

But it soon became clear that certain children needed a much higher standard of education than could be supplied in a Gurkha school and in 1954 authority was given for up to twenty children to be educated in British Army children's schools with a view to their eventual entry to the Royal Military Academy, Sandhurst. Admitted to a British secondary school in FARELF at 11 or 12 years of age, these Gurkha children would have to become 'enlisted boys' in order to continue at the school, until they were of an age to take the RMA entrance examination. It was found in practice that no Gurkha boy could reach the entry standard for a British secondary school without his first attending an Army primary school. Furthermore, as successive CEOs sought to provide better facilities for Gurkha children, more in keeping with rising educational standards in Nepal, and to realise the potential of each individual child, the numbers of Gurkha children attending the British Army children's schools continued to rise. This was to create problems in the future for both Gurkha and British children.

Handicapped Children. The education of handicapped children presented particular difficulties to the Army, but resolving them was worth all the time and money spent. Whatever success was achieved – and it was considerable – in helping these children was due to the extraordinary generosity and understanding extended to them by the local authorities and voluntary societies, and to the co-operation of Army Record Offices and of the regimental, medical and education officers who were in contact with parents at

186

home and overseas. Special mention must be made of two societies in particular – the Army Guild of St Helena, which was the chief annual contributor to the Director of Army Education's fund for handicapped children (which assisted parents with holiday and escort expenses, initial kit for boarding school, etc.); and the British Red Cross Society for their unfailing assistance with escorts between school and airports.

Section 34 of the 1944 Education Act required local education authorities to ascertain which children in their area needed special education treatment, and to make appropriate provision for them. Each local authority interpreted its obligation differently and the provision each made varied considerably, but over the country generally a pattern of special day and boarding schools was provided, some by LEAs, some by voluntary bodies, and individual tuition was arranged in hospital or at home.[7]

The Army's aim was to make it possible for parents to undertake their military commitments without seriously interrupting the special educational or training arrangements made for their handicapped children. These two conditions were contradictory since, as serving soldiers, the fathers had to expect family moves at frequent intervals, whilst the children needed a stable background. This stability of environment was important in the welfare of the whole family, since many parents were acutely aware of the often callous curiosity, even hostility, of neighbours to their handicapped children. For many civilian families the ordeal of moving into a new neighbourhood and gaining acceptance anew would have to be faced on only one or two occasions, but the Service family had to face this prospect frequently. Thus, whatever arrangements the Army made for its handicapped children had to be a compromise, which sometimes approached, but often fell short of, the ideal.

What facilities were available to handicapped Army children? The best arrangement was for such a child to attend a normal school, whether civilian or military, since it was in the child's best interests to give him no greater protection than his disability demanded. In this way, he would be better able to lead a normal adult life. Children who could not cope with life in a normal school needed special provision. There was no such special provision available in Army schools, but the generally smaller classes, compared with UK, often meant that a child, who was mildly educationally subnormal (ESN) or physically handicapped, could be successfully integrated into Army schools overseas. Parents, who contemplated taking their handicapped children abroad, were advised about local conditions immediately their posting was known. The Army had no wish to break up a family, nor had it the power to coerce parents to accept a given solution, however beneficial to parent or child. It tried first to win the family's confidence by presenting the facts and then to help parents decide what should be done to face their particular and individual problem.

The size of the Army's task was about that of the UK, namely, about 1·2 per cent of its school population was registered as being in need of special educational treatment.[8] This disregarded the fact that some 10–15 per cent[9] of children in both Army and LEA schools needed special remedial treatment for educational subnormality. To give advice to parents, and to help to obtain or to continue LEA facilities for their handicapped children, a special children's department was established in 1960 at the Institute of Army Education, Eltham Palace. When a Service parent was posted overseas, the problems of the handicapped child were handled at Eltham. Frequently, the best solution was to arrange for the child to be admitted to a residential school, but such places were too few in UK and not every LEA had access to them. Admittance almost invariably depended on whether satisfactory arrangements could be made for the child's school holidays, and guardians had to be found. Handicapped children were allowed two flights a year at public expense to join their parents overseas and for these escorts had usually to be found.

Overseas, in Germany and the Far East, the Army established a Child Guidance Service, composed of teams of an Educational Psychologist, a Social Worker and a Speech Therapist, which had access to medical specialists and were based on or located near a military hospital. There were three such teams in Germany and one in Singapore, each functioning on similar lines to an LEA Child Guidance Clinic. Handicapped children were identified and registered in the same way as in an LEA. The handicap of a pre-school child would be noticed first by the parents, the Army doctor or by the Sailors, Soldiers and Air Force Association (SSAFA) sister and the diagnosis would be confirmed by the Paediatrician or Child Psychiatrist in the nearest military hospital. If the child was of school age, the teacher would usually refer the case to the Doctor or Educational Psychologist. If ascertainment and registration were necessary abroad, similar medical and educational procedures were followed to those at home; the handicapped child's case file, showing the recommendations for special treatment, finally reached the Institute of Army Education, which was responsible for seeking LEA or voluntary help. In 1962 there were 225 such registered files of handicapped children: in 1966 there were 620, and in 1969 the number had risen to 1000, better diagnostic techniques largely explaining the increase.

What more could be done for the Army's handicapped children? The LEAs certainly need more resources, if they are to provide equal opportunities under the 1944 Education Act for all children, which means more and better facilities for social, physical and intellectual handicaps. In the Army, Record Offices continue to give the Institute of Army Education three to six months' prior warning of all postings (within or outside UK), of parents of handicapped children, although much shorter notice is not uncommon. Residential provision for the subnormal (MSM), who number 20 per cent of the Army's register of handicapped children (again in keeping with the national average), entails a long waiting period of 2–5 years for a static civilian child: a migratory Army child has, therefore, little chance of reaching the top of an LEA list and by definition cannot be educated in an Army school abroad. When a handicapped child accompanies its parents overseas, it is nearly always because that is the best course of even less attractive alternatives for the child and family as a whole, and the decision is always made as the result of intensive enquiries and consultations. The decision may present a Headmaster overseas with a problem in his school, which neither the staff nor the school is properly equipped to solve. It might be possible to provide more special remedial day classes for ESN children in the Army's schools overseas, where sufficient numbers of children could be concentrated, but that would mean more specially trained staff and resources. Two holiday flights each year to join their parents abroad at public expense are granted to all Service children. There are good reasons for a handicapped child to be given the third as a special concession to his incapacity, but such children cannot travel without escorts and this may involve their parents in considerable personal expenditure, despite escort and some financial help from voluntary bodies. Nevertheless, the arrangements made for the Army's handicapped children illustrate once again the need in the Army to provide welfare and educational services to help the soldier to concentrate on his primary combatant role and at the same time to ensure that he has the same opportunities for his children as any other citizen.

Recruitment of Teachers. Another function of the Institute of Army Education was the recruitment and selection of the teachers required to fill appointments in the Army's schools overseas,* and the briefing of successful candidates at a day's conference at Eltham Palace before they left UK. The Army's recruiting problems were similar to those of any LEA – a shortage of infant teachers and of some secondary specialisations, such as mathematics and science and remedial work generally. It was difficult to attract senior female staff, in their thirties and forties, for senior mistress and senior heads of departments in secondary schools. Perhaps the natural spirit of adventure burned more fiercely in the breasts of younger teachers, or perhaps they had fewer ties to hold them back. To this problem of recruitment had to be added the fact that the Army equated to a medium-sized county authority, in terms of number of children and teachers, but with a county area, which extended across the world.

Eltham Palace proved an ideal setting to introduce teachers to their future careers and to their Army employers. Their first sight of the Palace would be when they arrived to attend an interview board, in answer to an advertisement asking for 'progressive and enthusiastic, qualified men and single women teachers, with recent teaching experience in UK schools.' Their second would be when, as successful candidates, they came on a Friday or Saturday at the end of the term prior to flying out to join 2000 colleagues in Army children's schools overseas. At the briefing they would meet teachers going to the same Command, or even to the same school, since the Army recruited some 500 teachers annually. What was this Army educational service they were joining? Were Army schools very different from those they knew? Was it possible to take a car abroad with them and where would they be living? What was a Foreign Service allowance? Did they have to continue to pay superannuation and how could they get home if a parent were to become dangerously ill?

The day's briefing conference at Eltham was designed to answer these and many other personal and professional questions. A film showed them the schools, the children and the new environment.

---

* Since 1 April 1969 it has recruited and selected teachers for all three Service schools, as part of the Service Children's Education Authority.

Education Officers, with recent experience in the Command, talked to them about their particular school and about life in a military community. They were reassured by familiar things – the same school organisation, curriculum and examinations, the same experimentation with mixed ability groups, Nuffield science projects, and outward-looking sixth forms. They found they would be inspected by the same HMIs, with the Army's own inspectors thrown in for good measure, both of whom would help with in-Service training courses to explain the new teaching situations and to keep them in touch with developments at home.

They were invariably delighted by the conditions of work and staffing ratios (see Appendix B); perhaps even more so by the unrivalled opportunities for recreation and travel, since they had probably joined the Service 'to see the world', as much as to broaden their experience. If their ardour was slightly dampened by the unexpected realisation that, if not the modern equivalent of a James Bond or a Mata Hari, they were soon to be subject to security regulations, their spirits were quickly raised again by the free lunch and a bar – at UK prices! By the end of the day they were certainly well-informed and even more eager to start their new careers. They would each become, in turn, one of the Army's best recruiters for its schools overseas – a satisfied customer!

REFERENCES

1. *Hansard*, 29 July 1953. (The Grigg Committee (Report of the Advisory Committee on Recruiting, Cmnd 545, 1958), set up to enquire into factors affecting recruitment, confirmed the importance of first-rate provision for children's education.)
2. *Hansard*, 11 March 1954.
3. *Hansard*, 8 March 1955.
x. The convoy of 'coffins' (armoured vehicles with small shuttered windows, just large enough to take a child's neck) slowly winds up the 5000 foot mountain on its 40 mile journey. 'Please, Sir, can I go in Joe Smith's coffin?'—was the end of term cry!
4. Army Council Instruction 578/55.
5. National Board for Prices and Incomes, Report No. 116 (Cmnd 4079), HMSO, pp. 67–70.
6. 4th Report by the Council of Military Education for year ending 31 March 1866, letter dated Bombay, 22 December 1865.
7. S. S. Segal, *No Child is Ineducable*, Pergamon Guides.
8. Major W. G. Russell, RAEC, 'Handicapped Children in the Army'. *Torch*, May 1966.
9. Col. T. C. R. Archer, 'Problems of Handicapped Children in Military Communities Overseas'. *Proceedings of Royal Society of Medicine*, Vol. 62, July 1969.

APPENDIX A

Cost of Army Children's Schools

It is difficult to isolate the cost of the education of children from the Army Votes generally. The following table, the Pay of Civilians at Army Children's Schools, shows the rapid increase in the cost of one part of the service.

	£		£
1947/48	113,000	1956/57	1,683,000
1949/50	124,630	1957/58	1,865,000
1950/51	170,210	1958/59	1,900,000
1951/52	235,000	1959/60	2,295,000
1952/53	218,450	1960/61	2,432,250
1953/54	664,800	1961/62	2,653,500
1954/55	822,000	1962/63	3,205,000
1955/56	987,000		

The last separate estimate for Pay of Civilians at Army Children's Schools Overseas, 1968/69 was £5,537,180. With the merging of the three Services' schools under SCEA the civilian estimate for 1969/70 was £7,546,000 and for 1970/71 was £7,696,000.

APPENDIX B

BASIC STAFFING SCALES

The number of teachers authorised for the different types of schools is shown in the following table: modifications to this scale can be negotiated.

Serial (a)	Type of School (b)	Number of Pupils (Entitled and non-entitled) (c)	Number of Teachers authorised (including Head-teachers) (d)	Remarks (e)
1	Primary	Up to 15	1	In primary schools (or primary departments of all-age schools) of 200 or more pupils an additional locally entered teacher may be employed for the establishment of a progress class.
		16–45	2	
		46–75	3	
		76–100	4	
		101–120	5	
		For each additional 30 or part	1	
2	Secondary schools and departments	40–55	3	In all types of secondary schools and departments children over 15 years of age will count as two pupils for the purpose of assessing staffing ratios.
		56–75	4	
		76–85	5	
		86–100	6	
		101–115	7	
		116–135	8	
		136–150	9	
		Thereafter one teacher for each additional 20 or part thereof until 250	14	Locally entered part-time teachers may be employed in lieu of full-time teachers in secondary schools and departments at the discretion of the Competent Authority up to the equivalent of 25 teaching hours a week for each full-time teacher replaced.
		Thereafter one teacher for each additional 17 or part thereof until 624	36	Additionally, in secondary schools or departments of 700 pupils or less locally-entered part-time teachers of specialised subjects outside the range of teachers in post may be appointed to the equivalent of one full-time teacher (25 teaching hours a week).
		Thereafter one teacher for each additional 23 or part thereof until 1130	58	
		Thereafter one teacher for each additional 20 or part thereof		
3	Secondary boarding schools			Separate establishments will be negotiated for each boarding school.

16—T.A.C.

CHAPTER 13

The Years of Consolidation

Consolidation. If the first decade after the War was a period of improvisation and transition, laying the foundation for a new era in Army children's education, the years which followed proved ones of consolidation and solid achievement in all theatres. Numbers continued to grow, reaching 37,200 in 1966, representing a 50 per cent increase in ten years, as the detailed comparative charts on pages 214–215 show.

But let no one think that these were stable times. Political unrest was followed by troop movements, evacuation or reinforcement in one area after another. Schools had to carry on while military campaigns were under way. Schools continued behind barbed wire in guarded areas; school buses and train parties had to be escorted by armed troops, with armoured and air support. MELF suffered more of these upsets than either FARELF or BAOR, but there were periods of instability in all theatres. There was to be, in fact, between 1939 and 1967 only one period of four months (October 1961–January 1962) when British troops were not engaged in operations in some part of the world. The effect on teachers and children can be imagined. What needs to be recorded is the way teachers not only carried out their normal duties, but undertook tasks hardly expected of their profession. Breakdowns in school work and supplies were rare: morale was excellent and for this a tribute should be paid to the teaching staff and school administrators and to the Armed Services themselves.

By now the educational and financial authorisations of the early inter-departmental committees had been codified for the Army in the *Manual of Education*, Part XIII, 1956[1] and issued for the use of Commands overseas. The education to be provided in Army children's schools was defined as

'intended as far as possible to make up for the loss caused by absence from an educational system in the homeland. It will therefore, as far as possible, conform in type and scope to that being provided in England and Wales under the Education Act 1944. Provision will not necessarily be identical in all overseas stations and will always have regard to what is applicable in relation to local conditions and circumstances.'

Schools could be established, 'if no suitable and economical provision exists in civilian schools in the area', and the competent authority could authorise the opening of a primary or all-age school in any garrison for ten or more entitled children between the ages of 5–15. Where there were forty children or more of 11 years and over, authorisation was given for the opening of a separate secondary school or department. The principle was also laid down 'that one Service only will be responsible for each particular school'.

The responsibility for the efficiency and administration of Army children's schools was vested, as between the Wars, in the Commander-in-Chief, and the Command Education Officer was responsible to him for the 'standard of education provided in all Army children's schools within the Command'. These regulations gave guidance on the school curricula, on religious instruction, discipline and inspections, staffing scales and teachers' conditions of service; on the charges for the admission of non-entitled children, the arrangements for secondary selection, for medical inspections and school meals; they authorised the supply of audio-visual aids, educational stores, books and transport. In short, these regulations formed the basis of the Army's administration of its children's schools overseas for the next decade.

Since each Command's problems were different, the measure of achievement can best be seen by studying each Command separately.[2]

Far East. The easing of the situation against the terrorists in Malaya led during 1958–59 to the withdrawal of some 5500 troops, mainly British, in the Command as a whole, and the replacement of about 1000 British troops in Singapore by Gurkhas. This, together with the granting of independence to Malaya in August 1967, caused considerable movement of children, and educational plans once made had to be re-adjusted as troops were redeployed to meet the confrontation with Indonesia during 1962–66. Hong Kong was little affected by these political moves. The upward trend of the Command's school population continued, with increases mainly in the junior and secondary fields, especially in Singapore; but by 1962 there were signs of some levelling off in numbers for the first time since the War. The withdrawal of the Rhodesian-African Rifles and the establishment of a Royal Australian Air Force school on Penang Island (instead of their children attending the British Army school there) reduced the international character of some of the schools.

The early years of children's turbulence led to some attempts to standardise junior syllabuses and text books in reading and arithmetic. As more specialist equipment became available for the secondary schools, the technical, commercial and domestic science studies were strengthened, and 1958 saw the initial steps in FARELF secondary schools to implement the Duke of Edinburgh's Award Schemes. The supply and quality of the recently appointed school clerical staffs were proving satisfactory, but the recruitment of locally based European women for matron and assistant matron posts in the boarding hostels was proving wholly unsatisfactory. The Command was optimistic about the prospects of the planned new schools being available early in the 1960s, and the re-equipment of schools with metal and plastic furniture was proving very popular. The long delays in the ordering and supply of books, for years a source of frustration and impatience, had been largely eliminated by the increased use of air freight. With one or two notable exceptions, the school libraries were excellent. A new stationery scale, giving improvements in the quality of exercise books and a bigger range of stationery items, had been introduced.

In 1960, with the exception of St George's School, Hong Kong, housed since 1955 in fine new buildings, all the secondary schools were in improvised premises, either converted barracks, wooden buildings or Nissen huts. Consequently, standards of accommodation were generally unsatisfactory, especially in respect of laboratories and special-purpose rooms. Although improvements were constantly being made, the basic lack of purpose-built schools and the overcrowding made proper secondary education difficult. In Malaya, it was planned to concentrate all grammar school children in Singapore. Slim School, Cameron Highlands, would close and Bourne School, Kuala Lumpur, would become Malaya's central secondary modern school. The key to this plan was the availability of sufficient boarding places in Kinloss House, Singapore. In 1960, it could only accommodate 85 children and, until the additional boarding accommodation could be built, the plan would have to be delayed.

By 1962 these hopes had not materialised; Alexandra Grammar School still occupied its steeply sloping site, on which its premises were spread out at four different levels. The classrooms were still in makeshift premises and the children's movement from one block to another was often a long, hot and noisy climb. Numbers of children continued to fluctuate considerably, and in 1962 had reached 570 in the School (267 Army; 189 entitled civilians; 56 RAF; 37 RN; and 21 non-entitled civilians), with 43 children in the sixth form.

Turbulence was more marked in the Alexandra Secondary Modern School, whose numbers had risen from 287 in 1954 to 626 in 1962 and were still rising. It was noticeable that some of the older children arriving in the Far East had finished with schooldays in the United Kingdom, but once abroad they returned to school, since there were no prospects of local employment for them because of the labour regulations. Of the 626 pupils, 10 per cent had been at the school for over two years; 29 per cent for over one year and 61 per cent for less than one year. In three years there had been 57 new staff and 30 departures. Transfers to the grammar school sometimes took place at 13 years of age, which added to the disturbance. The lack of a hall and gymnasium was reflected in the open air assembly and outdoor PE, but twenty fair sized 'basha' huts made useful, temporary classrooms, well suited to the climate. The school met six days a week from 8.30 to 12.30 with extra curricula activities every afternoon, except Wednesdays, which had to remain voluntary because of transport difficulties.

At this time Bourne School, Kuala Lumpur, was still organised as a bi-lateral school of 394 pupils, of whom 232 were boarders. The converted hostel for girls and younger boys was excellent but the older boys' accommodation suffered by comparison. The school lacked a good library and laboratory accommodation but provided a wide range of options with a good teacher/pupil ratio. The afternoons were devoted to an equally wide range of club and outdoor activities. Its history was given in its magazine as follows:

'During the Malayan troubles in May 1954, General Bourne, the military commander of the British Forces, officially opened in Kuala Lumpur a group of temporary huts – our school.

'In September 1957, the first boarding houses were opened for the children of Service families stationed in other parts of Malaya. In that year also, Headquarters, Malaya Command, was moved to

197

Seremban and, as the families gradually followed, the need for boarding accommodation increased. Girls and junior boys were boarded in Arakan House near the School, and Istana Hostel, a former palace of the Sultan of Selangor, was taken over for the senior boys.

'With the ending of the emergency British military personnel in Malaya decreased and the School accepted fee-paying children of the many nationalities in Kuala Lumpur. Altogether, children of 22 different countries have attended Bourne School and about 5000 children, between the ages of 11 and 18, during its ten years of life.'

Singapore's *long term* plans, following the colony's independence, were intended to extend the primary schools in Nee Soon, Selerang and Pasir Panjang and to build new schools at Palau Brani and Nepal Circus. The existing secondary schools would be replaced by a bi-lateral mixed day school of 1000 pupils in Pasir Panjang. The Singapore Ministry of Education was persuaded to accept responsibility for the education of the children of Malay troops stationed in Singapore, but lacked accommodation for them. Classrooms were therefore loaned to them in the afternoons at Alexandra Junior School. In Malaya, the deployment of regiments and units in the early 1960s led to the closure of nine primary schools. Three continued with an increased capacity at Penang, Kluang and Johore Bahru. Three new primary schools were built at Fort George, Malacca, where was also opened in 1965 the new Slim School, Terendak Camp, a bi-lateral secondary school for 700 children, some boarding. Here, too, were concentrated all the Australian and New Zealand children in Malaya, both primary and secondary. Thus, at last, the Bourne (Kuala Lumpur) and Slim (Cameron Highlands)* schools were closed and, for the scattered children in the rest of Malaya, secondary education was concentrated in Singapore, with the opening of St John's secondary day (850) and boarding (150) school and the enlarged Bourne Junior High School for 1700 children, aged 11–14.

Long term plans in Hong Kong envisaged the enlargement of the Fort Stanley school and the building of a new infants' school at Victoria on Hong Kong Island. In Kowloon the primary school at the Gun Club site would have to be extended and Whitfield North primary school retained, until the long term numbers were stabilised. A new primary school would be needed in Sek Kong and a third school might be necessary, if and when all the families had been concentrated in the New Territories. St George's would

* Message from Field Marshal Viscount Slim on page 217.

remain the secondary school for all three Services in the colony, offering Comprehensive facilities.

An interesting link between the present Stanley and Victoria schools and the Hong Kong garrison schools of the past is provided by the following little historical cameo, written in 1924.

'About twelve miles from Victoria is the Chinese village of Stanley, near to which is the site of the first barracks, built for the British garrison after we obtained possession of this island. Only the foundations of the buildings remain, but the old barrack square can still be seen, and the well which supplied the garrison with water. A little cemetery lies just beyond the barracks, and here are the graves of those soldiers, women and children, who died in this "outpost of Empire", in the days when Hong Kong was a bare, rocky, fever-ridden island, and when nobody could imagine that in time it would become one of the busiest ports in the world. In this cemetery, situated amidst beautiful surroundings, is a pathetic link between the members of the Educational Corps in Hong Kong today, and their predecessors of eighty years ago, for one of the tombstones was erected in 1845 to the memory of the wife of Schoolmaster Sergeant John Home, of the 98th Regiment.'[3]

Such grim reminders of the hardships endured by the troops and their families, and by schoolmasters and mistresses, can still be seen in many garrisons overseas. They can still be seen recorded on the tombstones of the ruined church, overlooking the once malarial swamps and port of Malacca. They are recorded too, in the annals of the 15th Regiment (East Yorkshires), whose '102 wives and their children accompanied the Regiment to the West Indies to quell a negro insurrection. When the Regiment returned a few years later only 7 wives came back. Yellow Jack had killed the rest.'[4]

Gurkha children. The decade saw the introduction of many educational improvements for Gurkha children. For example, the conditions and standards of entry to British Army children's schools for bright Gurkha children were defined and standardised, and more boys were accepted into the schools, if they had the potential qualifications for admission to the Royal Military Academy, Sandhurst; girls were admitted as candidates for a nursing career with the Queen Alexandra's Royal Army Nursing Corps. But the bulk of the Gurkha children either returned to the Nepalese educational system or entered the Brigade of Gurkhas as 'Enlisted Boys' or adult soldiers. This meant, on the one hand, relating Nepal's primary school syllabuses to the Gurkha schools and, at the same

199

time, raising general educational standards so that the Brigade could recruit better apprentices and potential NCOs. These three differing aims considerably increased the provision of education 'of an elementary type', as originally authorised by the Treasury.

Standards of accommodation varied from permanent brick buildings to atap 'bashas', wooden huts and canvas tents. Only three schools occupied purpose-built accommodation. Numbers continued to rise as more married quarters were built, and the delay in deciding the long-term location of units meant improvisation and temporary expedients, since permanent buildings could not be authorised. In 1960 there were 14 schools, 1032 children and 50 staff located as follows:

	Schools	Children	Staff
Hong Kong	3	170	8
Malaya	7	584	29
Singapore	1	100	4
India	3	178	9

One of the major problems was the lack of continuity of education, which affected standards of attainment. Gurkha other ranks were only permitted to bring their families to Malaya every second tour of three years, but Gurkha officers could have their families permanently. The results were that classes for the former were determined by ability and not by age, and that the latter outgrew the secondary facilities available in Gurkha schools; 45 per cent of the children were, therefore, in the lowest Class and 20 per cent in Classes II and III of the infant schools. The remaining 35 per cent were spread over the three grades of the junior schools. Thirty-four of the fifty teachers were qualified. They were keen and interested in their children but their teaching methods were formal, academic and lacked imagination. The unqualified were normally put in charge of the lowest class, where numbers were usually the largest and the demands more exacting. Brought in to watch British infant teachers at work, they would watch, spellbound for the first twenty minutes, and then shyly whisper, 'When does the lesson begin?' The teaching of English, most important for the future careers of most of these children, suffered from a grammatical approach and the poor English language standards, especially oral, of most of the staff.

In 1967, the CEO, worried by the large numbers of secondary aged children still in the unit primary schools, tried to centralise secondary education in Singapore in a wing of the British Bourne Secondary School. Three teachers were borrowed from the Gurkha primary schools to teach the 60 children concerned. But the numbers of Gurkha children attending the British schools grew rapidly and in July 1968 there were 94 boys and 22 girls in the secondary schools (of whom 64 were boarders from Malaya), and 24 boys and 15 girls in the British Army's primary schools. The results were not always successful. At times there would be a conflict between western and Gurkha traditions and cultures; sometimes the language difficulties of the Gurkha children tended to hinder the British children's progress, in spite of the requirement for all Gurkha children to have a good standard of English before admission.

In 1969 the CEO revised the scheme, especially as the result of his survey of recent progress in the Nepalese educational system, where academic secondary high schools were being rapidly converted to multi-purpose vocational high schools. He obtained financial authority to establish in 1970 such a high school for 150 boys and girls in the New Territories in Hong Kong, where the Gurkha Brigade was to be eventually concentrated. Here, in addition to academic subjects, the boys would learn agriculture, building crafts and woodwork and the girls the home sciences of cookery, mothercraft, hygiene and home care. The better pupils would take their Nepalese School Leaving Certificate at the age of 15 or 16, after a four-year course.

Thus in future years, the great progress made in primary education for the Gurkha children will be matched by a stimulating new experiment in secondary education.

The Middle East. Children's education in the Middle East (1956–60) was greatly influenced by the continuous political unrest in all districts, and by such events as the Suez crisis (October/November 1956), the evacuation of families from Jordan and North Africa (1957–58) and the troubles in Cyprus (1955–59; 1963–64; 1968–69). This unrest, together with the continuing upward trend in school populations everywhere, and the uncertainty about the future structure of the Command, created conditions of change and instability, which were entirely inimical to the best interests of children's education.

'Solutions to many problems have to be found, often at short notice and by improvisation; considerable strain has been thrown upon

201

Head teachers and their staffs, as well as on the educational and administrative staff officers concerned, to which the response has been loyal and energetic',

wrote the Chief Education Officer.

The moves in the Command were almost bewildering – into the Canal Zone; out of the Canal Zone to Cyprus; the Cyprus build up; the Suez crisis and the evacuation of families from Libya; the Cyprus run-down. As a result schools opened and closed; there were acute shortages of staff and equipment; temporary expediencies had to replace long term planning, especially concerning the urgent need in the Command for a permanent boarding school. During 1955–56, the 10 schools in the Suez Canal zone (i.e. the Fayid and Moascar secondary, junior and infant schools, the Tel el Kebir 'all-age' school, and those of Suez, Port Fouad and El Ballah) were closed. The education staffs, moved from Egypt, had now once again to be redeployed, and more teachers recruited, as families, vacating the very limited accommodation in Egypt, found almost unlimited private accommodation in other areas and brought increasing numbers of children from the UK to be educated by the Army. In Cyprus, Kyrenia and Nicosia primary schools closed and two secondary schools opened – the King Richard School, Dhekelia (4 January 1960), and St John's School, Episkopi (11 January 1960), both comprehensive schools intended for the children of all Services in their respective catchment areas. Unfortunately, the initial accommodation provided at both schools was insufficient to meet all the secondary requirements of the island and some secondary departments were retained in primary schools. The boarding accommodation at Dhekelia had to be taken for military purposes and the plan to provide hostel accommodation for the sixteen secondary aged children at Homs and the thirty-three at Benghazi, together with the secondary-aged children at El Adem, had to be delayed.

Considerable military reorganisation followed the granting of Independence to Cyprus in 1960. The Army Command Headquarters remained in Cyprus but a new command, Near East Land Forces, covering Malta, Cyprus and N. Africa was created. Army and RAF troops were to be concentrated largely in the Sovereign Base areas of Dhekelia and Episkopi and there were consequent changes in the locations and numbers of children. The schools at Barce and Derna in Cyrenaica and Sabratha in Tripolitania had already closed in 1958. At Easter 1959 Tripoli All-Age School had to move out of the barracks in the centre of the town under an agreement with the Kingdom of Libya – a fortunate move since the school was safe from the riots which from time to time affected the city in subsequent years. The school grew steadily to more than 600 children and over 30 teachers before its final closure in December 1965, when the British garrison left Tripoli.

Benghazi School closed, opened and closed again, in the space of three years. Its final closure in 1967 was described by its Headmaster[5] in the following words:

'At 11am one morning in June, my telephone rang in the Queen Elizabeth II Coronation School. It was from Military Headquarters to say that the Israelis had bombed Cairo, that the town of Benghazi was in uproar and severe rioting had broken out. On no account were the children to be dismissed at 12.30, which was the hour when school normally ended at that time of the year. There were some 450 children of all ages in the school and hurried arrangements were made to provide for the mid-day meal and again for the evening meal, which the teachers prepared.

'By night-fall it was still impossible to allow the children home and they slept in their class rooms. Towards morning the Army families and those of the local British and American personnel began to arrive in D'Aosta Barracks and within 48 hours there were some 500 men, women and children living and sleeping in the school. Children were collected by their parents as they arrived and every corner of the barracks became a place of refuge.

'Machine guns were set up on the school roof and barbed wire entanglements hurriedly placed across the playground. The newly acquired Science Laboratory, for which the school had waited patiently for many, many months, became a Baby Clinic and Feeding Centre for Nursing Mothers. The school piano was man-handled to the open space in front of the NAAFI, which became the local village "pub". I was appointed Commander of this sector, except for military operations, and charged with the responsibilities of Chief Entertainments Officer and maintenance of the morale of the non-military population.

'It was a fortnight before school could again resume its normal function and then the children were brought to school in specially wired coaches and lorries and under armed escort for the last six months, until the school was closed for the last time.'

Cyprus. A team of HMIs and Army Inspectors visited Cyprus in 1960. They found the schools, in general, very satisfactory, despite the reorganisation difficulties. With few exceptions morale was high among Heads and assistants, who met frequently their other school colleagues and the Command Educational staffs to discuss a wide range of educational topics. Inspectors were very impressed by the appearance, behaviour and friendliness of the children. They appeared to have a completely healthy attitude towards school life, both in relation to work and to extra classroom activities. The Inspectors were broadly pleased with education in the primary schools, somewhat less so in the secondary schools, where the handicaps resulting from limitations of accommodation, equipment and appropriate courses were more apparent, and the frequent changes of staff and children more critical to attainment and progress. On the credit side was the breadth of experience which the children acquired, as a result of the kind of life they led – some compensation for the additional difficulties of learning, to which they were subjected. Their oral command of language was especially good, but there was a danger that this might lead to over-confidence and a superficial acquisition of knowledge.

Secondary education in Cyprus was provided by the RAF for children in the Episkopi-Limassol area at St John's School, while children in the Dhekelia cantonment and the town around attended the Army's King Richard Secondary School. It had 335 pupils (156 boys and 179 girls) in 1960 but building was in progress to raise the number to 500. The school became so overcrowded as numbers steadily increased that two temporary classrooms had to be taken into use some distance away in the old Garrison Church, two in a nearby married families hostel and one in a school bus.

Perhaps life in Cyprus during the period which followed can best be seen through the eyes of the Headmaster of Larnaca Primary School (Andrew Mathieson),[6] 1961–1967.

'I travelled to Cyprus from Tripoli School on Christmas Eve, 1961 and used the remainder of the holiday to take stock of the school, losing several pounds in weight as I did so. I was shattered. The main building – a former coffee house – still held the legend "Coca-Cola" on the wall: its classrooms were microscopic. Around it were 6 Nissen huts, embedded in a sea of mud, each with only one door and fitted with opaque, reinforced windows, which did nothing to dispel the gloom I felt.

'Term started. So overcrowded were some classrooms that I had to climb over desks to speak to the staff. There was no staffroom. The School-secretary worked in a draughty corridor, which did nothing for her bronchial condition. The school labourers obviously regarded their school duties as secondary to their other jobs, but always arrived on Fridays for their pay. The Turkish policeman, provided by the War Department, was killed by his fellow Turks for refusing to bear arms against the Greeks.

'Gradually we made progress. Rooms were enlarged by knocking down dividing walls; concrete paths and playing areas were built;

204

the school was painted and the gardens planted. A water cooler was installed. Clear glass, curtains and later blinds were fitted. Best of all, the house adjoining was rented to provide extra classrooms, a proper Staffroom and badly needed stockrooms. New books and a cine projector arrived.

'My turn-over of children was well over 100% per annum, since Larnaca was a "dormitory town" of families moving to permanent married quarters in Dhekelia. Many children had been to 8 or more schools. 20% of the mothers were not British and two children arrived at the school speaking only German. But, while the numbers on roll varied from 192 to 258, the pupil/teacher ratio was kept around 1 : 20. With the odd exception, the staff was excellent.

'By December 1963 a new school was started only to be brought to a sudden halt by the "emergency". I received an urgent call one night from 4 women teachers to say there were some armed Turks on their bungalow roof. The staff had tried to placate them by shouting "Turks very nice!" They were not amused. They were Greek! Children now had to be escorted to school by armoured vehicles and it should be recorded that, thanks to the troops, the school never closed.

'In one of my last Annual Reports I wrote "Teaching Army children and looking after the personal and social problems of members of staff is the most exhilarating, depressing, stimulating, frustrating experience I have ever had". Would I do it again? Gladly. What a wonderful life!'

In 1967 the military strength in Cyprus began to decline. Whereas by the beginning of the year there had been 1900 children in five schools, a year later there were less than 1300, shared amongst the King Richard Secondary School (450), and two primary schools in Dhekelia (360) and Ayios Nikoloas (440). A wide range of options could only be provided in the secondary school by over-staffing and the sixth form programme had to be curtailed. Primary education was easier to organise and standards were generally satisfactory, in spite of the in-built problems of turbulence and redeployment and a tendency in the schools to concentrate on the basic subjects, using a more formal approach than would be customary in the United Kingdom.

Malta GC. In Malta all three Services provided education at the primary level, each school having children of the other Services, while the Royal Naval school at Tal Handaq catered for the needs of all Service secondary children on the island. The Army had three primary schools – St Andrew's, Imtarfa and Tigne with 438, 84 and 280 children respectively in 1961. One pleasing feature of these schools was the full use made of the history and environment of Malta, at levels appropriate to the ages of the pupils. Local study enlivened the teaching of English, History and Geography and in nature study there were projects, 'pet' corners and school gardens. It was, however, difficult to provide, as adequately as in the UK, for the growth of some skills; for example, in instrumental music or in certain physical activities.

E. Africa. In East Africa the education of Service children was integrated with the civil system. In 1956 there were in the Command 862 Service children of school age, of whom over 500 attended civil schools spread over a wide area, which included Mauritius, Tanganyika, Uganda and the Central African Federation. Service schools were provided when civilian schools could not offer the UK facilities: for instance, the starting age in Kenya Government schools was 7 and primary education continued to 13, so some infant schools had to be provided: furthermore, Army schools had to be provided to supplement insufficient places in local schools, as, for example, in Nairobi. Nairobi, in fact, best illustrated this fusion between the local and Army schools. All Army children from the age of 10 followed the Kenya system of education and if they qualified in the State preliminary examination at the age of 12+ they were accepted into the Kenya secondary schools, which offered both academic and non-academic courses. Tuition fees were paid by the Army.

There were five Service primary schools in the area – Army children's schools in Nairobi (107 children), Gilgil (20), Nanyuki (98) and Mauritius (Vacoas) (26) and an RAF School at Eastleigh. The middle three provided non-academic secondary courses for children in their areas who had failed the Service selection procedures. For children outside these areas who needed non-academic secondary education beyond the age of 12, the only hope lay in attendance at a boarding school. If children failed the Service selection tests but qualified under the Kenya Government's system for secondary courses, their tuition fees were refunded but not their boarding fees, which many Army parents could not afford to pay. In Mauritius especially, Army parents were aggrieved at the lack of a full range of secondary education as assured under the 1944 Act, since there were insufficient places even for the local population and for Army children there were language difficulties as well.

By 1962, the build up of troops of the Strategic Reserve in Kenya and the encouragement given to all ranks to bring out their families resulted in steady increases in the number of school children. The Army schools at Nanyuki and Mauritius had closed in 1958–59 but increased accommodation was provided at Gilgil (206 children), Nairobi (234) and Kahawa (230). These were all primary schools with the usual handful of secondary-aged children. More children, too, were attending the Government schools, thus increasing considerably costs to the UK taxpayer, both by direct payments to the Kenya Government and indirectly by the new Army school buildings. But the educational problems of this Command were also to be solved by political decision, when Kenya was granted independence in 1963 and the British Army withdrew.

British Forces, Germany. In 1956 BFES was making its adjustments to match the redeployment of the forces in Germany resulting from the Federal Republic of Germany ceasing to be an occupied country and taking her place as an ally in NATO. It moved its headquarters from Dusseldorf to the new NATO Joint Headquarters at Rheindahlen. The Regional Offices were re-located at Herford and Rheindahlen, responsible for the northern and southern (including Berlin) sections of the zone respectively. This reduction of three to two regions was achieved by the amalgamation of the Rhine and Lubbecke military districts in April 1957 and the closure of Hanover district on 31 December 1957. The Zonal Board became the Services Board and met three times each year under the Major-General i/c Administration HQ BAOR, with the Air Officer i/c 2 Tactical Air Force as Vice-Chairman. The Board no longer included a Foreign Office representative after July 1956, when Foreign Office personnel in Germany ceased to be entitled to free education for their children.

The Command was thus faced with the termination of occupation costs, hitherto paid by the Federal Government, which meant that all expenditure, including deutschmark expenditure, became a charge to the British taxpayer. It had to make economies and yet at the same time provide for the considerable capital building programme, especially secondary, to meet BAOR's rising school population. The first to suffer these economies were the nursery schools, not obligatory under the 1944 Act, but a feature of the educational provision in post-war Germany. Nursery schools were officially closed in 1956, but continued on a 'self-help' basis under the management and control of Garrison and Station Commanders. Another economy was the adoption by BFES in September 1956 of the Army's world-wide scales for teachers, instead of the more generous Foreign Office scales allowed since 1946. In spite of the thirty-three teachers saved, the children/teacher ratio in July 1956 averaged 21·8 for Primary Schools. Nevertheless, there were still seventy-seven classes with more than thirty children at the beginning of the Summer term 1957 spread over seventy-three schools, and, because of the large number of Primary children seeking places, the age of admission had to be raised in some schools to 5+ and in Antwerp to 6+.

One cause for satisfaction was the generally high standard of attainment in the schools. This resulted from the good recruits being selected for the service, and the blend of experience of the senior staff (many of whom had been with the Command for 8–9 years), which with the generally satisfactory accommodation and equipment compared favourably with LEA standards at home.

Although the secondary schools were all comprehensive, the normal standard Army intelligence and attainment selection tests were taken each year by children over the age of $10\frac{1}{2}$ years. The battery consisted of the Moray House, followed by NFER tests (the latter introduced in the ̦Autumn of 1955). These selection procedures were chiefly useful for the information of LEAs at home in placing Service secondary children, but they were also useful for diagnostic purposes for children arriving from UK schools without record cards. They frequently showed the effects of constant changes of school, for the arithmetic quotients were invariably considerably lower than the IQs. Pressure on secondary boarding places, in spite of the opening of Queen's School, Rheindahlen, on 14 September 1956 for 400 children, was increased by the lack of a fourth boarding school – another victim of the economy drive – which remained until the separate boys' and girls' boarding schools were functioning at Hamm in 1960. These replaced one of the two original boarding schools, King Alfred School, Plön, which closed, the buildings being handed back to the German authorities for their Marine-unteroffizierschule (Naval Petty Officer School).

The annual building programme never matched the demand, in spite of the long list of projects completed – new schools, additional classrooms, new science and craft blocks, assembly halls, playing fields, boarding house adaptations, teachers' accommodation, etc. Only a proportion of the effort and money could be put into the provision of additional classrooms, etc., to meet the rising school population; there was a continuing need to replace unsatis-

33. *Bourne Secondary School, Singapore. Original barrack block in centre.*

34. *Beside the fountains of St John's School, Singapore.*

35.   *Panoramic view of St John's School, Singapore.*

36. Converting the Military Hospital into the Kent Boarding School, Hostert. The chapel is in the centre.

37. *Playground and classrooms. St David's Junior School, Rheindahlen.*

38. *St Christopher's Junior School, Rheindahlen. (Compare different style of Architecture with 37.)*

39. *The School Colours. Queen Victoria School, Dunblane.*
40. *Rt Hon. Edward Short visits Alexandra Junior School, Singapore, 1969.*

42. HRH The Prince Philip visits St John's School, Singapore, 1964.

41. A bouquet for a Princess. Paderborn Primary School, Germany, 1969.

43. *HM Queen Elizabeth II visits Eltham Palace, July 1970. Escorting her are the Author and the Director of Army Education.*

factory accommodation and to bring facilities up to Army building scales, and also to replace requisitioned property.

Another problem was transport. On 1 April 1956, the War Office had introduced a scheme whereby WD transport could be provided for educational visits and to playing fields and swimming baths within an allowance of 10s. per child aged nine years or over on roll at the beginning of the financial year. This scheme assisted all overseas commands, with the exception of BAOR, where a more generous scheme already existed, the cost being met by occupation funds. There were difficulties particularly in the boarding schools, where sports facilities were frequently some distance from the teaching and living accommodation, especially when the closure of the Suez canal necessitated a general petrol economy in the Command. A casualty would have been the BFES inter-school sporting and cultural exchanges, but for the generosity of parents and the use of non-public school funds. The secondary schools relied on these competitive sporting occasions, since their only alternative was to play local German schools or British adult units and neither was particularly suitable. Such visits also helped to build up a 'family spirit' within the schools in the Command.

The Director, BFES, was a member of the British Forces Broadcasting Network Advisory Committee. No regular educational broadcasts for schools in Germany were possible at this time, partly because of the lack of school reception equipment, partly the dearth of specialist writers locally, and partly the difficulties of timing the relay of UK school broadcasts because of copyright regulations. But special feature programmes for and about BFES schools, Christmas broadcasts, Sunday services, etc., became regular features on the British Forces Network, including a series of talks during 1956 on the various aspects of the work of BFES. In 1956 a team of boys from King Alfred's School, Plön, beat the UK winners of the BBC's 'Top of the Form' quiz series (The Royal School, Armagh), after having lost in the final the previous year by a narrow margin. 1956 also saw BFN organising its own 'Top of the Form' programme, the winners being Windsor Boarding School, Hamm.

BAOR had no school medical and dental service with doctors and nurses devoted solely to school work. Medical and dental officers of the Army and RAF medical services and SSAFA sisters included school health work as part of their normal duties. This had the advantage, except in the boarding schools with their own resident staff, of linking parent and child under the one doctor or dentist, and of linking the general practitioner directly with the hospital and specialist services. The main problem was the lack of facilities in Germany for handicapped children, because of their comparative lack of numbers and the wide geographical spread. Although BFES had a psychiatric social adviser who worked with the Service Psychiatric Services and whose advice was available to the school and to the parents, BFES had to wait until 1960 for the beginnings of a real diagnostic and placement service.

Generally, Army children were examined on admission to school, at 8, 11 and 15 years of age, and children who required special examination were usually followed up by the school doctor, in his capacity as family doctor. BFES boarding schools had a resident doctor, with a resident nursing sister in charge of each school sanitorium. A dental officer spent part of his school year in residence at each boarding school. Statistics show the heavy medical and dental load. In 1956, for example, 18,737 children were medically examined, whose health standards were graded: Good 15,308; Average 3324; Poor 105; referred to specialist 951; requiring education in special schools 17. Dental inspections during the year were 26,277; treatments 36,789.

Between 1960–63 Working Parties met in BAOR and at the Ministry of Defence to consider the long-term primary and secondary requirements of British Forces, Germany. Planning was made more difficult because of the long delay in the decision on the final force levels and resultant numbers of children to be accommodated, and uncertainty about the future of the Boarding School at Wilhelmshaven. In any event schools took about two years longer to plan, obtain the sites, place the contracts in Germany and build, than married quarters and multiple hirings, and temporary expedients were required to fill the inevitable gap.

The Working Parties agreed in 1961 that there were 2850 secondary places in permanent accommodation, represented by Queen's School, Rheindahlen (650), King's School, Gutersloh (500), Hamm (1050 boarding), Wilhelmshaven (650 boarding) and 100 places in W. Berlin. There were some additional places available, but these could only be considered as a short-term expedient. Some 2600 extra permanent places would be required, grouped by catchment areas around Dortmund, Hohne, Munster and Osnabruck. Day secondary schools of 450–500 places would be needed at each, and extensions to the schools at Rheindahlen and Gutersloh would provide the remainder. The first two schools and the Gutersloh extensions would be needed by September 1963, and the balance the following year. If PRS Wilhelmshaven closed, it would need to be replaced by a secondary day school either in the Hubbelrath or Minden areas (eventually sited at Rinteln), with some extra places at King's School, Gutersloh, to avoid unnecessary travel for some children.

Primary school planning and provision were easier, once the long term garrisons could be determined. Even so, a long list of new 4–6 classroom schools were needed at such places as Osnabruck, Hohne, Wulfenbüttel, Birgelen, Iserlohn, Dusseldorf and Hilden, with extensions at Fallingbostel, Hohne, Minden, Munster, Rheindahlen, Verden, Hameln, Celle and Gutersloh, to name but a few, and there were also the RAF requirements at Wildenrath, Bruggen and Laarbruch to be included.

I was myself concerned with the planning of these schools, as a member of the CEO's staff in Germany. Later, as Station Commander, Hohne, I helped to negotiate the secondary and primary schools there. I gave an impression of the schools and their problems at the time.

'Around the Northern Army Group's HQ in Rheindahlen were built 3 modern single storey primary schools for the children of the British and Canadian forces serving there. St George's School was typical of these attractively situated schools. It had 5 junior and 3 infant classes for the 216 children, under the care of a Headmaster, Assistant Master and 7 Assistant Mistresses, all qualified UK based teachers. The school, which opened in April 1955, was a show-place for its many visitors from NATO countries, all of whom were impressed with its lively and purposeful methods of teaching, its colourful rooms and its friendly atmosphere. To give added colour on festival days, it would have NATO Military Policemen on point duty outside, dressed in their national costumes.

'Nearby was the Queen's Secondary Day School, soon to double in size to 1000 children and operating on four sites. Next door to the main school was a comfortably appointed Ladies Mess for the teachers of the area, the men sharing an Officers' Mess not far away. Pressure on this school would eventually be relieved by the conversion of the nearby hospital at Hostert into the Kent Comprehensive Day School of 950 children, with boarding facilities for nearly 200.

'Kent School, Hostert, has a most interesting history. In 1909 two Franciscan monks set up a home, the St Josefsheim, for twenty (later fifty) mentally-retarded and handicapped boys. The

211

community was self-supporting, since the boys were taught a trade and helped in the kitchens, bakery, carpenter's, shoemaker's and metal-work shops, weaving mill and on the adjoining farm. The local inhabitants subscribed to the building of a chapel to avoid the long trek to attend Mass at the nearest church and to this day exercise their right to use it.

'In 1936 St Josefsheim was taken over by the Nazis; the monks were persecuted and imprisoned and many of the boys put to death under the practice of euthanasia. A veil of silence hangs over the war-time period. After the War it was used as an approved school for girls in need of moral care, and in May 1952 the school was handed back to its rightful owners, the Franciscan Monks. Without funds to restore it, they sold it to the German authorities, who leased it to the British in 1953 as a Military Hospital. In 1963 the Kent School opened in the converted hospital and today boasts seven laboratories, a spacious library, two large gymnasia, a splendid assembly hall and an examination record above the national average.

'Soon to be replanned were such schools as Scharfoldendorf – a Primary School of 3 small classes for 45 children, in its delightful chalet type building, situated high on a hill in the middle of beech woods; or the equally pleasant Hildesheim school, first opened in March 47 and transferred in 1959 to its skilfully converted barrack block, surrounded by a large playing field and paved playground, set with fixed agility equipment. I visited the Wunstorf Primary School, which illustrated one of the problems facing BFES in the provision of education for the children of isolated families. Here, 20 miles from the nearest Garrison, 34 children were taught in a house, originally built to accommodate an Officer and his family. The partitions between two rooms on the ground floor and on the first floor had been removed to allow two reasonable classrooms, a small paved court had been made in one part of the garden and some climbing apparatus had been set up on the lawns. I recall larger schools such as the Hanover Primary School, opened in 1955, but occupying new premises on a pleasant open site in a good residential suburb of Hanover. Its parent unit was the Headquarters of the Hanover area, largely a dormitory area, since most of the troops, apart from the military hospital, had been deployed elsewhere. Its biggest problem was the constant movement of children. In the year 1961–62, 183 children left and 229 were admitted in a school population of 280. Only 47 pupils had completed one year or more at the school, 85 had been two terms and 71 for only one term. Pressure of numbers had put a strain on the accommodation, necessitating the utilisation of all available accommodation—staff rooms, store rooms and two ground floor flats in a nearby residential block.

'I remember visiting a school of a different sort, one winter's day in 1962. Here at Ratingen 283 British children were sharing a building with a German school, which had formerly been a teachers' training college. Its barrack-like accommodation had been brightened, by the efforts of teachers and children, with paintings and models on the wide staircases and landings. This school was soon to be replaced by a new school, on a family site in the Dusseldorf area.

'While Hohne was waiting for its new secondary school to be built in the German equivalent of CLASP construction (Consortium of Local Authority School Planning), I had to find accommodation for the increasing numbers. I had my eyes on the Glyn Hughes hospital, named after the first British Medical Officer to visit Belsen, the Concentration Camp a mile down the road, whose staff had once lived in Hohne Camp. The Local Medical Officer complained that, once the School obtained possession of a couple of rooms in his hospital, it would not be long before it had the lot. He was right! I stayed long enough to take part one midday in the German workmen's "topping out" ceremony, when the roof of the new school was completed, and to arrange for these workmen to be quietly carried off military premises, as midnight approached, since they were obviously incapable of removing themselves after their liquid celebrations.'

One of the pupils described her school:

'I live at Celle, and Gloucester School is the nearest secondary school. My day starts by catching the school bus at a quarter to eight every morning here in Celle, and proceeding to Hohne, a journey of approximately 15 miles.

'It is a lovely big school with huge playgrounds, a tennis court, football field, race track, hockey pitch and several woods.

'The school building is all centrally heated, and the inside gives the impression of being fragile, as some of the classrooms are only separated by hardboard walls. There is always a lot of light as the school is nearly all windows; I feel as though I'm in a greenhouse at times!' (School Magazine.)

One school, which did not materialise, was Edinburgh School, Munster. It was a victim of the uncertainty over the ultimate deployment of troops in BAOR, and of the number of families to be accommodated. As negotiations continued over its future, the school existed in very poor conditions and the morale of teachers and children gradually deteriorated. Its Headmaster and staff, recruited at the same time as those at Hohne, battled under every conceivable difficulty and watched enviously the new secondary schools being built and opened around them.

Faced with the strong possibility of being unable to open his school on time, the resourceful Headmaster[7] enlisted the aid of the unit Provost Sergeant to hurry things up, and with the help of the prisoners awaiting sentence in the local guardroom, and innumerable packets of illicit cigarettes, he managed it. The Spring term was interrupted by the invasion of his premises by hundreds of

COMMAND	AREA	SCHOOLS	CHIL-DREN	STAFF			COMMAND	AREA
				UK	QAS	LET		
BFES	BAOR BELGIUM HOLLAND	90	13267	637	7	28	BFES	BAOR BELGIUM HOLLAND
FARELF	HONG KONG MALAYA SINGAPORE	33	6031	199	3	69	FARELF	HONG KONG MALAYA SINGAPORE BORNEO
MELF	CYPRUS CYRENAICA JORDAN TRIPOLITANIA	18	3196	83	4	38	MELF	ADEN CYPRUS
MALTA	MALTA	3	602	21	1	1	MALTA	MALTA LIBYA
EAST AFRICA	KENYA MAURITIUS	4	264	6	1	9		
WEST AFRICA	GOLD COAST NIGERIA SIERRA LEONE	7	636	11	—	19		
SHAPE	FRANCE	1	85	4	—	—	SHAPE	FRANCE
CARIBBEAN	JAMAICA	1	110	4	—	—		
BERMUDA	BERMUDA	1	41	1	—	1		
	TOTALS	158	24232	966	16	165		TOTALS

sheep, accompanied by a biblical character with cloak and crook and two black dogs, who insisted that he had inalienable grazing rights there, and had walked his huge flock fifty miles, as he did every Spring, to exercise that right. Nothing would move him, and lambing proceeded under the school windows, turning Maths lessons into impromptu biology sessions. What upset the Headmaster most was the harsh treatment of his first pathetic attempts to raise a few flowers and the loss of his vegetables from the 'school garden'.

It became, in course of time, a junior high school for 200 children, providing only the first three years of secondary education, in Army Barrack Blocks of bungalow type, lacking the accommodation necessary for physical education, music and general extramural activities, but possessing well-equipped science, woodwork and domestic science rooms. The older children of the garrison had to go to boarding schools elsewhere until 1970 when, at long last,

SCHOOLS	CHILDREN	STAFF UK	QAS	LET	COMMAND	AREA	SCHOOLS	CHILDREN	STAFF UK	QAS	LET
75	22559	963	—	152	BFES	BAOR BELGIUM HOLLAND OSLO	78	25679	1066	2	144
32	10895	402	2*	121	FAREAST	HONG KONG SINGAPORE MALAYA	39	16739	630	4†	179
6	2308	102	1	9	NEAREAST	CYPRUS EL ADEM TOBRUK PERSIAN GULF	16	6994	259	1	72
4	1156	50	2	3	MALTA	MALTA NAPLES TRIPOLI	9	2620	97	—	29
					MAURITIUS	MAURITIUS	1	143	4		4
					GHANA	GHANA	2	150			5
2	279	13	—	—		GIBRALTAR	2	715	22		6
119	37197	1530	5	285		TOTALS	147	53040	2083	7	439

Royal New Zealand Army Educational Corps † 2 RNZAEC 2 Royal Australian Army Educational Corps

it moved to new premises at Nelson Barracks to become a fully comprehensive school for 630 children, with all the modern facilities, including a single-teachers' mess. But by that time, the original Headmaster had moved elsewhere – to the new school at Hohne, which he had once watched grow with such envious eyes!

United Kingdom. We have followed the vicissitudes of the Royal Military Academy, Chelsea, from its foundation in 1801 as a boarding school for the sons of soldiers, through its removal to Dover in 1909 as the Duke of York's Royal Military School, to its more recent history in two world wars. Originally, the school was intended for boys who were expected to follow their fathers' profession, but now, although it still encourages them to join the Services, the boys are under no obligation to do so. Regularly inspected by HMIs, the school provides an education to GCE advanced and scholarship levels, which will fit young men to enter the universities or any other career, in an environment which retains what is best from the school's military tradition. It has recently added to its eight boarding houses, school chapel, sanitorium, swimming bath and classrooms, a block of eight well equipped science laboratories, a school theatre and a language wing. On its 150-acre site it now has a new sports pavilion and athletics track.

The staff, under an RAEC Headmaster (the post of Commandant was abolished in 1967), is half military and half civilian, with a resident medical officer and nursing sisters and the usual boarding school administrative and domestic staff. It is organised into two junior houses, each of 72 boys in the 11–13 age group, and six senior houses for the 312 elder boys. Applicants, who must be the sons of regular, or once regular, other ranks with at least four years' service, are selected after entrance examinations, which include Written English, Arithmetic and Verbal Reasoning tests, an interview and a medical. Account is taken of the father's (or mother's) service, of any special compassionate circumstances, and of the boy's suitability for the type of education provided at the school. After the first two years, which prepare them for entry to the senior school, the boys follow the normal courses of a comprehensive school and subjects appropriate to their interests and future careers. There is a wide range of clubs and societies, games and sports. The boys no longer wear military uniform, except when taking part in the compulsory CCF activities and on the Sunday parade, but the military virtues of smartness of bearing and appearance are encouraged. These can be seen at their best during the annual Trooping the Colour ceremony, which the boys command themselves.

The sister school at Dunblane has also had a fine range of new buildings added during recent years and is similarly staffed with civilian and RAEC teachers, all of whom live on the school campus. It has a Commandant and an RAEC Headmaster. The school is established for 250 boys, organised in a junior and three senior houses and prepared for the Scottish certificates of education, university entrance or Service colleges.

Her Majesty the Queen visited the school on 12 October 1967. One hundred and fifty boys stood at attention in their scarlet tunics, kilts and Glengarries in a single rank in front of the pipe band, facing the awning-covered dais from which Her Majesty presented the new colours to the school. After congratulating the boys on the smartness of their dress and drill, she said:

'The association between my family and the school has always been a close one. King Edward VII granted it the right to carry consecrated colours, presented first at Balmoral in 1909. King George V presented new colours in 1934 at Holyrood House. The ceremony today at Dunblane re-affirms and strengthens that association. Remember these colours are being consecrated. I give them to you in the belief that you will always do your best to care for them and to live up to the highest traditions of the school which you represent.'

REFERENCES

1. Superseded Provisional Regulations dated 1954.
2. Command Reports, 1950–1959, Institute of Army Education.
3. *Journal of the Army Educational Corps*, 1924.
4. John Laffin, *Tommy Atkins*, Cassell.
5. Mr C. R. Westcott, later the Headmaster of Edinburgh School, Munster.
6. Manuscript Report on Army Children's School, Larnaca, January 1962–July 1967 by the Headmaster, Andrew Mathieson. RAEC Archives.
7. Mr J. G. Tallack, BA, later Headmaster of Gloucester School, Hohne.

APPENDIX   A

Message from Field Marshal Viscount Slim

Windsor Castle
13 July 1964

Dear Mr Marchant,

It is sad to think that this is the last Speech Day that the Slim School will hold, but we must not be too depressed about it. After all the School does not die because changes in national administration close it. The School still lives on in all those boys and girls who have passed through it into the world and who carry with them the traditions and standards that they have learnt here.

Schools are like men; it is not so important how long they live but what they do with the years they are granted and Slim School has achieved a great deal. I have been very proud to have given my name to the School and to have known its achievements. I give everyone of you my very best wishes for happiness and success in the future.

Yours sincerely,
SLIM.

Headmaster,
Slim School, Cameron Highlands,
Malaya.

217

CHAPTER 14

The Present

Withdrawal from East of Suez. Economic retrenchment and stringency following the devaluation of the pound caused the Government to make financial cuts in January 1968 across the whole range of public expenditure. The heaviest were in defence. The Prime Minister stated in the House 'our security lies fundamentally in Europe and must be based on the North Atlantic Alliance'. Subsequently, the Defence White Paper[1] outlined the measures to be taken to curtail British defence commitments East of Suez and to wind up our military bases in the Persian Gulf and SE Asia. There would be a build-up of the strategic reserve in Southern England. The bulk of British forces would be withdrawn by the end of 1971 from Malaysia and Singapore (but not from Hong Kong) and from the Persian Gulf, and concentrated in Europe.[2]

This decision affected Army children's schools in two ways. First, it meant that there would be in Singapore and Malaya a gradual reduction of Service children, leading eventually to the closure of all schools there. Even greater than usual tri-Service consultation would be needed to decide which schools should remain to the last in a particular area and which should close: the teaching force would be redeployed and there would be some increases in children's education in Hong Kong, which would remain the long-term station in the Far East. Second, it would lead to the return to the UK educational system between 1968–71 of some 20,000 Service children, of whom approximately 14,000 would be Army children. The majority of these would be of primary age.

Plans were made for the repatriation of these children and for the future of the teachers. Each teacher was asked whether she (or he) would be willing to extend her current contract, until the final closure of the schools; if the contract had to be cut short through

218

the exigencies of the Service, would she be willing to transfer to schools in other Commands, or return to the UK with appropriate financial help?

In July 1968 the first Army children's schools were closed – the small school on Pulau Brani island near Singapore and the school at Ipoh Garrison. The following July, the school at Sea View, Malacca, the primary school at Taiping, and also the primary school at Johore Bahru were closed. In December 1969 Slim Secondary School at Terendak Camp closed, after a farewell performance of the musical play, 'Oliver', followed in March 1970 by the Mountbatten Primary School there, and the schools at Seremban and Kluang. It was decided to keep the schools in Singapore open, until the final withdrawal in 1971.

Mr Eldon Griffiths (Bury St. Edmunds) asked in the House of Commons[3] in February 1968, what preparations were being made to ensure that adequate education facilities were available to the children of Service families, on returning to the UK from posts abroad, during the following three years. Miss Alice Bacon (Minister of State for Education and Science) replied that local authorities would be kept informed by the appropriate Commands of impending movements of Service families into their areas. Mr Reynolds (Minister of Defence for Administration), enlarging on this reply, said that the 20,000 school children concerned and their families were likely to be stationed in the major garrison areas in UK, but that it was impossible to specify the actual numbers going to any particular area.

A newspaper article, under the heading 'Army Children on the March', discussed the problem.[4]

'Some of the LEAs most affected, in the traditional Army areas of the country, are hoping to take the increase in their stride. If returning families are put into existing married quarters, schools already exist: if they are put into quarters currently being built, then LEAs will have been informed at the planning stage, and having a new school ready for the moment when the new houses are occupied will present no more difficulty (but no less) than in the case of a new civilian housing development. Difficulties could arise, however, if the Army speeded up a phased married quarters' building programme under a District Council permission, in which case a village school might have to be urgently supplied with temporary buildings. There will be a problem, too, if old Army camps have to be re-opened as married quarters. The Army will inform the Department of Education and Science directly, if they intend to re-open an old camp for more than 500 people.

'Teachers in Army schools will not be redundant, since 500 teachers annually are recruited to fill the vacancies caused by 500 returning to the UK, and those wishing to complete their contracts can stay. Those teachers who wish to return will be all experienced teachers and should find jobs fairly easily. Those with posts of responsibility and Headmasters should also be readily absorbed into the UK system. It is significant that 19 Head Teachers in the summer of 1967 returning from BAOR have been appointed to Headships in bigger schools in Britain – possibly because all Army Secondary Schools are comprehensive!'

An interesting comment was made by the National Association of Head Teachers at their Annual Conference in 1968, during their discussions on the education of Service children in the UK.

'The problem should be causing more alarm than at present. It must be accepted that a Serviceman's life is naturally peripatetic, but we should see that the necessary brief periods that children spend in our schools are put to the best advantage. It is important that when children come to English schools, for however short a stay, their education should be up to the standards they have been accustomed to overseas.'[5]

Boarding Education. Another source[6] asked whether boarding places would be available in the UK for returning Service children, and pointed out the difficulty of assessing in advance the Services' need.

'Although the number of other ranks sending their children to boarding schools has doubled in the past five years, the total is still only 1225 compared with 6277 Officers' children. One of the largest and more convincing categories in Dr Royston Lambert's* statistics of need and demand for boarding is the Service child, whose parents are mobile. The Service man abroad is a case of need that no one will doubt. The Martin Report,[7] which LEAs take as their guide when they receive applications for assistance with boarding, bore heavily on the Service parents in one respect. They had to be overseas, or within 6 months of posting, to qualify. In fact, many parents, facing the strong probability of overseas postings, wish to start their children at boarding schools *before* they are actually notified of postings. On the other hand, the Martin Report's recommendation that membership of the Services should not in itself be a qualification gains added force now that more of the Forces will be permanently home-based. Within the UK Servicemen will still be a mobile category, but not necessarily more so than some other occupations that are not given financial assistance from public funds

* Dr Lambert had headed a research team, studying boarding education for the Department of Education and Science.

for boarding education. An increasingly mobile society should perhaps pay more attention to making the move from one part of the country to another less disruptive than it now often is in terms of syllabus, examination Boards, and age divisions. So far as boarding education goes, we need to help, and earlier than we have done in the past, those who really need it, while avoiding the creation of a special Army caste of boarders, where the mobility of their parents is no greater than those of various civilian categories.'

The possibility of the Services establishing their own boarding schools in the UK had been examined by the Lathbury Committee in 1954 without positive results. The cost was then established at £4m initial cost for 3700 children, with £180 per annum boarding costs per child. The cost of a Services' hostel scheme was estimated at £925,000 for the same number of children, with similar boarding charges. Later, as a result of the recommendations of the Grigg Committee, a boarding hostel was opened in conjunction with the LCC at Crown Woods in January 1965 for 120 boys and girls, who were attached to the comprehensive secondary day school; 90 per cent of these places were reserved for Service children and the remainder for children of Foreign and Colonial Office staff. So successful has this hostel proved that similar arrangements could be made to mutual advantage with other LEAs, many of whom need boarding facilities to make their own secondary schools viable, especially in rural areas.

Eight years later (in 1967), the Army gave evidence before the Government Commission on Public Schools.[8] It pointed out that wherever possible the Army built day secondary schools overseas. In some locations insufficient numbers of children within a suitably sized catchment area prevented the establishment of a workable day secondary school. In places such as Benghazi and Aden, secondary departments were attached to primary schools and consequently education was usually limited to courses suitable for non-academic children only. Grammar school children would not normally be taken to those stations. In some Commands there were large numbers of children in isolated areas, capable of being brought together to form a viable boarding school or to attend boarding houses attached to day schools.

All secondary schools were run on broadly comprehensive lines, but Army boarding schools overseas did not guarantee continuity of education for the children they served, since the children could only attend while their fathers were still serving in the Command. Where, however, a child was about to take a public examination, permission would be given for that child to remain at the school for the requisite period, after the parents had left the Command. There was a very considerable demand by Army parents for boarding places in the UK but the attitude of some parents towards Army boarding schools tended to vary, where they were *compelled* to board their children. Apart from such isolated cases, the demand for places at Army boarding schools exceeded the supply and in Germany it was almost always necessary to insist that, if a child lived within reach of a day school, he had to attend that school. In 1967 there were 2335 boarders at the following Army schools overseas:

Command	School	Place	Size	Number of Boarders
Germany	Windsor Boys'	Hamm	560	530
	Windsor Girls'	Hamm	570	550
	Prince Rupert	Wilhelmshaven	560	520
	Cornwall	Dortmund	450	120
	Kent	Hostert	810	175
Far East	Bourne Junior High	Singapore	1560	250
	St John's	Singapore	950	190

The major advantages normally claimed for boarding education were that it provided a greater opportunity for inculcating good community values and ethics, and for educating, influencing and training 'the whole child'; it provided more time and better facilities for games, organised cultural activities and hobbies, and boarding schools guaranteed continuity of education. The Army supported all these claims, except the last, since continuity was not possible in the Army's boarding schools overseas.

In the UK the majority of boarding schools were outside the control of LEAs: and it is interesting to note that the Army had a larger direct boarding commitment than any LEA.*

In the rather special environment of Army life, some of the benefits of boarding education took on a special significance. Children living in the area of a day school usually had excellent recreational and cultural facilities available, both at school and in the garrison. Without the boarding schools some children would lack these facilities, since they came from small isolated units, where social contacts with children of their own age and outlook were lacking. Most Army children settled quickly in a boarding

* The Army also had 700 boarders in its two military boarding schools at Dover and Dunblane.

school environment, benefited from it, and were loath to leave it to return to a day school. Cases of home sickness were rare and while this might in some measure be due to the adaptability of Army children from continually meeting new environments, nevertheless Army boarding schools were very contented communities. They covered the complete range of aptitude and ability. It was, moreover, Army policy to provide co-educational boarding schools and only two single-sex boarding schools existed, which were the result of accommodation problems in Germany. These schools at Hamm, being only two miles apart, fostered a full range of mixed social activities and some measure of integrated curriculum.

In June 1966 Dr Royston Lambert visited Army boarding schools in Germany, in connection with his research on public schools. He reported on his return that he considered

> 'the contribution, which the Army Department is making towards boarding education, is significant and any survey and report on boarding must take this into account. Army boarding schools are not simply schools with boarding facilities but boarding schools in their own right, with accommodation far better than the majority of schools in UK, while the food cannot be matched anywhere in my experience.'

Turbulence. The education of Army children is a topic always liable to spark off controversy in the national press. In 1963 a mother and teacher of Service children wrote complaining of the 'educational maltreatment, which many such children suffer', and started in the correspondence columns of *The Times Educational Supplement*[9] a series of charges and counter-charges, as each side marshalled its forces. The attackers blamed the children's frequent moves, long inter-tour leaves and their many changes of school and teacher. These factors, they claimed, were part of normal Service life, so remedies should be found in the standardisation of teaching methods, books and equipment. Why should one headmaster, for instance, ban streaming, homework, parent/teacher liaison, examinations and school reports and his successor reverse this policy? Why should a child be brought up on a diet of the three Rs and formal methods of learning in one school and change, willy-nilly, to a 'liberal' curriculum, project work and free-expression, when he moved to another. Teachers ought to concentrate on the basic subjects and surrender their own pet educational theories, however excellent these might be, to provide the long term stability which was so desperately needed by the Service children, temporarily entrusted to their care. Furthermore, the young teachers in Service schools should not let their 'hectic social life' obtrude into the classroom. 'Get on with your reading this morning. I'm too tired to struggle with you!' was a cry too often heard.

'Nonsense!' retorted the defence, composed invariably of head-teachers and assistants with years of experience in Army schools overseas. 'It is your child's twelve changes of school (presumably some in the UK), which is the principal cause of the trouble.' The Army is well aware of this problem and spends considerable time and money, trying to minimise educational disruption. It arranges for headteachers and staff to meet frequently through conferences of subject panels to develop common approaches. It represents the problems to LEAs and provides generous staffing scales to reduce the size of its classes and to promote specialist and remedial work with minority groups. Its capitation allowances for books, equipment and ancillary school services are well up to the best LEA standards. It hand-picks its teachers, not from the front row of the chorus[10], but from a large number of applicants from LEA schools all over the country. 'Not every teacher comes hollow-eyed to the blackboard from a ladies' night in the mess, although it would be idle to suppose that even the bluestocking does not get more attention abroad than she might at home.'[9] 'In my experience,' wrote one correspondent, 'repeated transfers of children do affect attainment and to counteract this is not easy. Even a child in a fixed location in UK has little guarantee of continuity of education, since the teacher shortage adds to the frequent changes of staff there, too. Furthermore, the Services receive their children from many different LEAs, retain them for a period in their schools overseas, and then return them to LEA care. It is the local education and private school authorities at home, which need to standardise methods and equipment.' As might be expected from such correspondence, not much of positive value resulted. But a retired Chief Education Officer[11], with a long experience of Army schools in the Far East, Germany and UK, had the last word. It was at least arguable, he suggested, that whatever temporary loss of achievement might be found in the usual classroom subjects was more than compensated by the social confidence, mental alertness and adaptability to be found in most Army children. As for the teachers, 'in the very great majority of cases they serve the children with conspicuous devotion to duty, in climatic conditions which can often be extremely trying, and in circumstances which not infrequently demand a cool head and sometimes an indifference to personal danger.'

In 1966, the Chief Education Officer of Wiltshire convened a conference to give an opportunity for the heads of both primary and secondary schools in areas with large Service populations to discuss this kind of problem with the officers of their LEAs, and with senior representatives of the Army and RAF. There were, he said, twenty-seven schools in Wiltshire with over 25 per cent of their children coming from Service families, totalling (in January 1966) 4331 pupils. These schools ranged in size from 636 pupils in a secondary modern school to thirty-four at Monkton Farleigh. Fifty other schools in his authority had a smaller ratio of Service pupils, numbering in all about 1000. Service children in all represented 10% of Wiltshire's school population. The rate of turnover in Service pupils represented admissions and transfer rates three, four and five times as great as would be normal. Three schools had admitted during 1964 more children than the highest figure ever reached in the year by their total roll. 'These statistics are enough to reveal the existence of a major educational problem, which presents a challenge to all concerned, if justice is to be done to both permanent and short-stay pupils.'[12]

To ease the situation, some of his larger primary schools in Service areas had been allowed to retain staff in spite of the temporary, but often lengthy, decreases in school rolls. The travelling expenses of teachers working in military areas, where no civilian living accommodation was available, as for instance Tidworth, had been paid. The committee had had its application for better staffing ratios for these schools turned down by the Department of Education and Science, but had been able to apply more generous scales for both clerical assistance and infant welfare assistants. Head teachers were maintaining for all children from Service families the record cards, used in all Service schools overseas. Peripatetic remedial teachers with special allowances were being appointed to the large junior schools at Bulford, Larkhill and Tidworth. They would work closely with the educational psychologists, since

'evidence of serious backwardness was incontrovertible. While appreciating the need for caution, it can be fairly said that the proportion of children with verbal ability quotients and English and Arithmetic scores below the County average is higher in schools serving Army areas, than in other areas in the County. This factor, coupled with the apparent increased tendency to maladjustment and emotional disturbance in schools serving Army areas, has led

Wiltshire to consider the establishment of a new and permanent post of a remedial teacher in many of the larger junior schools involved.'[12]

A feature of the county was the fact that Army families entering a garrison area might have two or three changes of address before settling into a permanent quarter, which could mean two or three classes for the children within a matter of weeks. For such children a boarding school or hostel might provide the answer. The LEA was also providing extra facilities for the youth service in the Tidworth and Bulford areas. There was a great need for nursery schools.

The headmaster at a county primary school in Colchester, with experience of Army schools overseas and similar problems in his present school, provided the following supporting evidence:

Number on roll	254
Number of staff	7
Number of Admissions (April 1954 to March 1963)	1391
Number of Withdrawals	1577
Total change-over	2968
Average yearly change-over	330

'It is not always realised,' he said, 'that the adjustment of a child to different methods of teaching, different teachers, and sometimes even different climates, is a difficult, delicate, and often long process. Army schools abroad have a much smaller teacher/pupil ratio and it is Army policy to return to the UK families having children who need special care (from physical, mental or moral reasons). Thus we have a much higher proportion of such "difficult" children than a normal school. I have found, in the main, over the last 9 years that Army children have at least as high an intelligence as their civilian counterparts. They need much more individual attention to bring their powers of fluent written expression into line with their intelligence.'

Prior to the assumption in 1948 by local authorities of responsibility for the education of Army children in the United Kingdom, the fact that the Army provided education facilities for its children, both at home and abroad, ensured a degree of uniformity of provision and afforded co-ordinated control and supervision. The result was a comparative ease of transition in a child's movement between schools at home or from a home school to one overseas. The subsequent integration of Army children's education at home into the national system has brought very great and self-evident benefits, but the change has also given rise to problems. Their education in the United Kingdom is now the responsibility of over

226

200 autonomous local education authorities, with a wide variety of practice in secondary selection and streaming policy, teaching methods, examination syllabuses, and attitudes towards Army children. There is now no direct central co-ordinating or supervisory agency. Children who, as a result of their fathers' postings, move frequently into and out of these schools are subject to the full impact of the variations between one authority and another, as well as between home authorities and those of the Army overseas. It must not be forgotten that as much movement can take place within the UK, as between it and stations overseas. Nevertheless, by the maintenance of UK standards in schools overseas, by providing machinery for the transfer of records to and from the UK, and by constant liaison with LEAs, the Army has done its utmost to reduce to a minimum the consequences of constant movement.

The problem of migratory children is, of course, not confined to the Services, since there is an increasing tendency in the UK for families to move with the father to new areas of employment. The Plowden Committee[13] recognised the need for priority treatment for special categories of children and specifically included Service children with gypsy and canal boat children as needing special consideration. The Plowden Committee tried to disentangle some of the principal influences which shaped the educational opportunities of children, to compare them and to assess their importance. It recognised that

'the task of abstracting these influences and measuring their impact when "all other things are equal" is the continuing concern of research workers. Parental outlook and aspirations: the opportunities and handicaps of the neighbourhood in which children live: the skill of their teachers and the resources of the schools they attend: their genetic inheritance: and other factors, still unmeasured or unknown, surround the children with a seamless web of circumstance.' The Committee saw "old buildings and poorly equipped schools, in which teachers will not work and to which they will not travel".'

There was the problem of migratory populations. The Committee criticised the LEAs for giving equality of educational opportunity, when what was needed was 'positive discrimination', by which extra resources should be given to priority areas and resources redistributed *positively* within an LEA.

Many of the Plowden criteria for these educational priority areas apply to areas and schools with large Service populations. 'There is evidence of serious backwardness among them and of high turn-over of pupils and teachers'.[13] It may well be that the answer is for the Services to persuade the Department of Education and Science and the LEAs that some of these garrisons need 'positive discrimination' and additional help from LEA resources. Numerically, Service children are only a tiny fraction of the nation's total population: nevertheless, they deserve something better of the society which the Services exist to defend.

There is much subjective conjecture, but little established fact about the nature and cause of these problems. Some research has been carried out,[14] but such research is limited in quantity and scope. One obvious difficulty is to isolate the influence of turbulence or discontinuity as an effect upon the child and his educational performance, from other relevant factors, such as varied environment (UK; alien; military; civilian; rural; urban; climate), family instability (absence of father, separation from relatives, tenuous friendships), varied accommodation (flat, house, furnished rooms, hotels, married quarters) and family insecurity (postings, courses, etc.). The question that really requires answering is what difference is there in the progress of comparable children, receiving educational experience equal in all significant respects, except for the element of discontinuity? In what ways must these two groups be initially comparable: intelligence, attainment, cultural environment, socio-economic background? And in what ways must the educational experience be comparable: type of school, type of home, efficiency of teaching, subjects studied? What constitutes discontinuity: change of home, school, teacher, class, syllabus, method?

Research to date indicates that there is no clear relationship between change of school or teacher and overall attainment in intelligence, arithmetic and English at the end of the primary school stage. Whatever a Service child has lost or missed in his primary career would seem to have been made up by the time his fitness for secondary education is assessed. A survey of Army teacher and parent opinion, however, confirmed a widespread conviction that changes of school had a detrimental effect upon a child's educational progress. A majority of headteachers consulted believed that reading skill was not affected by school changes and that oral expression was actually enhanced. But in all other respects the opinion was that each of the children would have reached a higher standard of attainment, if there had been a more stable educational background.

The failure to provide a scientifically based answer to the exact relationship between turbulence and depression of attainment may be due to other 'imponderables', such as the efficacy of remedial counter-measures, the assumption that continuity of education necessarily means continuity of *good* education, and that the standards of all schools and of all teaching are on the same level. Are losses of attainment more easily retrieved at the primary than at the secondary level and less easily in subjects such as Mathematics, History and Chemistry, which require the acquisition of knowledge in a more rigid sequence, than in Physics or English language? Is turbulence advantageous to some and disadvantageous to others – all the time, or at different times and under differing conditions?

The consensus of teacher opinion, supported by some scientific evidence, is that instability of home and school may have its effects on other aspects of the child's development, apart from academic attainment. Does constant uprooting develop a kind of insulation against close friendships and satisfy the need for affection and support from other children? At the same time, opportunities for play and easy mixing with peers may often be restricted, because of the location and standard of family accommodation. Is there equal evidence to suggest that the creation of stability of family separation by boarding education will eliminate the effects of family turbulence and lack of roots?

The answers to these questions are of great concern to Service parents and to all education authorities. Further research is urgently needed, since turbulence, as already stated, is not a Service problem alone. There is nothing to suggest so far that instability of school and home convey positive benefits, nor that the measures taken to counter turbulence by Army authorities – good pupil-teacher ratios, teacher selection and remedial teaching, etc. – are unwarranted. 'For while the effects may not yield as yet to objective measurement, there can be no doubt that they require to be countered by the most efficient teaching and the most secure and enriched environment that it is possible to provide.'[14] In this LEAs, the Service authorities – education, quartering, movements and administration – and parents have all a significant contribution to make.

Recent Developments. After the withdrawal of France from the military organisation of NATO in 1966, the SHAPE school in Paris, which had provided primary and secondary education for 274 British children, closed, and replacement international schools were built for the new HQs in Belgium and Holland. The new school at SHAPE HQ, Casteau, was sponsored by the Belgian Government and had a Belgian 'Directeur' in charge: it had five 'national' primary schools, each under a national Headmaster (Belgium, USA, UK, the Federal Republic of Germany and Canada) with an international secondary school on the same site. The AFCENT school, which opened at Brunssum in September 1967, was organised as four separate schools for British, American, Canadian and German children, with their own headmasters. The British school provides for children to GCE 'O' and CSE level. Students wishing to follow GCE 'A' level courses may go to BFES boarding schools. The first Director of the AFCENT school was a serving Colonel, late of the RAEC. The next Director will be an American.

1967 also marked the closure of the Army Primary School in Aden. From 1946 onwards school facilities for all Service children in Aden had been provided by the RAF, who had established a junior school for 400 children in air-conditioned bungalows on the airfield at Khormaksar, a bilateral secondary school nearby for 800 children and separate junior and infant schools at Steamer Point in former Turkish Army barracks. In 1963 the Army opened an all-age school for 350 children some 27 miles beyond the isthmus in 'Little Aden', a cantonment skilfully designed for a garrison of brigade strength and carved literally out of the sand. It was too far for the secondary-aged children to travel to Khormaksar, so the headmaster organised a purposeful course within the limits of his resources for the handful of secondary children in his school. The political events and the guerilla and terrorist activities of 1966–67 imposed a heavy burden on the military authorities trying to maintain normality for the families and their children. All credit is due to the Services, to the parents and to the teachers for facing the strain and physical risks so admirably that the schools were kept open and no child suffered educationally as a result.

In Germany BFES was reviewing its secondary development plans for the 1970s and considering the future location, size and viability of its school organisation, the cost-effectiveness of its schools, especially of the boarding provision. Experience teaches that all military plans must be subject to constant revision and educational ones are no exception, needing adaptation as family numbers and unit locations change.

The boarding school at Wilhelmshaven, isolated from the main garrison areas and hence costly to maintain, will probably be replaced by a larger day school in the Rinteln area. By 1972 the boarding requirement might be reduced to about 1000 places, and could be largely met by coeducational boarding schools at Hamm and Hostert, and 100 weekly boarders at Dortmund. Such weekly boarding annexes would help to make the small comprehensive secondary day schools more viable but would add to the cost. BFES may well experiment with middle schools, where circumstances permit: one such area is Berlin. For example, in 1970 the Gatow School had an infant department, a middle school for the 9–13 age group of the Gatow catchment area and also provided middle school facilities for the 11–13 year olds in the rest of Berlin. It might be possible to develop Gatow as a full middle school for the whole of Berlin's 9–13 age group, by turning the other schools into first schools and sending all the elder children to board at Hamm.

A major achievement in Germany was the provision of a youth service for the teenage population of the British Forces there. The recommendations of the Albemarle Committee (1960) had not received official support in the Services, but garrison and regimental commanders and the voluntary organisations in BAOR had established youth clubs, provided temporary accommodation, some equipment and funds and had organised a range of recreational activities. The RAEC and the secondary schools added their resources. But more was required. BAOR did not have a high teenage crime rate – quite the reverse, but there was much boredom, especially during holidays, when BAOR's school-aged population was increased by the UK boarding children, and there was the lack of a policy for the positive use of leisure.

In 1967, the Educational Services Coordinating Committee (SCESCO had been dissolved the previous year) appointed a working party, under the Director of Army Education, to consider the needs of BAOR's teenagers (14–20 year olds) and to make recommendations. Three LEA youth experts were invited to tour the Command to give their advice. As a result of the committee's report a youth service[15] was established for an experimental period of three years on 1 January 1969, 'to afford facilities comparable to those provided in Britain by Local Education Authorities.' Responsibility for control, organisation and administration, including public financing of the service, was vested in the Commander-in-

Chief, BAOR, and exercised on his behalf by the Chief Education Officer, BAOR, supported by a Youth Advisory Committee to represent the interests of the RAF and of the principal voluntary youth organisations operating in Germany. It was designed to be community and not school based, although the schools had their part to play.

A Chief Youth Service Officer was appointed to the CEO's staff, with three regional assistants (one female) to organise the scheme professionally, to coordinate the work of the voluntary organisations and of regimental helpers, and to train them. All clubs had to be registered, were given official accommodation, transport for their activities and for moving stores, some equipment, camping stores and furniture on loan, and financial help to supplement their own resources. It is intended that after the scheme has proved its worth in Germany the needs of youth in other Commands will be separately considered.

Thus, the CEO in BAOR, with youth added to his existing responsibilities for adult and children's education, has now all the duties of a Local Education Authority in the United Kingdom.

Except for a short period in occupied Germany, nursery education was not officially provided by the Army, although in every Command nursery schools were organised, administered and partly subsidised by local station or garrison commanders. These schools operated on a self-help, voluntary basis, parents paying small daily fees for their children to attend a couple of hours on two or three mornings a week. The Plowden report on primary education had supported the need for nursery education, a need enhanced in the Army by the constant movement of families and their children's lack of security. The new Army multiple hirings, 'islands in a foreign community', and sky-scraper flats in urban areas provided the same conditions of educational and emotional needs, which Plowden had described. So long as Parliament did not make it obligatory for LEAs to provide nursery education and while the majority of LEAs themselves did not promote it, the Treasury would not authorise such provision for the Army. The Director of Army Education, knowing the need, encouraged his CEOs to register all voluntary nursery groups, which ensured that nursery accommodation was adequate, sanitary conditions suitable, the staff were qualified or worked under the guidance of infant headmistresses, and that the schools' finances were properly administered.

The need to provide a stable environment for the Service child,

232

especially in infant departments, has led to experiments with full vertical or family grouping, so that a child could spend its whole infant life with one teacher. Usually infant schools were organised into three classes – a reception class for the 'rising fives': a middle class for the $5\frac{1}{2}$–6-year-olds and a top infant class for those soon to enter the junior school. But such was the pressure for admissions to reception classes that most children could only spend two terms there, sometimes only one. Moreover, such a wide ability and social range demanded very experienced and gifted teachers, devoted to this method of teaching. Recent practice has been to divide the family groups into two vertical classes – $4\frac{3}{4}$ to 6 plus and 6 plus to 7 plus. This provides stability and continuity of teaching and, at the same time, the teachers find little difficulty in handling the age range.

By the middle of 1968 more than 200 teachers' centres had been established in England and Wales. They varied in size and scope, but they had one thing in common; they provided evidence of the widely felt need among teachers for places where they could meet and discuss the new developments in educational thought and practice. In addition, they supplied a venue for regular In-service training, accommodated subject panel meetings and advisory groups, and acted as clearing houses for information and practical advice on the wealth of audio-visual equipment on the market. The demand for such centres came from the teachers themselves and, once formed, the centres were administered by them.

The military environment posed special problems for the establment of similar teachers' centres, because of the scattered nature of the Army schools and the greater distances involved. Nevertheless, a teachers' centre opened in February 1970 above the Mönchengladbach primary school in BAOR and one in Singapore, which the CEO, FARELF felt was justified, even though it would only have two years of life. There was no official authority for such a centre, but a site was eventually found, which had recently been evacuated by the Intelligence Security Unit, and furniture was made available from Units closing down in Malaya. It was ideally located to serve the two large secondary schools and five of the primary schools.

A strong teachers' committee, headed by the Deputy Headmaster at Bourne School as chairman, was formed to run the centre, which was officially opened in September 1969 with an exhibition of school textbooks, UK publishers responding magnificently, and producing over 3000 titles. Over 250 teachers joined, with membership open to teachers of the Naval and RAF schools and to members of the RAEC. Lecturers and courses were arranged two evenings a week, with a social night on a third. The centre was visited in 1970 by the Rt Hon Edward Short, Secretary of State for Education and Science, on his tour of schools in the Command. He told a gathering of teachers of the excellent impression he had gained of the Services' educational provision for their children, which compared very favourably with that made by LEAs at home, and of the excellent work being done by teachers and the educational staff.

Service Children's Education Authority. Before the Second World War both the Royal Navy and the Royal Air Force had children's schools of their own, but these were confined to a few stations. The Royal Navy had no married allowances, family passages and no quarters for its married personnel. The more junior ranks could not afford to pay out of their own pockets for their families to accompany them abroad, except to a station close to the UK, such as Malta, which became a popular family station with a school at Verdala. The RAF had married allowances but could only provide elementary education to the age of 12 for the children of a small number of married airmen. Since the war, both Services have made educational provision for their children under similar arrangements to the Army's. In 1968 the Royal Navy were responsible for 2735 children in 5 schools with a teaching staff of 134. The RAF had 11,723 children in 28 schools with 548 staff.

In 1968 the Ministry of Defence decided that the time had come to integrate under one central authority the separate responsibilities of the three Services for children's education. Accordingly, on 1 April 1969 a new authority, called the Service Children's Education Authority (SCEA), was established[16] to organise, direct and administer the education of Service children overseas and to deal with their problems in UK, in conjunction with the Department of Education and Science and the LEAs. It was also made responsible for the education of Gurkha children and of the Army's two boarding schools at Dover and Dunblane.

SCEA was placed in the Army Department, and was made responsible to the Director of Army Education for the 53,000 Service children in the 147 schools overseas and for the care of Service children with LEAs in UK. SCEA is staffed by officers of all three Services, with the policy-making section in central London and the selection of teachers, the central clearing for children's documents, and the placing of handicapped children with LEAs, made the responsibility of the SCEA department at the Institute of Army Education, Eltham Palace. Overseas, the 'major user' principle decided which Service should assume responsibility for the professional control of schools in a particular area, Army procedures for the provision of buildings, equipment and finance being used throughout. Thus the Royal Navy became responsible for Gibraltar (the Services took over the education of their own primary children from the Gibraltar Government in 1969), and Malta, the RAF for Cyprus and the Army for Hong Kong and Western Europe. Schools in Malaya and Singapore continue under their existing single Service management, until their closure in 1971.

The need to rationalise children's education was long overdue, and the LEAs will certainly benefit by the simplified control and single line of communication. SCEA will have organisational and administrative problems to solve: as more of its children return to the LEAs, it will increasingly have to concern itself with their problems in UK. It may also have to find new ways of financing children's education. At the moment such costs form part of the military vote. When savings have to be found in the Defence Funds, children's education has to compete for priorities with military manpower and equipment. When increases in national expenditure on children's education are considered necessary, provision for Service children may fall behind national standards, if the Services have to give priority to tanks before children. There is a strong argument for removing children's education altogether from the arena of defence finance and for funding it separately.

One result of the formation of SCEA was the abolition in 1970 of the Services Board of Education, Germany, one of whose chief responsibilities had been to ensure effective joint-service cooperation in children's education and to make recommendations, when necessary, to the respective Army and Air Force departments. The separate RAF link was no longer necessary, so there was no need for the Services Board. This was a natural and logical development. The Department of Education and Science, which was represented on the Board, still has a representative on the Ministry of Defence's Educational Services Coordinating Committee (ESCC) in London. This was a natural and logical development, following Service rationalisation. HMIs will continue to visit regularly

Service schools in Germany and the advice of the DES to be available at departmental level.

The Department of Education and Science, in concurring in this new arrangement, expressed appreciation of the way, over the years, the Services had taken account of the DES point of view and afforded every facility to the Inspectorate. Both looked forward to continued cooperation on a variety of matters affecting the education of Servicemen's children, both at home and abroad.

Thus ends, after nearly 300 years, the story of the Army's separate provision of education for its school children, a provision which has become merged in a wider responsibility for the children of all three Services. It is a continuing story of achievement and endeavour, by uniformed and civilian staff, sometimes pioneering but always seeking to equate its school facilities and policy with those of the nation at large.

REFERENCES

1. Statement on the Defence Estimates 20 February 1969 (Cmnd 3927), HMSO.
2. Keesing's Contemporary Archives, 22–29 March 1968, and Strategic Survey, Institute of Strategic Studies, 1968.
3. *Hansard*, 6 February 1968.
4. *Times Educational Supplement*, 4 August 1967 and 10 March 1967.
5. Ibid, 5 January 1968.
6. Ibid, 11 August 1967.
7. Report of the Working Party on Assistance with the Cost of Boarding Education. (Martin Report) HMSO, 1960.
8. Public Schools Commission Report, HMSO, 1968.
9. *Times Educational Supplement*, 26 April–24 May 1963.
10. *Sunday Graphic*, 13 February 1955.
11. Brigadier A. Nicholls, TD. MA.
12. *Education*, 23 September 1966.
    Another set of statistics from a Wiltshire Junior School of 533 children illustrates the problems. 150 children had fathers absent on duty and 128 fathers were awaiting posting orders; 227 had mothers at work; 94 left for school after the daily departure of both parents; 101 arrived home from school before a parent returned from work; 72 had foreign-born mothers; 22 had step-fathers; 23 came from homes which were breaking up.
13. Plowden Report, *Children and their Primary Schools*, HMSO, 1967.
14. For a summary of research to date and a commentary on it see Major R. C. R. Ritchie, BA, RAEC, 'The effects of school changes on Service children', *Torch*, the Journal of the RAEC.
15. Defence Council Instruction 184 of 1968.
16. Defence Council Instruction 198 of 1968.

APPENDIX A

List of Army Children's Schools 1968

British Forces, Germany

PRIMARY SCHOOLS (GROUP INDICATED)

BELGIUM   *Antwerp(3), Casteau (SHAPE)(3), Liege(1).

HOLLAND   Brunssum (AFCENT)(3).

BERLIN   *Charlottenburg(4), Gatow (5-13 yrs)(4), Kladow(2), Spandau(4).

FEDERAL REPUBLIC   *Bielefeld(5), Birgelen(2), *Bruggen(4), Buckeburg(2), Bunde (3), *Celle (Collingwood)(3), Celle (Grenville)(2), *Cologne (2), *Detmold(5), *Dortmund (Alexandra)(5), Dortmund (Victoria)(3), Dusseldorf(4), *Fallingbostel (Scott Infant)(3), Fallingbostel (Shackelton Junior)(3), *Geilenkirchen(3), Gutersloh (Haig)(4), *Gutersloh (Trenchard)(4), Hameln(4), Hamm(2), *Hannover(3), *Herford(6), Hildesheim(2), *Hohne (Montgomery)(4), Hohne (Wavell)(3), Hubbelrath (2), *Iserlohn(3), *Jever(1), *Krefeld(4), *Laarbruch(5), Lemgo(2), *Lippstadt(3), Lubbecke(2), Menden(2), *Minden (5), Monchen Gladbach(4), *Mulheim(3), Munster (Cambridge Infant)(3), Munster (Lincoln)(4), *Munster (Oxford) (4), *Munster (York Junior)(3), Munsterlager(2), *Nienburg (3), *Osnabruck (Clive)(4), Osnabruck (Cromwell)(3), Osnabruck (Marlborough)(4), Osnabruck (Wellington)(5), Paderborn (4), Rheindahlen – St Andrew's Infant(3), St Christopher's(3), St Clement's(4), *St David's Junior(3), St George's(3), St Patrick's(3), *Sennelarger(5), Soltau(1), Verden(3), Wetter(0), *Wildenrath(5), Wolfenbuttel(2), Wulfen(1).

SECONDARY SCHOOLS (DAY : BOARDING : GROUP)

     Cornwall Dortmund (D & B(6)), Edinburgh Munster (D(4)), Gloucester Hohne (D(7)), Kent Hostert (D & B(9)), King's Gutersloh (D(10)), Prince Rupert Wilhelmshaven (D & B(8)), Queen's Rheindahlen (D(10)), Windsor Boys (D & B(9)), Windsor Girls (D & B(8)), Gatow Berlin (Seniors).

Middle East

PRIMARY SCHOOLS

CYPRUS   Ayos Nikolaos(4), Dhekelia(4).

TRIPOLI   British Mission to Libya(1).

SECONDARY SCHOOLS

CYPRUS   King Richard, Dhekelia (D7).

---

* All-age schools in 1958.

Malta

Imtarfa (Infant (1)), St Andrew's(4), Tigne(4).

Far East

SINGAPORE   Alexandra (Infant(3)), Alexandra (Junior(5)), Johore (Infant(3)), *Johore Bahru(5), Nee Soon(4), Wessex (Infant (3)), Wessex (Junior(5)), Palau Brani(0), Selarang(3), Tanglin (Infant(2)), West Coast Road (Infant(4)).

MALAYA   Ipoh(0), Kluang(3), Highgate Hill(4), *Penang(4), Seaview(3), *Seremban(3), Sungei Patani(0), Taiping(0), Mountbatten(6)

HONG KONG   Gun Club Hill (Junior(4)), Sek Kong(4), Stanley Fort(3), Victoria (Infant(3)), Victoria (Junior(4)), Whitfield (Infant (4)).

SINGAPORE   Bourne (D & B(10)), St Johns (D & B(12)).

MALAYA   Slim Terendak (D5).

HONG KONG   St George's Kowloon (D9).

SCHOOLS CLOSED 1958-68

British Forces, Germany

*Ahlhorn, Borgentreich, *Brunswick, Cuxhaven, Degerndorf, *Delmenhorst, Dueren, Eindhoven (Holland), Essen, Goslar, *Hamburg (British School), *Hilden, Hook of Holland, Kiel, *Luneburg, Neumunster, Nordhorn, Oldenburg (Infant), Oldenburg (Junior and Sec.), Ploen, *Ratingen, Rotenburg, Scharfoldendorf, Schleswig, *Sylt, Wahn, Wilhelmshaven, Wunstorf, *Wuppertal.

King Alfred, Ploen (B), Windsor Mixed (B).

Middle East

CYRENAICA   *Benghazi (Queen Elizabeth II).

TRIPOLITANIA   *Homs, *Tripoli.

CYPRUS   Episkopi, Famagusta (Infant), Famagusta (Karaolos Jun. and Sec.) *Kyrenia, *Larnaca, Limassol, *Limassol (Berengaria), Nicosia.

Far East

SINGAPORE   Blakang Mati.

MALAYA   Alor Star, Kuala Lumpur (Infant), Kuala Lumpur, *Port Dickson, Sungei Adang (Malacca), Tampin,

HONG KONG   Minden Row (Junior).

SECONDARY SCHOOLS

SINGAPORE   Alexandra Grammar, Alexandra Sec. Modern.

MALAYA   Bourne, Kuala Lumpur; Slim, Cameron Highlands.

PRIMARY SCHOOLS

CARIBBEAN   *Up Park Camp, Jamaica.

E AFRICA   Nairobi, Kenya: *Vacoas, Mauritius.

W AFRICA   Nigeria – *Zaria, *Kaduna, *Lagos.
Sierra Leone – *Freetown.

FRANCE   International School, Paris (SHAPE).

SCHOOLS CLOSED 1951-58

British Forces, Germany

PRIMARY SCHOOLS (most had nursery depts).

Bad Honnef, Bad Oeynhausen (Infant), Bad Oeynhausen (Junior), Bad Salzuflen, Berlin (Herthastrasse), Berlin (Davoserstrasse Nursery), Bremervarde, Buxtehude, Fassberg, Gottingen, Hannover (Nursery), Hannover, Hamburg (Altersdorf), Hamburg (Blankenese), Kiel-Holtcnau, Luneburg Nursery, Rothenburg, Thorsdorf, Utersen, Warendorf, Westerland.

SECONDARY SCHOOLS

Hamburg (British School Sec Dept).

Middle East

PRIMARY SCHOOLS

CYRENAICA   *Barce, *Derna, *Tobruk.

EGYPT   El Ballah, Fayid (Infant), Fayid (Junior), *Moascar, *Port Fouad, *Suez, *Tel-el-Kebir.

TRIPOLITANIA   *Sabratha.

TURKEY   *Ankara, Istanbul.

SECONDARY SCHOOLS

CYPRUS   Nicosia.

EGYPT   Fayid.

E AFRICA   *Asmara, *Gilgil, *Mackinnon Road, *Nanyuki.
W AFRICA   *Accra, *Kumasi, *Takoradi, Tamale.

Far East

PRIMARY SCHOOLS

MALAYA   Batu.
HONG KONG   Whitfield Barracks.
BURMA   *Rangoon.

PRIMARY SCHOOLS

AUSTRIA   *Graz, *Klagenfurt, Spittal, Vienna, Villach, Zeltweg.
BERMUDA   *Garrison School.
JAMAICA   *Newcastle.
TRIESTE   *Trieste.

SCHOOLS CLOSED BEFORE 1951

BURMA   Mingaladon.
CEYLON   Colombo, Diyatalawa.
GREECE   Athens.
ITALY   Rome, Naples.
JAPAN   *Miho, *Iwakuni, *Hiro, *Eta Jima.
PALESTINE   Sarafand.

240

Index

Main references are indicated by bold type

245